Paradise Lost

G. K. HUNTER

Professor of English, Yale University

London

GEORGE ALLEN & UNWIN

Boston   Sydney

George Allen & Unwin (Publishers) Ltd,
40 Museum Street, London WCıA ıLU, UK

George Allen & Unwin (Publishers) Ltd,
Park Lane, Hemel Hempstead, Herts HP2 4TE, UK

Allen & Unwin Inc.,
9 Winchester Terrace, Winchester, Mass 01890, USA

George Allen & Unwin Australia Pty Ltd,
8 Napier Street, North Sydney, NSW 2060, Australia

First published in 1980
First published in paperback in 1982

British Library Cataloguing in Publication Data

Hunter, George Kirkpatrick
  'Paradise lost'. – (Unwin critical library).
1. Milton, John. Paradise lost
1. Title
812' 4   PR3562   79–41772
ISBN 0–04–800004–3
ISBN 0–04–800007–8 Pbk

Set in 10 on 11 point Plantin
and printed in Great Britain by
Richard Clay (The Chaucer Press) Ltd,
Bungay, Suffolk

GENERAL EDITOR'S PREFACE

Each volume in this series is devoted to a single major text. It is addressed to serious students and teachers of literature, and to know-ledgeable non-academic readers. It aims to provide a scholarly introduction and a stimulus to critical thought and discussion.

Individual volumes will naturally differ from one another in arrangement and emphasis, but each will normally begin with information on a work's literary and intellectual background, and other guidance designed to help the reader to an informed understanding. This is followed by an extended critical discussion of the work itself, and each contributor in the series has been encouraged to present in these sections his own reading of the work, whether or not this is controversial, rather than to attempt a mere consensus. Some volumes, including those on *Paradise Lost* and *Ulysses*, vary somewhat from the more usual pattern by entering into substantive critical discussion at the outset, and allowing the necessary background material to emerge at the points where it is felt to arise from the argument in the most useful and relevant way. Each volume also contains a historical survey of the work's critical reputation, including an account of the principal lines of approach and areas of controversy, and a selective (but detailed) bibliography.

The hope is that the volumes in this series will be among those which a university teacher would normally recommend for any serious study of a particular text, and that they will also be among the essential secondary texts to be consulted in some scholarly investigations. But the experienced and informed non-academic reader has also been in our minds, and one of our aims has been to provide him with reliable and stimulating works of reference and guidance, embodying the present state of knowledge and opinion in a conveniently accessible form.

C.J.R.
University of Warwick,
December 1979

PREFACE

The present book owes its beginning to the suggestion of Professor C. J. Rawson that I should contribute a volume to the series of which he was to be General Editor. I remembered the fun I had had running a staff seminar on *Paradise Lost* in 1965 and therefore suggested that I might try to write something about *Paradise Lost*, hoping that I might be able to recapture for others the sense of power and liveliness I found in the text. The actual writing has been greatly aided by student responses to lectures and seminars I have given on the topic, both at Warwick and at Yale. The finishing has been made possible by a grant by the John Simon Guggenheim Foundation. The text of *Paradise Lost* used throughout this book is that edited by Alastair Fowler (Longman, 1968 and 1971). The textual principles of this edition (modern spelling but original punctuation) cannot everywhere be defended; but the commentary is so full and so well focused that I cannot do less than invite my readers to consider that mass of evidence which my own book draws on (in agreement and disagreement) at every stage in the argument. Milton's prose works are normally printed from the text of the Columbia Milton (CM), though in some designated cases translations from the Student's Milton (SM) or the Yale edition of the prose works (YM) have been preferred.

CONTENTS

CHAPTER 1

Introduction: The Manipulations of Genre

John Milton saw himself as a poet, as a Christian poet, as an English poet and as a 'just' (i.e. classical) poet. I believe that it would have been very hard for him to retain his sense of himself if he had self-consciously betrayed any of these 'callings', central and vital to his sense of his identity as they were. But for us these separate callings have a tendency to pull in separate directions; and, though I think the order of the epithets I have given is probably enough the order of their importance to Milton, Milton's belief seems to have rested on an assumption that from first to last they were never incompatible, so that he never need sacrifice the lesser to the greater. The rhetoric, strategy and technique of his major works can be seen to be working to maximise the coherence of this group of self-identifying characteristics, and to minimise their inner contradictions. Some of these potential contradictions are well known: the problem is particularly obvious in the apparent clash between humility and certainty, his own voice and God's voice (his by inspiration), Biblical and classical allegiances, Hebraism and Hellenism. This book about *Paradise Lost* takes as the central spine of its treatment of this great inexhaustible poem the problems of continuous adjustment to these alternative pressures that the writing of an English Christian epic imposes not only on the author but also on the reader.

Milton, given his position as self-dedicated poet, and Humanist imitator of the Classics, was inevitably wedded to the idea and the practice of genre. His Latin and Italian poems spell out the nature of this allegiance in their very titles (elegia, sonnet, canzone, epitaphium); and the allegiance of his English poems is equally clear in text and often in title – *Paradise Lost*, an epic; *Paradise Regained*, a 'brief epic'; *Samson Agonistes*, a tragedy; *Comus*, a masque; 'Lycidas', a pastoral elegy. The modern reader tends to dismiss such labelling as either obvious or irrelevant, and to take it at best to refer only to outward and accidental form, not to animating spirit or central claim to significance. But in so far as the modern critic does this he separates himself from Milton and the kind of audience he chiefly wrote for, whose assumption seems to have been that the perception of genre was a first statement of the type of meaning to be expected and the type of framework upon which the actual structure observed would have to be erected.

Milton's attitude to the epic poem he regarded as the crown of his life, the work he could leave behind and which others would not willingly let die, marks out not only his relation to the models of epic writing – Homer, Virgil, Tasso – but also his sense of himself and his relationship to the English language. To erect a poem in the mid-seventeenth century on the framework left by Homer and Virgil was of course to make a claim about English, about the chosen subject-matter, and about the poet himself, which particularities of treatment could modify but hardly transform. And to offer this in English and in 1667 (the date of the first edition) invites an audience to contemplate the epic vision remade in terms appropriate to that culture and its assumptions. The epic genre is in this sense not to be seen as a straitjacket into which the poet squeezes his inappropriate modernity, but rather as a challenging model against which he has to invent or imagine a modern equivalent, whose modernity is no less vital than its equivalence. In what follows I shall be discussing the role of a number of the formal techniques of epic poetry as they appear or disappear in Milton's poem – the proposition, the myth, the narrative, the episodes, the similes, the high style, the divine causes, the flashbacks – but I do not seek to suggest that the relationship of *Paradise Lost* to the epic tradition can be described wholly in terms of such formalities. One has to ask what such formal techniques are *for* in the classic poems. Only when we know that shall we be able to see how far the presence or absence of the same formal characteristics links the deeper structures of the several model poems. In many cases the resonance of similarity is only there to mark the nature of a departure from the tradition or the assertion of a rebellion against the tradition. Milton's statement in Book IX that his poem is 'not less but more heroic than [*The Iliad, The Aeneid, The Odyssey*]' is only one of many such assertions that the poem is joining the tradition in order to transform it, or even to *save* it. The invoked presence of Homer and Virgil is, in these terms, only present to mark the rejection of their meanings and the reinterpretation of their style. The Renaissance doctrine of imitation was merely sterile if one went on copying the mannerisms of (e.g.) Cicero or Horace; in the end, if it was to find fulfilment, imitation had to lead the pupil 'to make something of his own' which would nevertheless be irradiated by the virtues of his model. When the expectation of genre is attached to the doctrine of imitation we see that new material is continually having to be found appropriate to the genre, not simply as new wine in old bottles, but so that the genre is continually reinvented in response to the pressures of a different culture.

The modern assumption is that the doctrine of genre sees literature essentially in terms of a static set of boxes or containers; what I am suggesting is that it was essentially dynamic, as new material took over the function of old forms and demanded a realignment of relationships. The nature of this demand exerts, I think, a continuous pressure on *Paradise Lost* and a continuous pressure on the reader to manipulate the frameworks supplied and interpret the stylistic implications. But perhaps, if one is to make the general point, it is easier to begin, not with *Paradise Lost* but with the much shorter 'Lycidas', a poem whose specific generic claim (to be a pastoral) is made dynamic by the pressure on the reader of other generic possibilities (eventually sharpened and focused on as heroic). Milton represents the occasion of the poem, the death of Edward King, as making a primary demand on a pastoral poet for a kind of poetry he is too immature to write. Autobiography or quasi-autobiography is used to encourage us to relate alternative generic frameworks. A traditional point about pastoral is that it was young man's poetry; Virgil's career – pastorals in youth, Georgics in middle life, and epic in maturity – is enshrined in the lines placed at the beginning of the *Aeneid* in all editions throughout the Renaissance:

> Ille ego qui quondam gracili modulatus avena
> Carmen, et, egressus silvis, vicina coegi
> Ut quamvis avido parerent arva colono,
> Gratum opus agricolis: at nunc horrentia Martis.   (Ia–d)

(I am the man who used to turn out graceful pastoral poems, and then, emerging from the thickets, I so charmed the neighbouring fields that they were totally submissive to the zealous ploughman. That was a poem the farmers liked. But now I am going to deal with the horrors of war.)

Spenser, the English poet Milton was most willing to acknowledge as his own model, was similarly explicit. At the beginning of his epic poem *The Faerie Queene* he also refers us back to his pastoral beginnings:

> Lo I the man whose Muse whilom did mask
> As time him taught, in homely shepherd's weeds
> Am now enforced a far unfitter task
> For trumpets stern to change mine oaten reeds.

Milton makes no such point at the beginning of his epic; but in his pastoral 'Lycidas' he dramatises, in what we will come to recognise as typical Miltonic fashion, the expectations that genre raises (and conceals from modern eyes), concentrating our attention on the poet's effort to write the poem, presented (here as in *Paradise Lost*) as the focus for the tension between the conflicting 'schemata' (to use E. H. Gombrich's useful phrase) within which he might write it.

'Lycidas' begins with a statement that the poem is going to be a failure. The situation demands a crowned poet, a *laureate*, great emotional charge, the high style; but Milton is not yet mature, and in his efforts to assume the crown he will spoil the poetry. And yet he may not refuse 'the mead of some melodious tear' to the external representative of spoiled poetry, the poet Lycidas 'dead ere his prime'. So, in spite of his premonition, he has to press the switch, tell the Muses to begin and even 'somewhat loudly sweep the string'. The point of this somewhat enigmatic line I take to be the sense it gives of pressure to make an effort, not to relax into immature prettiness. But the poem does keep relaxing ('aye me, I fondly dream'); the irregular stanza form permits tightening and slackening of emotional pressure to be represented by extended paragraphing and run-over lines. The formal structure of the poem mirrors the poet's on-and-off responses to the high demand that the situation makes upon him. The base-line, as it were, is that of pastoral reminiscence and nostalgia:

> Together both, ere the high lawns appeared
> Under the opening eye-lids of the morn
> We drove a-field, and both together heard
> What time the grey-fly winds her sultry horn . . . .   (25–28)

'The form is that of a pastoral, easy, vulgar and therefore disgusting,' says Dr Johnson, making precisely the right responses, though apparently unable to formulate aesthetic reasons why they are right. The pastoral form is intended indeed to appear *easy. Otium* is a characteristic not simply of fictional shepherd life, but also of verses about shepherd life, and the delicious delicacy of Milton's vein of pastoral has blinded most critics to the extent to which Milton is placing his own skills inside the larger framework of possible forms, theatrically manipulated across the scene of the poem to represent the various pressures of the occasion. Milton knows as well as Dr Johnson or the modern reader that 'they never drove a field, and . . . had no flocks to batten'; but the leisure that this fiction creates enables the poet to represent the problems of genre and so of interpretation of the meaning of King's death that the whole poem moves round. Again and again the sections shift from humble acceptance and ease at the beginnings of the 'stanzas' to angry questioning of destiny and lofty denunciation of its workings at the ends. These resonant tones first appear in the report of the death of Orpheus:

> What could the Muse herself that Orpheus bore,
> The Muse herself, for her enchanting son,
> Whom universal nature did lament,
> When, by the rout that made the hideous roar,
> His gory visage down the stream was sent,
> Down the swift Hebrus to the Lesbian shore?   (58–63)

Then, having made this effect, Milton allows the emotion to break, and returns, as it were from an anacoluthon, to the quiet beginning of another section:

> Alas! what boots it with uncessant care
> To tend the homely, slighted, shepherd's trade. . . ?   (64–65)

But this too, in its turn, rises beyond the pastoral to an impressive and non-pastoral dignity – the oracle of Apollo:

> Fame is no plant that grows on mortal soil,
> Nor in the glistening foil
> Set off to the world, nor in broad rumour lies,
> But lives and spreads aloft by those pure eyes
> And perfect witness of all-judging Jove;
> As he pronounces lastly on each deed,
> Of so much fame in heaven expect thy meed.   (78–84)

The ethical and eventually Christian assurance of these concluding lines takes us far from the frieze of goat-foot gods. But having reached this *O altitudo* Milton breaks off again, and self-consciously returns his poem to its pastoral base-line:

> O fountain Arethuse, and thou honoured flood,
> Smooth-sliding Mincius, crowned with vocal reeds,
> That strain I heard was of a higher mood.
> But now my oat proceeds. . . .   (85–88)

Again we reach resonance, in

> It was that fatal and perfidious bark,
> Built in the eclipse, and rigged with curses dark,
> That sunk so low that sacred head of thine   (100–102)

and again the form allows a break, and we return to simplicity with the quiet and unstrenuous Camus. But not for long. The wave-movement has been gathering momentum, and now it throws up the most terrifying figure in the whole poem. With the entry of St Peter the poem leaves altogether the *dorique delicacy* that Sir Henry Wotton thought wholly characteristic of the young Milton and takes on the heroic accent of Juvenalian satire and the prophetic splendours of Jeremiah-like denunciation. The pastoral deities are so frightened that they have to be coaxed back into the poem (or so Milton tells us):

> Return Alpheus; the dread voice is past
> That shrunk thy streams. . . .   (132–33)

Only then can the poem move towards its slow *decrescendo* conclusion. Once again Dr Johnson showed himself accurately responsive to what was happening: 'With these trifling fictions are mingled the most awful and sacred truths, such as aught never to be polluted with such irreverent combinations.' The tension between the *trifling fictions* and the *awful and sacred truths* is not one that Milton was liable to miss. The difference between Milton and Johnson is not that one saw what the other missed, but that what Johnson judged to be destroying the poem was employed by Milton to support it. Johnson's idea of excellence depends on a congruity of materials held together as decorously appropriate to a single point of view. Milton, I shall argue, writes far more like a metaphysical than this, and is far more the impresario of his poetry, manipulating the fiction of the poet and the generic status of his work to secure striking effects. The form is that of a pastoral. True! But Milton shows us the poet making pastoral gestures only to exploit the judgements that might be made about a person so doing, and to pose us questions about the meaning of such gestures, and why these were chosen from the larger repertory of gestures conceivable. There is a traditional question about Milton's 'sincerity' in writing about Edward King, and a traditional worry that he is more interested in himself than in his alleged friend, or interested in King only as a surrogate Milton. From the angle I am proposing these alternatives look no longer really alternative. Displaying himself writing a poem about King, Milton gives equivalent reality to both figures. The death of King poses an artistic problem whose solution raises the whole issue of poetic vocation and the poetic progression that leads from the poetry of irresponsibility (pastoral) to the poetry of responsibility (epic) demanded by the fact of death. At the end of the poem the 'uncouth swain' is seen tuning his Doric instrument and presumably completing the poem he has just written. The mood is more relaxed and confident than at the beginning. *Uncouth* he may still be, but his *forced fingers rude*, now *touch the tender stops of various quills* with something like expertise. It is, of course, a limited expertise. It is only the starting-point for a journey into the poetic future's 'fresh woods and pastures new'. Precisely what this line means is not clear in the poem. A poetic destiny is looked forward to but not described. But given the polarities within which the poem has operated it seems obvious that the 'poetry of responsibility' where death is faced as the poet's meed, and fame claimed as his right, is in view. There is the sense at the end of the poem of leaving an enclosed world and moving out into one more open and less protected. This movement is forced by necessity on the swain Lycidas, but it can also be chosen by his *alter ego*, the swain Milton. Lycidas is moved out from the Cambridge meadows to outface the terrors that killed him:

Henceforth thou are the Genius of the shore. . . .

So Milton moves out from the restrictions of an enclosed pastoral world where loss has *large recompense* to one where loss may be for ever – the world of *Paradise Lost.*

The end of 'Lycidas' is extraordinarily like the end of *Paradise Lost,* when Adam and Eve are forced to leave the garden:

> The world was all before them, where to choose
> Their place of rest, and providence their guide.

The meaning of the departure from *this* enclosed world is, of course, very different. But the manipulation of generic levels is very similar. At the end of 'Lycidas' we leave the pastoral enclosure, which has been continually threatened throughout the poem. At the end of *Paradise Lost* we have left, says Mrs Anne Ferry, 'the true pastoral world of Eden and have entered the true heroic world of perilous yet glorious choice' (*Milton's Epic Voice* (1963), 42). In the sense in which I use the generic terms, nothing could be more wrong. When we place *Paradise Lost* beside 'Lycidas' we can see, I hope, that at the end of the epic poem we leave the literary mode and world of epic – heroic challenge and response, huge fates held in balance in once-for-all situations, continual interventions of the divine – and come face to face with what one may call the world of the novel, the world of individual destinies, minimal epiphanies, human psychology. And the mode of the epic has been threatened by such intrusions of 'real life' throughout the length of *Paradise Lost.* The model of fallen human feelings and human behaviour has been used by Milton throughout the epic as a way of expressing states and actions actually beyond human comprehension. And the poem continually offers us the possibility of mismatch between what can be said and what needs to be said, as between epic ambition –

> That with no middle flight intends to soar
> Above the Aonian mount, while it pursues
> Things unattempted yet in prose or rhyme   (I, 14–16)

– and human frailty:

>   unless an age too late, or cold
> Climate, or years, damp my intended wing
> Depressed. . . .   (IX, 44–6)

> In darkness, and with dangers compassed round,
> And solitude. . . .   (VII, 27–8)

As I will be saying again and again, the epic mode offered Milton in *Paradise Lost*, as the pastoral mode offered him in 'Lycidas', a set of audience expectations which he saw it as his business to exploit, deny, reinterpret, approach and turn away from. Less centrally important than in 'Lycidas', but still crucial, is the impression he creates of the poet himself assuming responsibility for what he writes; and once again he shows himself in the act of choosing how he will write it.

Of all the major epics *Paradise Lost* most intrudes the author or narrator on our attention. Ancient rhetoricians described the epic as a mixed form which showed both the direct communication of narrator to reader (as in lyric) and also the exclusion of the narrator, in the soliloquies and dialogues that characterise drama. Homer and Virgil show us men talking to one another, but also tell us directly about the contexts in which men say these things. In their own voices they describe actions at length and remind us of events both before the present of the story and subsequent to it. What is more interesting, however, than the mere co-presence of these alternative modes of telling us what is happening is the effect that the overlapping of narrative and dramatised voices has on our sense of the poem. In general one might say that Homer makes nothing of the personal presence of the narrator. He is present as an objective witness and a presenter of standards that everyone else shares (with the exception of constitutional outsiders like Thersites and Dolon). The Homeric mode, indeed, seems designed to play down genuine differences of attitude. Helen and Paris (improbably enough) think the same of Helen and Paris as everybody else does. It is not conflict of attitudes that separates Hector and Achilles, Trojans and Greeks, but a conflict of destinies. This being so, the narrator can only be supererogatory if he inserts his own attitudes. Even in the *Aeneid* the narrator has hardly any more personal function. He is a Roman and he sees Augustus at the end of the action; but this is a teleology so compelling for everyone in the poem that he need not make anything of his special position, or any special or personal interpretations of what he sees or hears. The situation of the narrator of *Paradise Lost* is very different. Not only is he fallen like the reader and unlike much of the world of the poem, but he is also the sole connection we have between the things we know ('real' life) but do not really understand and the things we understand (as Christians) but do not really know. And he is capable of making this connection only as an individual whose personal experience expresses his capacity for essential understanding. The story of the Fall of man is a story which can be represented as occurring through a sequence of events in time; but an understanding of it depends also on experiencing it as a sequence of events in the psychological space of our individual life. To express the effort to write the poem is one way of depicting what the poem is about, reminding us of the continuous present of the author's emotional struggle to find a language (which is also our language) in which these mysterious events can be embodied.

The obvious places where the author shows himself in *Paradise Lost* are at the openings of new sections of the story, at the beginnings of Book I, of Book III (where the story moves from Hell to Heaven), of Book IV (where it reaches the Garden), Book VII (where the poem moves into its second, earth-bound, half), Book IX (when the 'comedy' of the Creation gives way to the tragedy of the Fall). In all these passages certain recurrent attitudes appear. The comparison of the Christian and the Classical epic is a constant. Milton presents himself caught in the painful truths of a Christian perception and yet aware (as in 'Lycidas') that the question 'Were it not better done as others use?' is continually posed by the material and the revered tradition. There is constant invitation to relax into the traditional language and so the traditional valuation. But the constant answer must refuse. Even if the poet proves inadequate, Man's fall must at least be more splendid than that of the Classical Bellerophon who only fell 'from a lower clime', for Milton's muse soars 'Above the flight of Pegasean wing' (VII. 4). As always in Milton, the classics are invoked only as a procession of splendid captives, dragged in to grace the Christian triumph (and then be put to death). The poet is present in these episodes as a believer praying, in the context of a pagan invoking his muse, and this again gives rise to statements of contrasting pride and humility, pride at being the vessel of this truth, appalled humility at the thought of his own unworthiness, together with a revaluation of the classical poems that provide the form of the rejected and re-embodied tradition. Milton also recurrently represents himself as caught in the experience of his characters. Sometimes the point being made is the achievement of an astonishing fusion between the Christian life of the narrator and the experience he is narrating. When, at the beginning of Book III, his narrative reaches the realms of light he writes as if it was Milton rather than Satan, the subject rather than the object, that has been

> long detained
> In that obscure sojourn, while in my flight,
> Through utter and through middle darkness borne
> With other notes than to the Orphean lyre
> I sung of Chaos and eternal Night. . . .   (III, 14–18)

The sense of soaring release in 'Hail Holy Light' identifies the poet with the poem and allows us to experience with him the Christian meaning of the poetic achievement, in an ecstatic coincidence of present and past, myth and psychology. Likewise, later in Book III, when Milton tells us of the angels hymning the beneficence of the Son's self-sacrifice to redeem man, the poet himself joins into the hymn:

> Hail, Son of God, saviour of men, thy name
> Shall be the copious matter of my song
> Henceforth, and never shall my harp thy praise
> Forget, nor from thy Father's praise disjoin!   (III, 412–15)

This passage raises in an interesting way the question how far we should take these authorial intrusions as autobiographical, how far we are invited to bring to our reading our awareness of Milton's thought. It is often said that Milton takes, in the poem, as he certainly does in his theological treatise *De Doctrina Christiana*, an unorthodox 'Arian' view of the Son as not the equal of the Father. The author's intrusion at this point in Book III indicates the danger of too passive an acceptance of these stiff doctrinal positions. If the passage here contains any Arianism (or anti-Arianism), it is not in order to impress such views upon us as true (or false), but to dramatise the alternatives seen to be available to the poet. Milton perhaps implies that he has in the past 'disjoined' the Son from the Father; but perhaps he is only saying that *Paradise Lost* in its earlier books has dealt with the Father rather than with the Son. In either case he will *Henceforth* make up for it by a particular devotion to the Son. The intrusions, it would seem, are not there to divert our attention from the artefact to the artist but to use the interrelation of artist and artefact to enlarge our sense of the poem as *chosen* out of the potential alternatives available, though in such a way that all the alternatives remain visible.

My last example of Milton's intrusions is also explained, almost universally, as the imposition of personal views on top of artistic practices, in terms of the man rather than the poem. In Book IV we hear of Adam and Eve going to bed. Milton uses the event as an excuse to condemn

> Whatever hypocrites austerely talk
> Of purity and place and innocence,
> Defaming as impure what God declares
> Pure . . .   (744–7)

and then he turns from negative to positive, and again offers his own hymn:

> Hail wedded love, mysterious law, true source
> Of human offspring. . . .
> Far be it, that I should write thee sin or blame,
> Or think thee unbefitting holiest place,
> Perpetual fountain of domestic sweets. . . .   (750–60)

It is natural for commentators to remember Milton the celebrator of the mutuality of marriage, the divorce pamphleteer, the Protestant scorner of holy celibacy. But the strategy of this passage relates to the poem at least as much as to the man. Here, as elsewhere, the paradox of the fallen celebrating the unfallen is expressed by a complex pattern of interrelationship between the survivals and the defacements of that pristine age. The hymn of the fallen Christian author reflects the undimmed capacity of the believer today to respond to the idea of vanished innocence which Scripture has preserved for us. But his vision is only complex enough to be convincing if it finds itself among competitors; we are conscious of the need to argue and interpret, and of the poem as constructed out of these arguments and interpretations.

By and large one can say that Milton's intrusions raise our consciousness of the uncertain nature of the boundary between subject and object, author and poem. They indicate that that was 'a way of putting it, not very satisfactory'. A powerful transition of this kind appears at the end of that famous and beautiful passage in Book I which ascribes the splendours of Pandemonium to the workmanship of someone elsewhere called Mulciber:

> Nor was his name unheard or unadored
> In ancient Greece; and in Ausonian land
> Men called him Mulciber; and how he fell
> From heaven, they fabled, thrown by angry Jove
> Sheer o'er the crystal battlements; from morn
> To noon he fell, from noon to dewy eve,
> A summer's day; and with the setting sun
> Dropped from the zenith, like a falling star,
> On Lemnos the Ægæan isle   (I, 738–46)

Milton continues:

> Thus they relate,
> Erring; for he with this rebellious rout
> Fell long before; nor aught availed him now
> To have built in heaven high towers; nor did he scape
> By all his engines, but was headlong sent
> With his industrious crew to build in hell.   (746–51)

The crucial and delicate placing of the *erring* here marks an extraordinary moment of authorial intervention and audience correction. The becalmed and static beauty of Mulciber's fall, like thistledown seen on a perfect summer's afternoon, is suddenly transformed from aesthetic approval to ethical condemnation – a condemnation that marks the lost beauty of Greek myth (and Greek architecture) almost as much as the loss of righteousness. For Stanley Fish (*Surprised by Sin*, 1967) such transitions mark the change from wrong to right attitudes, a chastening revelation of how wicked the aesthetic response has been, with an indication of how the reader should do better in the future. The point I am trying to make is rather different. The interventions of the narrator seem to me to mark the recurrent focus of the poem on the alternative modes its material demands, alternatives which may be clearly ranked in terms of judgement (as here) but clearly continue to co-exist without denying one another's poetic power. The unresolved problem of applying judgement to such material seems to me the issue that arises from the accumulation of instances. Satan's heroic energy, set against his theological status, is an issue of this kind throughout the poem and deserves a fuller treatment at another point, but it is worth noticing now (for a sample) how the author intervenes at the end of Satan's first fine Achillean speech so as to challenge the genre:

> So spake the apostate angel, though in pain,
> Vaunting aloud, but racked with deep despair. . . .   (I, 125–6)

The Christian inside of the hero is summoned up to confute the Homeric outside; but it does not wholly confute it, and I cannot believe it was intended to neutralise the aesthetic effects that have been pains-takingly achieved.

I have noticed above Milton's St Peter-like interventions to denounce alternative modern responses to the past. It is worthwhile noticing the relation of what happens in these cases to the model of 'Lycidas' I discussed earlier. The unfallen Adam and Eve offer the reader a picture of goodness so transparent and uncomplex that it seems to demand unmediated presentation, simple and direct. It would seem to be the role of the narrator to melt into the bushes, leaving us alone in benevolent contemplation. This is not the Miltonic mode, however. Contemplation quickly turns to judgement and judgement to controversy:

> Nor those mysterious parts were then concealed,
> Then was not guilty shame, dishonest shame
> Of nature's works, honour dishonourable,
> Sin-bred, how have ye troubled all mankind
> With shows instead, mere shows of seeming pure,
> And banished from man's life his happiest life,
> Simplicity and spotless innocence!   (IV, 312–18)

The choice to tiptoe away and leave the 'objective' picture standing by itself would have been a doctrinal choice and, in literary terms, a generic choice. The material Milton is here dealing with has a natural tendency to the idyllic and the nostalgic. Nostalgia for the vanished beauties of Eden flourishes on a passive acceptance of the gap between then and now. But Milton's aim is to express not only the gap but also the bridges across it. What he says about honour, 'honour dishonourable', is a key to his manipulations. It was a standard pastoral *topos* to deplore the coming of 'tyrant honour', which had imposed shame on the natural sexuality of the Golden Age. Milton describes the sexuality of Eden, however, as already accompanied by ideas of honour. Eve behaves in a manner not inappropriate for a coquette, 'With coy submission, modest pride,/And sweet reluctant amorous delay' (IV, 310–11); and when she first sees Adam she turns away, as by erotic calculation:

> Not obvious, not intrusive, but retired,
> . . . she what was honour knew. . . .   (VIII, 504–8)

At first sight this looks like the 'honour dishonourable' of the *topos*, but but at a second look it becomes clear that Milton presents the 'honourableness' of marriage as already part of unfallen Nature in the Garden, so that the coquettish behaviour of Eve is already held inside the honourable bonds of matrimony, seen here not as restricting but as spiritualising. The denunciation of modern distortions does not point us in the direction of nature, as the *topos* does, but in the direction of spirituality (which, before the Fall, *was* nature). The idyllic and nostalgic mode offered its readers an assumption that one could escape the ravages of 'tyrant honour' by a change of social convention (for example, by leaving the court and going into the country). Milton corrects this by indicating that there is no return to the Garden for fallen man; the only route towards innocence lies ahead, through Jesus Christ. And yet the vocabulary and the mode of projecting innocence cannot escape from the dream of nature, which is all that the poetic vision can use, the only material it can build with. Again, the authorial intervention marks the need to achieve a double focus, a sense both of the generic meaning of what is said, and of the limitation that must be imposed on any such expression by a proper awareness of the limits of human (or fallen) expressiveness. Milton's generic design upon us is, I am suggesting, a way of drawing our attention to the essential duplicity of what he can say, in his fallen language, about the state of heaven, the unfallen earth and the possibility of salvation. The manipulation of genre combines with the revelation of this poet as the manipulator to give an *as if* status to what he says, and to the way in which we respond to what he says.

CHAPTER 2
The Epic Mode

(i) AN ENGLISH CHRISTIAN POEM

The dominant English poet in the decade of *Paradise Lost*, John Dryden, noted when he introduced his most sustained and possibly his most influential work, his translation of the *Aeneid*, that the heroic or epic poem was 'the greatest work which the soul of man is capable to perform' (*Essays*, ed. Watson, II 223). There can be little doubt that Milton shared this sentiment, which was, after all, only the cliché of the age. He had from early on in his rather self-conscious and deliberate cultivation of himself as an English poet (or rather *the* English poet) hoped that an epic might, in some form, crown his life. As early as 1628 (when Milton was twenty) he expressed his aspiration to

> . . . sing . . . of kings and queens and heroes old,
> Such as the wise Demodocus once told
> In solemn songs at king Alcinous' feast,
> While sad Ulysses' soul and all the rest
> Are held with his melodious harmony
> In willing chains and sweet captivity.
>
> ('At a Vacation Exercise', 45–52)

And in 1641–2, when the Civil War loomed over everything else in England and Milton was already embroiled in controversial pamphleteering, he took the opportunity to remind his audience that 'I should not choose this manner of writing [i.e. prose] wherein knowing myself inferior to myself, led by the genial power of nature to another task, I have the use, as I may account it, but of my left hand' (CM, III, 235). He sees himself, and wishes others to see him, as a man propelled forward by 'an inward prompting which now [in the period before the Civil War] grew daily upon me, that by labour and intent study (which I take to be my portion in this life) joined with a strong propensity of nature, I might perhaps leave something so written to aftertimes, as they should not willingly let it die' (CM, III, 236).

The task Milton had set himself as his natural aim was not only to write an epic poem, but also to write one which, as I have noticed above, encompassed his two abiding passions, patriotism and religion. The patriotism that applied to such a venture was, of course, linguistic as well as political. Though in the juvenile 'Vacation Exercise' quoted above Milton had fluently hailed his 'native language' as quite suitable for 'some graver subject', when it came to the actual writing of the definitive epic he saw himself (as did other Renaissance poets of large pretension) to be making a self-sacrificing choice. The success of his early writings that pleased him most (if we are to judge by the frequency with which he refers to it) was the success his Latin poetry enjoyed in Italy. But he felt the call, he tells us, 'to fix all the industry and art I could unite to the adorning of my native tongue; not to make verbal curiosities the end (that were a toilsome vanity) but to be an interpreter and relater of the best and sagest things among mine own citizens throughout this island in the mother dialect. That what the greatest and choicest wits of Athens, Rome or modern Italy, and those Hebrews of old did for their country, I in my proportion, with this over and above, of being a Christian, might do for mine; not caring to be once named abroad, though perhaps I could attain to that [understand 'if I wrote in Latin'], but content with these British islands as my world' (CM, III, 236–7). What we should notice here is Milton's concern that the language, as he says, 'of monks and mechanics' (English) should be thought capable of carrying the cultural weight of the epic tradition. But Rome, after all, had made Latin a great language by exercising it in the great matters of epic, taking on the Greek world in its greatest monument, Homer; and modern Italy, in the person of Tasso, had taken on the splendours of Virgil and matched them in the vulgar tongue. So the new nation cannot hope to emerge from provinciality until it has achieved its own monument in its own language. Whatever the risks, the task can hardly be avoided. It is interesting to notice the extent to which Milton may be assumed to have succeeded. Dr Johnson (no Miltonolator) remarks in his 'Life of Milton' that there is a danger in setting out the faults or weaknesses of *Paradise Lost*: 'What Englishman can take delight in transcribing passages which, if they lessen the reputation of Milton, diminish in some degree the honour of our country?'

Milton aimed in his epic to vindicate not only his country and his language but also his faith. In the passage quoted above Milton speaks of the great advantage he has in 'being a Christian'. The Greeks, the Romans, the Hebrews of the Old Testament, the Roman Catholic poets of modern Italy may have to be conceded some built-in cultural advantages – though Milton hopes he can overcome these – but they have one common disadvantage: they do not know God's truth. He did not, of course, think of his patriotism and his religion as separate; one existed to reinforce the other. He intends his poem to be, as he says, 'doctrinal to a nation'. The office of the poet is to preach to his countrymen:

These abilities . . . are of power beside the office of a pulpit to inbreed
and cherish in a great people the seeds of virtue and public civility, to
allay the perturbations of the mind, and set the affections in right tune,
to celebrate in glorious and lofty hymns the throne and equipage of
God's almightiness, and what he works and what he suffers to be
wrought with high providence in his church; to sing the victorious
agonies of martyrs and saints, the deeds and triumphs of just and pious
nations, doing valiantly through faith against the enemies of Christ; to
deplore the general relapses of kingdoms and states from justice and
God's true worship.   (CM, III, 238)

Milton writes here as if he expected the great poet to handle political
and historical material quite literally. *Paradise Lost* does not do so, of
course. But the retreat from the explicitly political does not necessarily
imply a change of attitude to the heroic. *Paradise Lost* spells out the
inescapable conditions within which 'virtue and public civility . . . affections in right tune . . . victorious agonies of martyrs and saints . . . deeds
and triumphs of just the pious nations' must take place. The poet whose
inspiration is the Holy Ghost cannot easily descend to particular institutions but he can powerfully promote modern institutional and national
virtue by pointing to its unique and solid base in the knowledge of God.
The declared aim of the poem, to

> assert eternal providence,
> And justify the ways of God to men   (I, 25–6)

provides a touchstone by which the true destiny of England can be set
against 'the general relapses of kingdoms and states'. The distinction is
the same as that which Christ points to in the fourth book of *Paradise
Regained*, putting the pagan Greeks (once again) in their places. These
men were

> statists indeed,
> And lovers of their country, as may seem;
> But herein to our Prophets far beneath,
> As men divinely taught, and better teaching
> The solid rules of civil government . . .
> Than all the oratory of Greece and Rome.
> In them is plainest taught, and easiest learnt,
> What makes a nation happy, and keeps it so,
> What ruins kingdoms, and lays cities flat;
> These only, with our Law, best form a king.

>   (IV, 354–64)

It is sometimes argued that the condemnation of Greece and Rome in
Book IV of *Paradise Regained* marks a change of attitude from that

found in *Paradise Lost* with its multitude of Greco-Roman imitations. At no time, however, does Milton seem to have noticed any incongruity between doctrinal condemnation of Greece and Rome and formal endorsement of its systems. The aesthetic doctrine of the gilded pill (sour doctrine in sweet language) allowed, of course, that social penetration had to be achieved by whatever means were available. Milton sees the necessary poem as one

> Teaching over the whole book of sanctity and virtue through all the instances of example with such delight to those especially of soft and delicious temper, who will not so much as look upon Truth herself, unless they see her elegantly dressed. . . . What a benefit this would be to our youth and gentry may be soon guessed by what we know of the corruption and bane which they suck in daily from the writings and interludes of libidinous and ignorant poetasters, who having scarce ever heard of that which is the main consistence of a true poem, the choice of such persons as they ought to introduce, and what is moral and decent to each one, do for the most part lap up vicious principles in sweet pills to be swallowed down, and make the taste of virtuous documents harsh and sour. (CM, III, 239)

Milton, like other Humanist critics, sees the 'moral and decent' organisation of 'a true poem' as possessing a natural affinity to personal and national virtue in spite of the fact that the best exemplars (the classics) are poisoned by impiety. That he continued to have these attitudes, to the end of his life, is clear from the headnote on 'The Verse' which he set before the second edition of *Paradise Lost*, published in his last year (1674). His appeal here is still to the 'judicious ears' that will approve 'the learned ancients both in poetry and all good oratory' and particularly 'Homer in Greek and . . . Virgil in Latin'. These are set against the preferences of 'vulgar readers' and the practice of the 'wretched matter and lame metre . . . of a barbarous age [that is, the Middle Ages]'. 'The true poem' is assumed to provide not only a model of elegant writing but also a paradigm of lucid and just organisation, indicating what is appropriate to the separate parts, what to the present and what to the past, what to narration and what to dialogue, what to character and what to plot. And this lucidity is seen as not only aesthetic but also ethical. Thus the distinction between the unrhymed verse of the classics and vulgar clinking of barbarous medieval verses soon shades into the distinction between 'ancient liberty' and 'modern bondage' — a distinction that makes perfect sense if not obliterated by the light of the Gospel. That Milton was willing at some times or at some levels of his thought to shield his aesthetic and ethical distinctions from this religious obliteration is clear from many passages. In *Reason of Church Government* he

speaks of the models provided by Homer, Virgil, Tasso, the Book of Job,
Geoffrey of Monmouth, as if the choice was wholly a formal matter.
He is dubious, he tells us, whether to write in

> that epic form whereof the two poems of Homer and those other two
> of Virgil and Tasso are a diffuse, and the book of Job a brief model
> . . . and what king or knight before the Conquest might be chosen in
> whom to lay the pattern of a Christian hero . . . in our own ancient
> stories. (CM, III, 237)

It seems clear that Milton in this 1641–2 period thought of his epic as
centred on a 'king or knight' in the manner of Tasso's *Jerusalem
Delivered*, in which Geoffrey represents the king as hero and Rinaldo
the knight as hero. This is the kind of subject which would have allowed
him to keep the double aim of patriotism and piety in good view. He
speaks of the figure of Arthur in his poem to Manso, Tasso's patron, in
terms which raise the possibility that Arthur was the 'king . . . before
the Conquest' referred to above. He says in his poem:

> . . . indigenas revocabo in carmine reges,
> Arthurumque etiam sub terris bella moventem;
> Aut dicam invictae sociali foedere mensae,
> Magnanimos heroas et (O modo spiritus ad sit)
> Frangam Saxonicas Britonum sub Marte phalanges. (80–4)

(In my poems I shall resurrect the kings of my own country, and even
Arthur who conducted war under the earth; or I will speak of the great-
hearted knights of the round table, kept unconquered by reason of their
fellowship; and (if I can find the impulse) I will beat down the Saxon
ranks under the military might of the Britons.)

Arthur had indeed considerable advantage for his purposes. As neither
Saxon nor Norman it could be claimed that he represented the unadulter-
ated purity of British life. He could also (even more importantly) be
seen as representing the primitive purity of the British church, before
the Papistical intrusions of Rome and the Normans defaced it; and therefore a model for the Reformed purity of the seventeenth-century church.
Other figures from early British history had of course similar advantages;
and the hold that this area had on Milton's imagination is well indicated
in the list of topics which appear in the manuscript notebook in Trinity
College, Cambridge. Alongside sketches of the actual subject-matter of
Paradise Lost, and many Biblical stories, we find here also no less than
thirty-three British subjects, as well as five that he refers to as 'Scotch
stories or rather British of the north parts'. The British stories all
belong to the period 'before the Conquest'.

It may be significant that the list of 'British Trag[edies]' written down in the Trinity manuscript does not mention Arthur. Certainly by the time Milton wrote his *History of Britain* (published in 1670) he was prepared to scorn Arthur as a mere fable; for 'he who can accept of Legends for good story [sc. history] may quickly swell a volume with trash, and had need be furnished with two only necessaries, leisure and belief, whether it be the writer or he that shall read' (CM, X, 128). I take it that the question of Arthur's historical truth was important to Milton when he thought about his actions as the substance of an epic poem, and that the blot on his historicity came to seem also a blot on his appropriateness for serious poetry. This was not a relevant issue in the one English poem Milton thought of as a possible model for his own epic: Spenser's *The Faerie Queene*. In *Areopagitica* he adapted to Spenser Horace's celebrated reference to Homer –

> Troiani belli scriptorem . . . relegi:
> Qui quid sit pulchrum, quid turpe, quid utile, quid non,
> Planius ac melius Chrysippo et Crantore dicit   (*Epistles* I, 2 : 1)

(I have been rereading the narrator of the Trojan war, who speaks more clearly and better than Chrysippus and Crantor about which things are beautiful, which vile, which useful, which not.)

– writing of Spenser as one 'whom I dare aver a better teacher than Scotus or Aquinas'. But the role of Arthur as the 'hero' of Spenser's *The Faerie Queene* is in a mode which not only makes historicity unimportant but also runs counter to most of the poetic values Milton made central to his poem. In *Paradise Lost* Milton aims to 'justify the ways of God to men' by reporting what the Holy Spirit tells him:

> Instruct me, for thou know'st; thou from the first
> Wast present.
> . . . what in me is dark
> Illumine. . . .   (I, 19–23)

The Holy Spirit is treated here in the manner of the witnesses on whom Milton relies in his *History of Britain*. Geoffrey of Monmouth is not to be trusted in the matter of Arthur, for he came five hundred years after him. But 'thou from the first/Wast present'; the matter of *Paradise Lost* is true, in the sense of deriving from a wholly reliable witness. Spenser cannot give this kind of truth to Arthur, nor does he seek it for him. Like the other characters in Spenser's poem Arthur is important for what he means rather than what he is. He stands for a quality of *megalopsychia* or magnanimity ('Magnificence' is Spenser's word) which may be assumed to reappear in British history and which Arthur must have had if he had existed. A discovery that the historical figure had never existed would hardly affect the force of the figure in Spenser's poem. But the discovery that the Garden of Eden was only a myth, that Adam never existed (or was an orang-utan) cannot be equally compensated for by an assertion of meaning. Milton is everywhere an enemy to allegory, which he sees as a typically Popish obfuscation of Biblical clarity and literal truth. Spenser himself, we should remember, represented Anglicanism as the Una of single inescapable truth, and Papistry as the Duessa of double meaning. But Milton pushes this perception much farther. His principal characters – Adam, Eve, Satan, God, Michael, Abdiel, Beelzebub, Christ – do not represent anything beyond themselves. Their meaning derives from their existence, not their existence from their meaning.

If it is right to suppose that the search for literal truth is a central element in the dislodging of Arthur, then I think one must go on to say that it dislodged equally all the other British histories noted in the Trinity manuscript. For the truth which is not only factual but also significant for all human life can only be found in one place – in the Bible. Arthur is significant, but not true: 'Athelstan exposing his brother Edwin to the sea, and repenting' may be true, but is not significant. Only the workings of God are factually true and universally significant. Moreover, in choosing to write the Christian story Milton could see that he was not in fact deserting the ambition to glorify his countrymen. I have suggested above that Englishness could be defined by spiritual as well as geographical co-ordinates, by a position in God's providence as well as one in European history. In *Paradise Lost* Milton describes God's Englishman in essence when he describes the freedom and the struggle that belong to the truly Christian soul, the Adam, the Satan and the Christ that is within us all (potentially at least).

Reliance on the literal actions of these divine and quasi-divine characters to give meaning to the poem lands Milton in some obvious difficulties. Humanist imitations of the classical epics had normally proceeded on the basis of human beings and quasi-human gods, as in the originals. The readers' responses operated inside an understood system. In a poem like Vida's *Christiad*, a telling of Christ's life in Virgilian hexameters, the Christian supernatural is expressed wholly inside the vocabulary of the classical pantheon, God appearing as *regnator Olympi*, *pater omnipotens*, *aeternus genitor*, etc., locutions which indicate the issue of power and its movement of ebb and flow as the central point of reference for the reader of the story. Milton, in deserting the history of action for the issue of judgement, Arthur for Adam, is inevitably opting out of the main stream of Humanist imitation of the classics. His morally divine and physically human characters can express power-struggle only to a very limited degree. And he has set his face, as I suggested above, against the obvious way out of this dilemma – the use of the traditional allegory of warfare as a way of talking about the Christian struggles of the spirit. St Paul, after all, had given a lead, which Spenser and Tasso were happy to follow, in suggesting that the soldier's armour can represent 'the whole armour of God' in the Christian struggle against evil. But Milton's characters are meant to be understood in terms of intention rather than action, the over-arching of Providence rather than the immediate struggle. Dryden, as so often, shows himself in close touch with the Humanist assumptions which surround Milton's choices and give them their particular resonance. He complains, in his 'Discourse Concerning the Original and Progress of Satire', that 'his heavenly machines are many, and his human persons are but two' (*Essays*, ed. Watson, II, 84). The remark is usually dismissed as the irrelevance of a Rules-besotted pedant; but we should notice that Milton was such another. The domination of the poem by the Divine Intention was certainly deliberate choice; but it was a choice which carried Milton far from the traditional material of the epic poem, the heroic combat of warriors in battle.

Milton's literalism of temperament and aesthetic preference required him not only to repudiate allegorical warfare but also to bring into issue the undoubted fact that real warfare is both confused and inconclusive. His poem specifically repudiates

> Wars, hitherto the only argument
> Heroic deemed, chief mastery to dissect
> With long and tedious havoc fabled knights
> In battles feigned; the better fortitude
> Of patience and heroic martyrdom
> Unsung;   (IX, 28–32)

The Humanist disdain of war, of which Erasmus is the most famous exponent, was complicated in Milton's case by his deep involvement in an armed struggle in which thousands of his countrymen died. Clearly he admired the generals of his own side in the English Civil War, but his praise is regularly accompanied by clear reservations. In his sonnet to Cromwell (1651) he allows that Cromwell has achieved his power by battles, but he is careful to set the verbal battles against controversy ('detractions rude') in parallel to those against soldiers, and to make as climax not the fact of victory but the question of what you do with victory. If peace is not used for moral triumph, then the war has been lost: 'peace hath her victories/No less renowned than war'. Again in the sonnet to Fairfax: 'For what can war but endless war still breed'.

Perhaps the fullest statement of these views and the closest to *Paradise Lost* appears in his exhortation to the English nation in his *Second Defence*:

War hath made many great whom peace makes small. If after being released from the toils of war, you neglect the arts of peace, if your peace and your liberty be a state of warfare, if war be your only virtue, the summit of your praise, you will, believe me, soon find peace the most adverse to your interests. . . . Unless you will subjugate the propensity to avarice, to ambition and sensuality . . . you will find . . . a more stubborn and intractable despot at home than ever you encountered in the field . . . let these be the first enemies whom you subdue; this constitutes the campaign of peace; these are triumphs, difficult indeed, but bloodless; and far more honourable than those trophies which are purchased only by slaughter and by rapine. Unless you are victors in this service, it is in vain that you have been victorious over the despotic enemy in the field. (SM, 1155; CM, VIII, 241 is a different translation)

The alternative Milton offers in place of traditional heroism, 'the better fortitude/Of patience and heroic martyrdom' (IX, 31–2), imposes a passive reading on an active subject. The need to express the superiority of endurance to achievement explains much in the structure of Milton's poem. Milton, with one eye on Homer and Virgil, begins with something very close to the tradition: Satan as hero can draw on the traditional rhetoric of 'bloody but unbowed'; and we deny Milton's art if we do not respond to the magnificence of the military commander and political leader. The degree of self-consciousness that is involved is nicely illustrated in a passage towards the end of the great expression of Homeric energy in Books I and II. After the parliamentary debate in Book II the fallen angels retire to various places and pursue their pleasures – their fallen pleasures, I need not add. Among the higher solaces of this fallen world Milton notes the activities of those who

> sing
> With notes angelical to many a harp
> Their own heroic deeds and hapless fall
> By doom of battle; and complain that fate
> Free virtue should enthrall to force or chance.
> Their song was partial. . . .   (II, 547–52)

D. H. Burden has noted (*The Logical Epic* (1967), 58 ff.) that this is precisely the mode of the Homeric epic in which the tribe or nation celebrates its own heroism in battle ('Their song was partial') and defines heroism as resistance to fate or chance, the refusal to bow down before necessity. Once again *Paradise Regained* gives us a more precise gloss on the events of *Paradise Lost*. Christ's rejection of Greek culture includes in its broad scope the Stoics or philosophers who

> in themselves seek virtue; and to themselves
> All glory arrogate, to God give none;
> Rather accuse him under usual names,
> Fortune and Fate, as one regardless quite
> Of mortal things.   (IV, 315–18)

This characteristic classical definition of virtue as the power of the self to resist the tyranny of the other lies behind the persuasive rhetoric of Satan's famous heroic speeches:

> What though the field be lost?
> All is not lost; the unconquerable will,
> And study of revenge, immortal hate,
> And courage never to submit or yield:
> And what is else not to be overcome?   (I, 105–9)

The devils, in their conception of providence as fate, freedom as self-will, justice (the elevation of the more worthy) as tyranny, and heroism as individual resistance, easily reproduce the vocabulary and so outlook of the *Iliad*. C. S. Lewis reports that Goethe made a related point: '[the *Iliad*] shows that on this earth we must enact Hell'. So Satan in Book II sets up the political situation by which he has to be called upon as the strong man to rescue the diabolical parliament from its confusion and impotence; and Milton finds it easy to give him here the famous sentiments of Sarpedon to Glaucus in lines 310–21 of the twelfth book of the *Iliad* (a passage Milton quotes elsewhere: CM, VII, 112). Satan asks the same rhetorical questions:

> Wherefore do I assume
> These royalties, and not refuse to reign,
> Refusing to accept as great a share
> Of hazard as of honour, due alike
> To him who reigns, and so much to him due
> Of hazard more, as he above the rest
> High honoured sits?   (II, 450–6)

Sarpedon's sentiments are generally supported by the whole value system of the *Iliad*; but Satan's rhetoric is undercut not only by the political chicanery which lies behind it, but also by the parallel offer of the Son in Book III, to rescue mankind from the 'achievements' of Satan. In the demonstration of opposite qualities which appears in this conjunction – self-sacrifice against self-aggrandisement, sincerity against hypocrisy, love against hate, obedience against defiance, the search for fulfilment against the spoiler's negative art – we see the old heroism absorbed into 'the better fortitude/Of patience and heroic martyrdom'.

The Son offers a conception of freedom as choice to fulfil for love more than is asked for. Heroism emerges as the saving creativity which redeems what is lost and joins what is broken, not that which is defined by separation and opposition. There is an obvious danger in the idea of Milton 'placing' and 'repealing' Homeric heroism in his poem. If we say that the structure first of all exposes the old heroics in Books I and II and then swallows them up in Book III, we might naturally be taken to mean that the thing swallowed up disappeared from sight and mind. From angel's ken this may be true enough, when the whole action is compacted into a single vision of God's providence. But the human reader reads otherwise. In a poem the length of *Paradise Lost* the reader comes to identify with certain attitudes; and though these may be modified or even contradicted by the total experience of the poem they do not disappear and cannot really be disowned. One might as well argue that humanity is swallowed up in the poem because what finally matters is not man's response but God's plan. It has been pointed out many times in recent years that *Paradise Lost* illustrates the Christian paradox of 'the fortunate fall' or *felix culpa*: if the Fall of Adam and Eve 'caused' the Incarnation, the showing forth of the Love of God through the sacrifice of His Son, then we may say that the Fall was fortunate in that it called forth this inestimable benefit. At the end of the poem, when Michael has shown Adam the full range of human history and divine intervention, he points to the fulfilment of the process not as a re-entry into the Garden but as the achievement of

> A paradise within thee, happier far   (XII, 587)

The comparative is obviously deeply meant by Milton; even though the poem begins with a promise to 'regain the blissful seat' (I, 5), the result of the Fall is not simply a recovery but a replacement of the good by the better. To push this to the ultimate is to discover that the whole of *Paradise Lost* is, like Dante's poem, a Divine Comedy, loss, sorrow and waste being merely temporary incommodities resulting from a failure to look far enough ahead. At the level of whole-poem generalisation it is hard to deny the force of this logic; but it is equally hard to feel its relevance to the act of reading page after page. The Providence which governs the poem is like the curvature of the earth, indisputable but also invisible. And so our sense of the perspectives that we use to see cannot be thrown away. To know about the better things to come hardly mitigates the emotion that is generated by the waste of the good. As we observe the necessary destruction of Eve's beauty, of Adam's dignity, even of Satan's potential, our response is to tragedy not comedy. Our gratitude for the sad stilled humanity of the final lines –

> They hand in hand with wandering steps and slow,
> Through Eden took their solitary way

– must embody, if it is to affect us, the strong sense of present loss as well as the distant glimpse of redemption.

The Christian heroism which the reader can accept as capable of eventually swallowing up the heroisms of Homer and Virgil must both show forth the literal actions described in the Bible and also convey meanings that are relevant to the modern world. Simply to assert the truth of Scriptural statement is to retreat from any useful interaction with the rest of human experience. Scripture in that case becomes some kind of *mantra* by which the mind is emptied of all other (and so irrelevant) thoughts. This was hardly Milton's way; and his discussion of Bible-reading in his *Doctrine and Discipline of Divorce* (1644) indicates the extent to which he is prepared to go in claiming necessity and freedom of interpretation. In Book II, chapter 19, of that work he tells us that

> there is scarce any one saying in the gospel but must be read with limitations and distinctions to be rightly understood; for Christ gives no full comments or continued discourses but (as Demetrius the rhetorician phrases it) speaks oft in monosyllables, like a master scattering the heavenly grain of his doctrine like pearl here and there, which requires a skilful and laborious gatherer, who must compare the words he finds with other precepts, with the end of every ordinance, and with the general analogy of evangelic doctrine: otherwise many particular sayings would be but strange repugnant riddles.
>
> (CM, III (2), 491)

There may be some degree of special pleading here; Milton was seeking to prove a doctrine of divorce that had few precedents. But in fact there is little necessary contradiction between this and his other statements. He is not arguing for a free licence of interpretation. The mind of the interpreter, he sees, must always be locked in a pious contemplation of the text as well as a scrupulous examination of the self. In his theological treatise, the *De Doctrina Christiana*, his emphasis is rather on the limits of interpretative freedom, but his views are not incompatible with those quoted above from his pamphlet on divorce. Speaking in the *De Doctrina Christiana* of God's shape and character he says that all we can know is that 'he has that form which he attributes to himself in Holy Writ. God, then, has disclosed just such an idea of himself to our understanding as he wishes us to possess' (YM, VI, 136). Bible-reading is seen as a dialogue between God, who speaks through His book, and the modern, sometimes cultivated and classically trained, reader, who brings to the dialogue all of himself that proper devotion and humility can allow. The words of Scripture are undoubtedly true

and literally true; but the question how these sacred words come to have
the meaning that the Holy Spirit implants in the devout heart is a matter
for discussion with the Author. The nature of Bible-reading which I
discuss at a later point (pp. 45ff) – the need to collate evidence from a
wide range of separate texts and see meaning in a mosaic of fragments
– undoubtedly promoted this habit of searching for the voice of unifying
inspiration. But even in respect of a single text we can see that Milton
presses on every shred of literal fact to yield the meaning that his
cultivated sensibility (and that of his reader) could allow. The actual
words of the Fall story in Genesis, chapter 3, are, for all their simplicity,
very mysterious:

Now the serpent was more subtil than any beast of the field which
the Lord God had made. And he said unto the woman, Yea, hath
God said, Ye shall not eat of every tree of the garden?
2 And the woman said unto the serpent, We may eat of the fruit of
the trees of the garden:
3 But of the fruit of the tree which is in the midst of the garden, God
hath said, Ye shall not eat of it, neither shall ye touch it, lest ye die.
4 And the serpent said unto the woman, Ye shall not surely die:
5 For God doth know that in the day ye eat thereof, then your eyes
shall be opened, and ye shall be as gods, knowing good and evil.
6 And when the woman saw that the tree was good for food, and
that it was pleasant to the eyes, and a tree to be desired to make one
wise, she took of the fruit thereof, and did eat, and gave also unto her
husband with her; and he did eat.
7 And the eyes of them both were opened, and they knew that they
were naked; and they sewed fig leaves together, and made themselves
aprons.
8 And they heard the voice of the Lord God walking in the garden
in the cool of the day: and Adam and his wife hid themselves from
the presence of the Lord God amongst the trees of the garden.
9 And the Lord God called unto Adam, and said unto him, Where
art thou?
10 And he said, I heard thy voice in the garden, and I was afraid,
because I was naked; and I hid myself.
11 And he said, Who told thee that thou wast naked? Hast thou
eaten of the tree, whereof I commanded thee that thou shouldst not
eat?
12 And the man said, The woman whom thou gavest to be with me,
she gave me of the tree, and I did eat.
13 And the Lord God said unto the woman, What is this that thou
hast done? And the woman said, The serpent beguiled me, and I did
eat.

14 And the LORD God said unto the serpent, Because thou hast done this, thou art cursed above all cattle, and above every beast of the field; upon thy belly shalt thou go, and dust shalt thou eat all the days of thy life:

15 And I will put enmity between thee and the woman, and between thy seed and her seed; it shall bruise thy head, and thou shalt bruise his heel.

16 Unto the woman he said, I will greatly multiply thy sorrow and thy conception; in sorrow thou shalt bring forth children; and thy desire shall be to thy husband, and he shall rule over thee.

17 And unto Adam he said, Because thou hast hearkened unto the voice of thy wife, and hast eaten of the tree, of which I commanded thee, saying, Thou shalt not eat of it: cursed is the ground for thy sake; in sorrow shalt thou eat of it all the days of thy life;

18 Thorns also and thistles shall it bring forth to thee; and thou shalt eat the herb of the field;

19 In the sweat of thy face shalt thou eat bread, till thou return unto the ground; for out of it wast thou taken: for dust thou art, and unto dust shalt thou return.

These words have haunted Western thought for so long that it is hard now to see that they are saying anything at all. But they were quite likely designed to haunt rather than inform. The vivid clarity of the moments that are present in the text catch the interpreting mind and draw it into the black spaces between the present elements. But nothing in the text actually supports interpretation. The power of such writing is without question, but it is of a kind that was particularly useless to Milton's immediate purpose. Its power is in its blankness, its rejection of interrelations. But Milton's mode of writing (if I am right in my description of it) arises from his capacity to set up divergent inter-relations, converging points of view, multiple choices for the reader. As suggested elsewhere, established habits of Bible-reading, in which the Old Testament stories were seen through the web of references that the New Testament and the commentators had piled on top of them, supplied something of this missing complexity. But Milton shows us manipulations of the actual words of Genesis, chapter 3, without drawing on glossators; he remains narrowly faithful to the inspired words, and yet renders them amenable to his epic purposes. A central part of his strategy in this matter is his art of repetition and variation. Thus, the crucial moment in the Fall of Eve is played over twice, once in dream and again in reality. The version 'in reality' moves the weight of responsibility from where it is found in Scripture. In Scripture the most important passage of the argument for eating the apple belongs to the woman herself. The woman first says there is a prohibition; in a brief general statement the snake denies the prohibition, and the woman's own sensory powers then take over and carry her the rest of the way. In the Bible then, the actual eating of the apple comes at the end of a rather stop-and-start process – there is no clear continuity between what the snake says and what the woman thinks. In Milton's version of the eating, however, the woman's emotions are expressed inside Satan's persuasions, and she has little to do but fulfil his proposals. It is he who speaks of 'this fruit divine/Fair to the eye, inviting the taste/Of virtue to make wise' (IX, 778–80). Milton does not turn his back on the Genesis version, of course; he gives it literally in Eve's dream of the Fall. There 'the pleasant savoury smell/So quickened appetite that I methought/ Could not but taste' (V, 84–6). The archaic prototype of Scripture is thus preserved; but the intellectualised modern Eve is also allowed to be present. Genesis's explanation of the action in terms of instinctive appetite belongs to Eve, just as the regressive version of our selves that appears in dreams belongs to each of us. But the action that bears the weight of moral responsibility is (as it must be for Milton and other modern readers) an act of intellectual response to Satan's temptation, and so a free moral choice by the whole of human nature, by a figure adequately respresentative of modern religious life.

Another way in which Milton stays faithful to the Scriptural text, and yet renders its action fully representative of modern heroism in Christian struggle, appears in his taking the words of Genesis as not only literal but also metaphorical. Genesis tells us that the first effect of the eating was that 'the eyes of them both were opened and they knew that they were naked'. Pregnant with symbolic meanings these words may be; but in Milton's more abstract vocabulary a literal presentation of them is bound to seem a rather lame and bathetic representation of the much prepared-for knowledge of good and evil. Milton rings a series of changes on the contexts within which the idea of eyes being opened appears. The promised opening and the experienced reality, the equi- vocation of the fiend who spoke both true and false, are thus developed in a series of alternative ways of expressing the mystery; and so the literal nakedness merges into its moral analogues. The apple is repre- sented as a species of aphrodisiac-intoxicant. Adam and Eve burn with sexual greed, and when that is satisfied their queasy guilt is powerfully projected both in terms of psychological realism and in terms of an abstract commentary on that, so that an alternative after-image is imposed on top of the mythological Fall described by Genesis:

> . . . up they rose
> As from unrest, and each the other viewing,
> Soon found their eyes how opened, and their minds
> How darkened; innocence, that as a veil

Had shadowed them from knowing ill, was gone,
Just confidence, and native righteousness
And honour from about them, naked left
To guilty shame. . . .
. . . destitute and bare
Of all their virtue. (IX, 1051–63)

The simple idea of a physical nakedness that is looked at is turned into
a psychological nakedness that looks, a stripping away of the innocence in
which nakedness was also a veil between their eyes and 'knowing ill';
the physical eyes are opened indeed (as Scripture says) but the mental
interpretation of what the eyes see is 'darkened'. An identical change of
focus appears later when Eve hides herself for shame, but not simply
the natural shame of being seen, which Genesis strongly implies in its
statement that 'Adam and his wife hid themselves from the presence of
the Lord God amongst the trees of the garden' (verse 8). Milton's Eve
instead asks that the trees

> Hide me, where I may never see them more (1090)

– where *them* refers to *those heavenly shapes* (1082) who are visiting
the garden. Once again the shame has been internalised and intellectualised, made more that of a complex modern individual and less a
natural physical reaction. The separation between heaven and earth is
measured by the mode of perception that the individual is able to bring
to bear.

The techniques that Milton brings to the rendering of Scripture have
an obvious relation to that traditional handling of Biblical texts that went
under the name of 'accommodation', the name being derived from an
assumption that Biblical statements are set out as they are because they
are 'accommodated' to the understanding of their human readers. The
theory is referred to specifically enough in Book V of *Paradise Lost*
where Raphael tells Adam that, in the narration of heavenly events he
is about to begin, the 'facts' have been simplified for human ears:

> what surmounts the reach
> Of human sense, I shall delineate so,
> By likening spiritual to corporeal forms,
> As may express them best. . . . (571–4)

Milton is, however, not only anti-allegorical in his own writing but also
staunchly anti-figurative as a reader of Scripture. He is unwilling to
allow any large gap to appear between the corporeal forms it presents
and the actual truth it conveys, and he makes Raphael conclude his
statement of 'accommodation' with a caveat:

> though what if Earth
> Be but the shadow of heaven, and things therein
> Each to other like, more than on earth is thought?   (574–6)

Temperamental and doctrinal preferences seem to have pushed Milton in the direction of likeness rather than unlikeness between things mortal and things divine. If we set him beside a thinker like Calvin, we can see that the same texts produce in another temperament quite a different emotional response. Calvin, like Milton, was an enemy to figurative reading of the Bible. But it is clear that Calvin has in addition a particular abhorrence of the attribution of human qualities to God, 'lest the introduction of any thing unseasonable should afford an occasion of calumny to the malicious, or of error to the ignorant' (*Institutes*, I, XIII, 28). Anthropomorphism in scripture he explains by the graphic notion 'that God lisps, just as nurses are accustomed to speak to infants' (I, XIII, 1); but it is evident that he finds it distasteful that there is need for such accommodation, 'to accomplish which the Scriptures must necessarily descend far below the height of his majesty' (I, XIII, 1). Milton, on the other hand, neither in terms of his beliefs nor of the function of his poem, can properly pursue this distinction between what is and what men can say about it, for his poem is bound to be a tissue of the things that men can say, and which they are justified in saying, because God says them also, in the Bible. Milton's attitude to accommodation can thus be seen as an extension of his attitude to Bible-reading, which I have discussed above. Raphael's 'What if . . .' hypothesis allows him to stay close to the anthropomorphic mode of telling, which he contemplates less for the great unknowns that lurk behind the presented facts than for the alternative responses that human minds can bring to bear. At one level, as I have noted above, this means being willing to bring into contact with the text all the rhetorical skill in analysis that Renaissance schoolboys learned to apply to Virgil and Ovid. His aim, it would seem, is not to deny literary sophistication but to assert that its true object should be the Hebraic and not the Hellenic writings. In *Reason of Church Government* Milton speaks of 'those frequent songs throughout the law and prophets', describing them as 'incomparable . . . not in their divine argument alone, but in the very critical art of composition' (CM, III, 238). Likewise in *Paradise Regained*, Christ, though he rejects Greek culture, speaks of 'Our psalms with artful terms inscribed'; he presents Greek art as a mere imitation of the Hebrew, bearing the same relation to that as 'varnish on a harlot's cheek' bears to God-given beauty. The point being made is not that literary culture must be rejected, but that 'true tastes' (347) will always prefer the literary culture of the Scriptures, whose beauty is the natural expression of wisdom, not false colour on a vile face.

Milton's 'accommodation' is thus never a departure from the letter but rather a preservation of the options on what the devout heart and the rigorous intelligence can make of that letter. Speaking of typology in the *De Doctrina* he says somewhat darkly that 'Each passage of scripture has only a single sense, though in the *Old Testament* this sense is often a combination of the historical and the typological' (I, xxx; YM, VI, 581). This sounds like a model of how to have your cake and eat it: all passages are unitary, though some have two senses. I think the problem may be understood if we remember Milton's concern with the reader. Scripture makes unitary statements, but human weakness is such that we have to grasp at the meaning from two sides. This is not to say that there are two meanings; it is simply that it is difficult to express the one in less than two terms.

The inspired simplicity of Genesis read according to the letter, the lucid structures and proprieties that Homer and Virgil show us, the spiritual responsiveness of the modern reader – these are the three points between which Milton has to steer his poem, keeping in touch with all of them all the time and avoiding the shoals that attach to each of them. The problems of navigation that arise are the principal subject of this book. We can see Milton having to tack back the forward through parallel presentations, double meanings and a circuitous delaying style both of writing poetry and of telling the story. In my next section I shall concentrate on the problems of 'telling' that Milton and the reader have to share. In Chapter 4 I shall pick up the parallel problems of writing poetry.

(ii) NARRATIVE AND MEANING

Milton, like other literary artists, aims to tell a story and to give us a sense of meaning which will tell us why this story is important. A widely diffused if not much argued modern assumption is that the ideal way to achieve this end is to combine the two aims as closely as possible – as, for example, by dwelling heavily on the meaning which the events have for the sympathetic characters who participate in them, and whose choices determine the way the story will go. Milton's classical models, however, as well as his Biblical sources, made this kind of unity difficult if not impossible for him. The nature of his central characters – God, Christ, Satan, Adam, Eve – is such that human empathy with them has to be at most sporadic. The meaning of these events cannot be presented as merely inherent in the human choices that lead to action, but has to be presented to us separately from the action, which can then be seen to embody it. The classical models no less than the Biblical subject-matter require such a separation. The 'meaning' of the *Iliad* is not to be encompassed by the story of Achilles, though the story of Achilles is certainly a central example of the meaning; the interpretation of life that the poem offers is evidently larger than any of the lives that embody that interpretation. Homer's gods, unlike Milton's, are irrational and haphazard. The meaning of life, under these conditions, must be created by the human individuals themselves and, though the individuals vary, the story will always be much the same. It will always be a story about death, about the choice to purchase glory though the price is death – a story whose meaningful issue is essentially momentary in its demonstration, and whose moments are isolated from one another, hardly accumulative and without any promise of change. Troy *will* fall; that is the vanishing-point of the story of the *Iliad*. But beyond the fall of Troy the Gods will remain the same and the conditions of human life will continue to present only the same chances and the same restrictions for all men.

This means that the non-progressive structure of meaning in the *Iliad* imposes severe limitations on the story that we follow. It means that meaningful actions in the poem tend to follow one another by a system of open variation rather than one of closed sequence. Critics have always noticed that the *episode* is the characteristic unit of the *Iliad*'s structure. Achilles quickly sinks into the background of the narrative, and the action progresses by retailing the *aristeia*, or prowess-episodes, of one hero after another, arranged rather like pictures in an exhibition, with only the occasional 'marker' to point forward to the sequential necessities of the Achilles story. There is no necessity in the mere story that Milton has to tell that prevents organisation along these lines. Reading through the Old Testament we find a not dissimilar set of *aristeia*, narrated in respect of one character after another. The meaning of these separate lives, arranged in a chronological row rather than the geographical framework of the *Iliad*, is again dependent on an external system of interpretation that is given by divine fiat and only exemplified by human choices. The choice of Adam-and-Eve (obedience or dis-obedience) is recapitulated in Cain-and-Abel, Abraham-and-Lot, in Isaac-and-Ishmael, Saul-and-David, etc.; as the choice of Achilles (honour or survival) is recapitulated in Hector, Sarpedon, Patroclus, etc. The repeat of the situation takes away, of course, in both cases, the particular psychology of the choice and makes the individual representative rather than unique. But there is an essential difference: the Bible stories can be read (and were so read by Milton, as by other Christians) as progressive and leading to real change. The later examples (culminating in Jesus Christ) exemplify the meaning more completely than the earlier ones. The earlier ones are seen as *types* or foreshadowings of the Christian examples; and thus they have a meaning beyond that inherent in the original choice, a meaning as preparatives for the full and radical change that the Incarnation brings about. *Paradise Lost*, Books X and

XI, show this system in full flower and I will talk about it again when I come to deal with the structure of these books. The stories of the Bible are thus, for the Christian reader, both like and unlike those epic stories that appear in the *Iliad*. The combined Hellenic and Hebraic pressure on Milton to show life as a series of detached episodes inevitably came to him accompanied by a Christian counter-pressure, obliging him to admit into his system such a degree of *cause* or *motivation* as would hold together the whole story, and everything attached to it, inside a single progressive or developing revelation. *Paradise Lost* is both a story through time and a story out of time; in the former dimension it shows development, but in the latter dimension it is essentially static (though even this is not entirely true, and I will offer some qualifications at a later point). This juggling feat is accomplished in part by substituting (as has often been noticed) the dimension of space for the otherwise scarcely apprehensible dimension of static time.

Marjorie H. Nicolson has said that '*Paradise Lost* [is] the first modern cosmic poem in which a drama is played against a background of interstellar space' ('Milton and the telescope', reprinted in *Science and Imagination*, 81). Movement through space in *Paradise Lost* has certainly some of the qualities of modern 'space epics', and it is worth noticing that in such examples of the genre as *2001* or *Star Wars* the dimension of time is largely usurped by that of space. More pertinent to my purpose here is the point that *Paradise Lost* is held within the circumference of God's infinite patience and unity. From His point of view all bodies are equally present in time. In their simultaneity He sees spatially the time the narrative will take to bring them into collision. When God in book III sees Satan flying towards earth 'coasting the wall of heaven on this side night' (III, 71) it is in spatial terms that the future is realised, thus combining in one perception man's future and God's present:

> Him God beholding from his prospect high,
> Wherein past, present, future he beholds,
> Thus to his only Son foreseeing spake. . . .   (77–9)

The interaction of these two pressures on Milton's poem, towards diversity and unity, dispersion and development, can be studied in a number of ways and observed at a great variety of points. We can see that the gesture towards episodic interest which we find in such characteristic epic moments as Satan's journey to earth, Eve's dream, Raphael's survey of astronomy is normally accompanied by a doctrinal understanding of the material which tethers it to the central concerns of the poem in a quite un-Homeric way. Even in what may seem most formally imitative of the classical mode, in such a passage as the catalogue

of devils in Book I, lines 356 ff., the formal imitation tends to become
absorbed into the overall interpretative scheme and so is rendered
unepisodic. The catalogue of devils derives from the catalogue of ships
and warriors in Book II of the *Iliad* and the catalogue of Latin generals
in *Aeneid*, Book VII. It is usually assumed that the original epic purpose
of the catalogue was to provide for later listeners a sense of which
ancestor, whose tribal hero, was in at the great event. The catalogue
provides a map, as it were, of the lands that were involved, and so a
link between the listeners' present sense of themselves and the vanished
world of the epic action.

Milton's catalogue is, like Virgil's, a list of enemies, and of enemies
whose names and meanings have survived into more modern times.
These are

> Powers that erst in heaven sat on thrones;
> Though of their names in heavenly records now
> Be no memorial blotted out and rased
> By their rebellion from the books of life.
> Nor had they yet among the sons of Eve
> Got them new names . . . .   (I, 360–5)

The names and deeds that follow in the list are, we are given to understand, further examples of *accommodation*, not realities but modes of
belief that superstitious men have invented. The powers of evil that
appear in Milton's Hell are described and have meaning *as if* such names
were real. But the names, the list and the self-sufficiency of the episode
are all on the surface only. Beneath the surface is the doctrinal understanding that links this passage to the centre of the story. The catalogue
is for Milton rather more an occasion for judgement than for accumulation of morally neutral data (proper for an episode). The exposed
fictional nature of the data – the names and stories – throws our
attention on to what is more truly real, the moral (that is, human)
meaning of the activities by which false gods make themselves known,
and by which men give importance to fictional selves, separate from or
opposed to God, whose parasites and parodies they are:

> yea, often placed
> Within his sanctuary itself their shrines,
> Abominations; and with cursed things
> His holy rites, and solemn feasts profaned. . . .   (388–91)

At the level of the doctrine which the poem requires us to bear in mind
the self-proclaimed self-sufficiency of the devils is undercut in advance.
If it were true, it would allow them an episodic existence, such as, from
time to time, they believe they could have, when they would

rather seek
Our own good from ourselves, and from our own
Live to ourselves, though in this vast recess,
Free, and to none accountable. . . .   (II, 252-5)

But it is the punishment of the Devils to take images and fictions as realities, to confuse subjective and objective, what is seen with what exists. The inhabitants of Hell, like the inhabitants of the *Iliad*, live on the assumption of their own historical importance; and within this assumption the catalogue of devils is a true episode. But from the point of view of the pious believer it is all characteristically Satanic, 'self-begot, self-raised'. Just as Death, a non-shape (II, 666-70), acquires substance only by what he feeds upon, so the other inhabitants of Hell are mental constructs waiting for the will of the malign believer to give them reality, history and the right to their own episodes.

The changed status that 'episodes' are bound to have in a poem suffused by doctrinal unity is shown in Virgil's imitation of Homer as well as Milton's. Homer's poem has an ending which is, for all its individual brilliance, an unsatisfactory conclusion for the narrative. In the last book Achilles and Priam achieve something like a *katharsis* of emotion; but the other heroes, still alive, are left dangling in limbo. Something of this epic inconsequence is also found at the end of the *Aeneid*. But the culmination of the whole movement of that poem in the figure of Augustus imposes (at one level at least) the same kind of compelling forward drive as the parallel figure of Jesus Christ gives to *Paradise Lost*. The foundation of Rome, the mastery of the world, the invention of law and order – these may be seen as giving meaning and interconnection to all the episodes, to Palinurus and Amata and Helenus and Dido, as well as to the principal characters involved in the ending. But the *Aeneid* cannot be described as a progressive narrative carrying us through time from cause to effect, any more than the *Iliad* can. Its progressions and its discontinuities are designed to give us, the readers, a sense of space between story and meaning, between what happened and what was meant to happen, and Milton was able to draw on its example to create his own variation on the epic tradition.

The relation between the narrative sequence and the doctrinal meaning in both the *Aeneid* and *Paradise Lost* imposes on the author the need to balance the two interests by breaking up what is continuous in time, 'placing' events in a relation to one another opposed to that of mere sequentiality. The most obvious technique to achieve this end is that of flashback, the reminiscence of past events in a present to which they are thematically related. Milton's extensive use of this method takes him behind the *Aeneid* to its model, the *Odyssey* of Homer. The forward pressure of destiny in Virgil's poem uses for its own purpose the legacy left by the *Odyssey*, but the mode of the earlier poem is entirely visible through the structure of the later one. Aeneas is shipwrecked near Carthage as Odysseus had been at Phaeacia, and is helped by the royal lady Dido as Odysseus was by the royal lady Nausicaa. In the court he tells the story of his wanderings (as Odysseus does, in Books IX, X, XI), and the marvellous tale he tells, up to the point where we first met him in Book I, is an important part of the fascination he exerts over us as readers, as over his original courtly audience.

The disruption of time in the *Aeneid* is less extreme than in the *Odyssey*. The flashback occupies only two books, and the narrative quickly picks up in Book IV what it dropped in Book I. This might be thought to show that Virgil's progressive poem has no functional use for flashbacks. In the *Odyssey*, however, they are their own justification. Odysseus' return is continually cross-cut, first of all by the story of Telemachus' search for his father, and the brief retellings of his history that occur in the courts of Nestor and Menelaus. In Book VIII Demodocus, the official bard of Alkinoos of Phaeacia, sings about Odysseus, but Homer cuts him short to allow the hero himself the major flashback. The cross-cutting technique of the *Odyssey* is as fitting to its subject-matter as it is foreign to the *Aeneid*. The *Odyssey* is a poem of *NOSTOS*, return, focused by the backward glance. Men's minds are here dominated by the past, by what happened at Troy, the great emotional experience of their culture, in whose shadow they pass the rest of their lives. It is not surprising that the poem is structured as a series of attempts to recover and use the past. The *Aeneid* is, on the other hand, a poem pressing forward, in doctrine if not always in the narrative. The first half is dominated less by the reminiscence of what happened at Troy than by the prophecies of what will happen in Italy, and by the model of the future that the present holds – Dido as Carthaginian foreshadowing Hannibal, and as African queen foreshadowing Cleopatra.

Paradise Lost is, in its own way, a poem dominated by its past, by the question 'How did we get to this point?' The question here cannot be answered, of course, by mere story-telling about the route taken. It is also a poem about the way forward. The Fall of man is a beginning of one story as well as the end of another one. The subject-matter thus encourages the poem to be liberal beyond example with both flashback and prophecy (or anticipation). In fact, the story-line virtually disappears under the cross-hatching of these alternative perspectives. The amount of attention Milton's poem gives to retrospect (Books V–VIII) and prophecy (Books XI–XII) establishes these as of comparable weight to present-tense narrative. In the Homeric and Virgilian poems it remains clear that the narrative is the real spine of the poem, and the present-to-future of the hero the principal focus of our interest. But in *Paradise*

Lost our attention is split not only between widely separated places and yawning differences of time but also between different contenders for the hero-ship (Satan, Adam, Christ), not only the history of man being related but also that (more parallel than precedent) of the fallen angels. The core of the poem, the central four books, gives us a vast series of retrospective reconstructions of the past, by which Adam builds up the experience and knowledge he needs in order to justify the second half of the poem in which he will, like Aeneas, journey forward from myth to history (though he proceeds by loss to his earthly city, as Aeneas proceeded by gain). Odysseus and Aeneas conduct their own retrospectives, but Adam is listener or questioner, not speaker. The flashbacks here offer us (as I say) intellectual precedents rather than narrative ones. Odysseus' narrative tells us that he lives in a magical world which differentiates him from other men; Aeneas' retrospect establishes him as a Man of Destiny carrying the burden of the past into a realisation of the future. But neither of these flashbacks establishes a context of meaning by which alone we know how to judge the hero. Adam is seen as to some extent the double of Satan on one side and of Christ on the other side, and the poem of *Paradise Lost* may be said to turn on the relationship of these three figures, who never meet (or, if they do, only under the most straitened circumstances). The recapitulations and variations in destiny that flashback and prophecy allow make it possible for Milton to establish a sequence which is not handled primarily as a narrative, but as a set of variations, differentiated chiefly by the meanings that can be extracted from parallel situations.

Retrospect and prophecy are two of the traditional techniques of setting out the meanings of epic actions, as against straight narrative sequence. And in these terms we can see how prodigally Milton takes over and transforms the methods he inherited. He uses these techniques, we may say, to set out his events in an order which does not deny a narrative construction but which places in front of such a structure a set of alternative methods of construing the material, noting variant sequences and parallels, thematic designs and interpretative arrangements of the action. One of the most obvious ways in which he does this is through the order of the books.

Once again it is possible to see that Milton found a model for his technique in the classical epic structure that he took to be the *just* shape that the civilised poet was bound to imitate. And once again one can note that the Humanist doctrine of imitation allows Milton to start with the form but to go beyond it in adaptation to his Christian meaning. Milton first published *Paradise Lost* in ten books (1667), but in the second edition he revised and divided into twelve (1674). The new number links his poem with the *Aeneid*, and through that with the twenty-four-book forms of the *Iliad* and the *Odyssey*. But the connection

with the books of the *Aeneid* has more to it than mere number.* It is
fairly clear in reading the *Aeneid* that Virgil designed his poem as a
symmetrical structure. In this, as in other matters, he follows Homer.
In the *Odyssey* the basic four-book divisions build up into a binary

.

*The perception that the 1674 (twelve-book) version of *Paradise Lost* is
related to the twelve-book structure of the *Aeneid* creates some difficulties,
which need to be exposed and discussed. For the points that I take to indicate
symmetrical arrangement are present in the original ten-book version (1667)
no less than in the twelve-book version. The centrality of Book VI, which
is the most obvious feature of the *Aeneid* structure, seems to be self-consciously
incorporated into the structure of *Paradise Lost*, other evidence being capped
by the proem to Book VII where we hear that 'half yet remains unsung'.
In the ten-book version, however, these words seem misplaced, whether they
refer to the whole poem (as I assume) or simply to Raphael's narration (as is
sometimes supposed), since six books are behind but only four books ahead –
Books VII (later VII and VIII), VIII (later IX), IX (later X), X (later XI
and XII). If one believes that the symmetries are really there, one must face
the problem of describing a ten-book structure which incorporates and exposes
the symmetries which are described above in terms of the twelve-book version.
To be plausible such a structure must be reasonably simple and bear some
relation to the background of the poem.
    The history of the writing of *Paradise Lost*, beginning with plans for a
five-act drama and only subsequently developed into an epic poem, creates an
initial probability that the ten books bear some relation to an original set of
five acts. The simplest version of this would be a structure in which each
two-book unit equalled one act. This does not, however, produce meaningful
divisions, and the obvious symmetries are destroyed by it. A slightly more
complex version of dramatic form, however, avoid these disadvantages. This
assumes a Greek dramatic structure, with prologue, three episodes, and exode
or epilogue. The two books in Hell create the obvious prologue for this form.
The narrative of human history from the Fall to the Second Coming supplies
the exode. The 'action proper' runs therefore from the hymn to light at the
beginning of Book III to the bickering twilight of Adam and Eve after the
Fall. The difficulty of the form is that it assumes that each 'episode' in this
vast drama is in two parts, one before the Fall of the Angels and one after.
Thus Book III is joined to Book X (Book IX in the ten-book numeration),
Book IV joins Book IX (Book VIII in the ten-book version), and Book V
joins Books VII and VIII (Book VII in the older numbering). Book VI is
then seen as a central or transitional moment in the poem (as numerically – in
terms of line-count – it *is* the centre of the poem). The form described may
be represented diagrammatically by some shape such as the following:

		Prologue in Hell: Books I and II	
Book III	Heaven/Satan	Book IX (= X)	Heaven/Satan
Book IV	The Garden	Book VIII (= IX)	The Garden
Book V	Satan's Revolt	Book VII (= VII and VIII)	Man's creation
		Book VI The War in Heaven	
		Exode into history: Book X (= XI and XII)	

If this diagram is compared with that given in the text on p. 40, it will be
noticed how many of the symmetries of one version reappear in the other.

structure, 12 books of wandering (4+4+4), followed by 12 books of life in Ithaca. So also in the *Aeneid* we find four books of wandering at the beginning and four books of fighting at the end. But much more significant is the binary form centred on Book VI, the descent into Hades, which is not only the centre of the poem in numerical terms but the hinge in a structure of descent and ascent. The prophecy of Anchises at the end of Book VI represents the climax of the prophetic voices that have sounded throughout the preceding books. Now the nature of the Roman destiny is made clear. The rest of the poem must put this vision into effect. The poem thus breaks into two equal halves, which are set against one another in complementary balance, a Troy half and a Rome half, a recovery half and a discovery half, an *Odyssey* half and an *Iliad* half, a voyaging half and a warfare half – and no doubt many more.

It is possible to argue further that the material in the two halves of the *Aeneid* is so disposed as to mark a symmetry perceptible to individual readers, but difficult to imagine as perceptible in the bardic conditions of Homer – a symmetry of events marked as related by their position in terms of descent down one side of the poem and ascent up the other side. Thus the false succour that Aeneas receives in Carthage, the invitation to repose in the false Rome, the City of Juno not of Jupiter, in Book IV, is matched at the corresponding point on the upward slope (Book VIII) by the succour Aeneas receives in the true Rome, the city of Evander, the city of humility and not of luxury. It is, indeed, possible to argue this; but it is by no means clear how far Virgil intended such detailed correspondences to be necessary to our sense of the poem. What is clear is that Milton, beginning with imitation of the two-part structure of the *Aeneid*, went on to devise a much more elaborate overall plan, whose symmetries are clearly intended to be part of the meaning.

The structure of the *Aeneid* offered Milton a model of symmetry which included some suggestion of ways in which symmetrically placed but sequentially separated events could be made to refer to one another. Milton's disposition of his story seems designed to allow an even sharper use of the same technique. His Book VI occupies a role similar to that of Book VI in Virgil's poem. The proem of Book VII speaks of a change of focus now due to be put into effect:

> Half yet remains unsung, but narrower bound
> Within the visible diurnal sphere;
> Standing on earth, not rapt above the pole,
> More safe I sing with mortal voice. . . .   (21–4)

In the first half of the poem the narrative has been 'rapt above the pole', visiting God in Heaven as well as Satan in Hell and hearing of heavenly actions in Raphael's narrative. Only Book IV, set in the Garden, fails to fulfil the distinction made. And in Books VII–XII we are constantly on earth, hearing of the creation of the planet, of the animals, man and eventually woman, as well as the actions of the temptation and fall, the guilt, the expulsion, and Michael's narrative of Biblical history leading to the Atonement and the Second Coming. Only the narrative's return to Heaven and Satan's return to Hell in Book X really interrupt this earthbound progress (as the visit to Eden interrupted the first half). Thus in *Paradise Lost*, as in the *Aeneid*, we have six books of violent movement and change followed by six books of more restricted movement, concentrated on a particular and crucial area of struggle. If one sets out the twelve books of *Paradise Lost* in terms of a descent followed by an ascent, one finds oneself with a diagram that points to many of the central connections in the poem:

Book I }	Fallen life	Book XII }	Fallen life
„ II }	in Hell	„ XI }	on earth
Book III	Heaven/Satan	Book X	Heaven/Satan
Book IV	The Garden	Book IX	The Garden
Book V }	Gabriel's	Book VIII }	Gabriel's
„ VI }	narration	„ VII }	narration

In explicating this diagram we can conveniently begin with the central four books of narration. Moving up one step from this, we come to Book IV on one side, facing Book IX on the other. The relationship of these two books is one of the most obvious things in the poem. In Book IV we arrive with Satan in the Garden and see him make his first moves of temptation and seduction. After the giant interruption of Raphael's narrative, we pick up his action again in Book IX, and see there the completion of those things begun before. The Fall completed, we return to Heaven in Book X to hear God's epilogue on the Garden, as in the corresponding place in Book III we heard His prologue. In Book III the Son had offered to descend and redeem man; in X He descends to condemn him. In III Satan enters into the world; in X he leaves it. In III the Heavens celebrate the Son's self-sacrifice to redeem man; in X Hell celebrates Satan's victory in debauching man. Beyond these correspondent books lie four more, Books I and II on one side and Books XI and XII on the other. Both belong together as continuous narrative, in one case the narrative of Satan's post-Fall survival among the ills of Hell and the recovery of a heroic sense of self in warfare against man and God; in the other case the narrative is of man's post-lapsarian survival among the ills of the World and the achievement of a blessed sense of self as still capable of salvation through the inter-cession of the Son. The two falls, that of Satan and that of Man, are not simply preceding and subsequent parts of a central narrative line; they are also two contrasting versions of the same theme, by which we learn from one what has been avoided or unstated in the other. And this thematic, spatial rather than chronological, relationship of inter-woven plot and sub-plot is characteristic of the whole poem. Milton's necessary avoidance of the episodic structure of Homer has not com-mitted him to simple progressive narrative : the complexity of relationship from part to part revivifies, to some extent, the openness of relationship between the parts that we find in the Homeric form. The poem is not only, or even chiefly, in terms of its effect, a progression from beginning to end; it is also a series of static tableaux, thematically related and as capable of being read backwards as forwards. We the readers are not being asked, of course, to read any other way than from beginning to end. It is only in this arranged perspective that we see the correspon-dences and relationships as we are meant to. Let us notice, in these terms, how we enter into the poem and respond to the new things we meet.

The very opening of the poem combines meaning and chronology in an interesting way. The Argument to Book I sketches for us the kind of backward drift of meaning (towards an ultimate 'cause') that has to be invoked before we reach the point where a proper forward movement can begin. This sketch, as I say, indicates the outline of the movement, but not the minutely devious means by which Milton organises the transitions from one period of time to another:

The first book proposes . . . man's disobedience . . . then touches the prime cause . . : the serpent, or rather Satan in the serpent; who revolting from God . . . was . . . driven out of heaven. . . . Which action passed over, the poem hastes into the midst of things, presenting Satan with his angels now fallen into hell. . . . here Satan with his angels lying on the burning lake, thunderstruck and astonished, after a certain space recovers. . . .

The poem itself largely avoids the explicit chronology which sustains the Argument and moves, rather, by altering our perspective. It begins, as it must, with meaning – a meaning identical for *him* then and for *us* now : 'man's first disobedience and the fruit . . . death . . . till one greater man/Restore us'. Most obviously the time is the reader's present moment; but it is also the eternal present of the Holy Spirit, who spoke the same truth at the Creation, to Moses on Sinai and through Jesus at the Pool of Siloam. As the lines progress, however, the focus narrows from the eternity of such truth to the particular moment of *this* inspiration, Milton writing this poem at a particular point in time, contemplating the eternal, but also hoping to be granted the starting-point of a particular vision. We are made aware that we are sharing the viewpoint

of the creator of the poem as his imagination scans the abyss of time
for a beginning to his narrative. From eternity he closes in on Adam
and Eve, but the meaning of their crucial action has to be sought for
even before that beginning. The movement of the poem reflects the
movement of its author's mind through the material; but gradually, as
he stretches towards a true beginning, the house-lights (so to speak)
begin to fade; we cease to be so aware of the scene as one being inspected
for its meaning, and more and more it assumes the quality of a narrative
reality which we are absorbed into. The change of focus is largely
achieved by subtle changes in the verb-tenses. The narrator in the present
first seeks inspiration in the present ('say first . . . who first . . .') to reach
an event in the past and a causal figure in the past – 'The infernal
serpent: he it was who . . . deceived'. Having reached the figure of
Satan the narrator can begin to elaborate his context. He asks the
question *When* this happened and offers an answer in terms of a continuous 'life-span' for the devil, 'What time his pride/Had cast him out
of heaven'. Like a composer establishing a new key-signature, he brings
extra reinforcement to the new centre of attention, building up a complex
of relationships around it. He tells us more about the Fall of the
angels. But Milton himself is still part of our picture, showing himself
telling the story. 'Him the almighty power/Hurled headlong flaming
from the ethereal sky' he says of Satan. He does not say 'had hurled',
which is the action seen from the point of view of Satan; the language
points back to the author. But not for long. As we are told about Satan
lying in the pool for nine days we begin to feel ourselves lying there with
him. By the time we get to the *now* in line 54 we are sharing a present
tense which is all Satan's, not Milton's and not the Holy Ghost's:

> for now the thought
> Both of lost happiness and lasting pain
> Torments him. . . .

We see what he sees, and feel with him while he feels it. We are now in
a position to progress along a straight narrative line with our secured,
even if only short-term, guide. With only minor adjustments we can
move forward through two books of continuous time. The memory of
the fall, the rallying cries, the recovery from the pool, the infernal
council, the decision to send Satan, and his voyage to the earth – all
these follow one another in the expected order. It is only when we reach
the beginning of Book III that we have to face again the problem of the
poem's time-sequence and the possibility that it consists of a series of
giant discrete blocks rather than a continuous fabric.

But this is to advance too quickly, and to oversimplify. The relation
of the end of Book II to the beginning of Book III is typically

ambiguous. At the end of Book II we leave Satan, newly arrived out of chaos, contemplating Heaven and Earth. Book III begins with the famous apostrophe to the element Satan has finally achieved:

> Hail, holy Light, offspring of heaven first-born!

We might, for a moment, think that Satan was still speaking. The hint of one continuity and the quick correction of it by an alternative phrasing of the material is typical of Milton. For at the beginning of Book III we find ourselves, in fact, removed from the world of Satanic utterance, back to the opening of Book I, with the author, his Inspirer and the start of all things, when

> the voice
> Of God, as with a mantle didst invest
> The rising world of waters dark and deep,
> Won from the void and formless infinite.   (III, 9–12)

The poem now undertakes the very pattern of these lines in its large-scale handling of the material. The voice of Milton (like that of God) wins back from the moral *void* of the Satanic books a renewed sense of a world bathed in light and truth and *mantles* it in his understanding of providential protection. Continuity with the moral chaos of the Satanic past is not thrown away, however, though the point of view is shifted so radically that at first we might think so. The shift of focus shows us narrative transformed into meaning. We learn that the view-point on action is at least as important as the continuity of the action. God looks out of his light-drenched empyrean and sees, from his position far above, the action we have just left – Satan's voyage. There we saw it all at the level of Satan's eyes and in terms of Satan's intention. Satan looked at the Earth and saw it as a tiny object, apparently smaller than the moon:

> This pendent world, in bigness as a star
> Of smallest magnitude close by the moon.   (II, 1052–3)

Now the image of the big Satan and the small world – which is another way of saying the powerful Satan and the powerless world – is transformed. God comments:

> Only begotten Son, seest thou what rage
> Transports our adversary, whom no bounds
> . . . can hold; so bent he seems
> On desperate revenge, that shall redound
> Upon his own rebellious head.   (III, 80–6)

We look down on the tiny, self-important and self-ignorant figure with something like infinite condescension. And then (with God) we turn away. It is only after four hundred lines of celestial beatitude that we return to Satan, and yet another two hundred and fifty elapse before he speaks. Even then the disguise of 'a stripling cherub . . . Not of the prime, yet such as in his face/Youth smiled celestial' (636–8) prevents him and us from reassuming the infernal point of view. The continued presence of celestial beings and celestial landscape makes Satan a stranger in Book III, centres our interest in a region distant from and hostile to his purposes.

The disposition of the material of *Paradise Lost* into blocks separated by time, space and point of view is most obvious, as I have said above, in Milton's use of retrospection and prophecy in Books V–VIII and X–XI. It is in the vast back-narration in the middle of the poem that Milton is able to hide what turns out to be on further inspection the chronological beginning of the whole story (V, 577). The War in Heaven which follows (Book VI) bears something of the same relation to Book I as we have seen Book III bearing to Book II. In Book I we saw the Fall from the angle of the fallen. Now, some thousands of lines later, we can 'correct' that view by seeing their Fall from God's angle in a 'comic' version of their earlier 'tragic' picture of injured merit. But here the narrative continuity is even more vestigial than there. Milton hardly encourages us to go back and join together what he has so painstakingly put asunder. The effect aimed at is, I take it, one of perceived correspondence and renewed judgement, so that we learn the complexity of the moral design that is held within the infinite spaces of God's Providence. Milton must have known well that mode of narrative which occurs in much Romance (and particularly in Ariosto), where stories are regularly cut off at their most intense moments so that the denouement can be held over our heads while other stories build up to *their* climaxes. Milton gives us something of the moral cliff-hanger in moments like that noticed above where Satan is brought within sight of Earth and then (narratively speaking) whisked away again. But the generation of narrative excitement is low in the scale of Milton's concerns. He is more interested in using pause and delay to allow us to notice the variety of alternative attitudes inherent in the situation, so that the eventual Divine closure can be understood on the widest possible front.

From a God's-eye point of view the poem is a vast spatial *stasis*, stretching from everlasting to everlasting. But this doctrinal truth, while it can be evoked – and it is continually evoked by the methods I have described above – can hardly be told, and certainly cannot be narrated. For narrative depends on a sense of time; and the poem cannot be read except in the expectation of change, process, development. Not only

Adam and Eve, but also God (Father and Son) and Satan, Sin and Death, all use the language of past, present and future (and, using English, have little alternative), speaking as if grammatical tense also established causal relation. The Father foresees the Fall, the Son forecasts the Atonement; Satan invites the Devils to consider a future of revenge to recoup a past of defeat. We the readers not only attend to the local passage of time when characters leave, arrive, begin, continue, conclude, propose, achieve, but also read the whole poem as progressing to events in time – to the Fall and the Expulsion in the real events of the narrative and the First and Second Coming in the larger time-scale of prophecy and understanding. The observation that the Fall is a psychological myth which repeats itself in the developmental history of every individual does not stop it being apprehended in the poem as an event placed in time. The thematic connections provide a 'sub-plot' in the sense that they comment on and alter the significance of a 'main plot' reading which could stand meaningfully without them, though less richly.

The relationship between story and meaning that Milton deploys, each infringing the other, but neither denying the other, is close to the relationship that Milton, as Christian reader, found in the Bible. I have made this point in general already (above p. 26), but it is worth while looking at it again to note just how it works. The Old Testament was read as a repository of *true* stories (such as the Genesis story of the Fall of Man). But the truth of the Old Testament narratives only became complete for the Christian reader when they were viewed through the non-narrative doctrinal spectacles of the New Testament. The Pauline Epistles (especially that to the Hebrews) offer a series of superimposed commentaries on the basic Hebraic events. Their concern is to interpret what the reader already knows rather than describe new events. A mode of reading is thus sanctified as basic to religious practice. God's dealings remain much as they were told in the original stories; but our perception of the pattern in which the events and images of the Old Testament separate and cohere thickens and deepens as we read not only the Epistles but Midrashim and commentaries and lectures and glosses of Rabbis and Fathers, Exegetes and Reformers and Councils. And this was, of course, a powerful part of Milton's reading. Let us take one example of the way in which a part of the original Garden of Eden story acquired significance by being seen through the layers of subsequent reference (or apparent reference) – the meaning of the *serpent* who appears in Genesis 3 : 1–15 : 'Now the serpent was more subtil than any beast of the field which the LORD God had made . . . said unto the woman. . . . And the serpent said unto the woman. . . . And the LORD God said unto the woman, What is this that thou hast done? And the woman said, The serpent beguiled me, and I did eat. And the LORD

God said unto the serpent, Because thou hast done this, thou art cursed above all cattle, and above every beast of the field; upon thy belly shalt thou go, and dust shalt thou eat all the days of thy life: And I will put enmity between thee and the woman, and between thy seed and her seed; it shall bruise thy head, and thou shalt bruise his heel.' At this point the serpent slinks out of the story of Genesis, never to reappear.

What does it all mean? It would be easy to suppose, reading this story by itself, that we have here a series of observations about real snakes and an aetiological myth to explain why they are as they are – subtle or convoluted and twisted, cursed or disadvantaged (to conflate old and new vocabularies) by having no legs and so having to 'eat dust', frightening to women. But if one reads the verses not as an isolated myth, a fairy story or anthropological specimen, but within a doctrinal explanation of the whole of human experience, the *serpent* cannot be simply itself; it must stand for a more generalised enmity to mankind, not simply an enemy, but the Enemy *(Sathanas)*. To suppose that Moses (or God) wished us to understand this when he wrote Genesis (and how could He have wished anything less?) is to suppose that the key to the meaning is found elsewhere in His writings (or Scripture). The Enemy appears elsewhere, of course, in the Bible, and with especial force for the Christian reader appears in serpent-like or related contexts in the New Testament. In Revelation, 12:3-11, St John the Divine describes the battle between Good and Evil as between God and the Dragon, the Dragon appearing in verse 9 as 'that old serpent called the Devil and Satan which deceiveth the whole world' (cf. Revelation, 20:2). But the key connection is probably that supplied by Paul in Romans, 16:20. Paul has been exhorting his brethren to be 'wise unto that which is good, and simple concerning evil', and goes on: 'And the God of peace shall bruise Satan under your feet shortly.' It seems likely enough that Paul and John were consciously picking up the Genesis story and giving it a new Christian meaning. But they were also making it impossible, of course, for the Christian reader to think of Genesis 3 without the other parts of the total design adhering to it. The natural Christian assumption is that these meaning were inherent in the story of the Fall from the earliest (Mosaic) telling; they were not clear to the bleared sight of Old Testament readers, but were finally clarified – not added – by those who had received the revelation of Jesus Christ. Reading the Bible (under instruction) is thus an accumulative experience, as the same ideas, images, phrases, echo and re-echo and move towards clarification and total coherence.

This process, by which the several separated parts of one reading experience gradually accumulate a meaning, is one that we would expect to find imitated in Milton, and indeed *Paradise Lost* does seem to offer both narrative dispersion and narrative accumulation in a way that separates it from its classical models, though its method is not, of course, precisely similar to that of Scripture (see above, pp. 27 ff). Take the crucial moment in the story when Adam first meets Eve. This is told us twice, at widely separated points. In Book IV, lines 449–89, Eve tells Adam her earliest memories, how she awoke 'under a shade of flowers', how she looked into a pool and saw a beautiful creature, how an invisible voice led her towards Adam, and finally how, frightened by his manly looks, she tried to fly away but was prevented by his claims and his hand. In Book VIII we hear the other half of the same story when Adam (in his turn) tells to Gabriel the story of *his* beginning. Now we learn how Adam besought God for a mate, and God made Eve out of Adam's rib. We see the same process of meeting as described in Book IV, but with a different interpretation. Eve saw Adam and was frightened:

> I espied thee, fair indeed and tall,
> . . . yet methought less fair,
> Less winning soft, less amiably mild,
> Than that smooth watery image; back I turned . . .
>
> (IV, 477–80)

For Adam the turning back is, however, a symptom of the quality of female virtue, and the scene is described in terms not of sensory adjectives but of abstract nouns. Her turning away is now said to have been due to 'innocence and virgin modesty,/Her virtue and the conscience of her worth'. Her yielding is likewise seen in terms of abstract characteristics:

> I followed her, she what was honour knew,
> And with obsequious majesty approved
> My pleaded reason
>
> (VIII, 508–10)

How are we meant to read the relationship between these two passages? Are we meant to take each separately as an expression of the character of the speaker, and as part of individual memory rather than shared event? Or are we meant to collate the two, noting what is common and what is different in the two accounts (as I have done above)? Since Eve's version precedes Adam's, are we meant to take the former into account when reading the latter, but not vice versa? Such questions seem significant for the modern reader, but seem to be significant for the poem largely by their irrelevance to its own processes. The first meeting of Adam and Eve (like their going to bed: IV, 736 ff; VIII, 510 ff.) is one of the events in which the circuit of the poem suddenly brings the careful reader face to face with the divergent points of view within which the action is held. The effect sought is presumably a transfer of attention from action to contemplation, from what happens to the meaning behind that happening, seen differently by different observers. What looks like progression from one point of view seems more like stasis when plotted from several points of view. And this perception is procured by innumerable small interactions rather than a few large ones.

One large-scale effect of Milton's way of ordering the material of his poem is that he can delay introducing the Garden of Eden and its inhabitants until he has accumulated around it the complexity of alternative attitudes. Even the 'Argument' set before Book IV reveals the pressure of what we have learned on what is before us:

The Argument

Satan now in prospect of Eden, and nigh the place where he must now attempt the bold enterprise which he undertook alone against God and man, falls into many doubts with himself, and many passions, fear, envy, and despair; but at length confirms himself in evil, journeys on to Paradise, whose outward prospect and situation is described, overleaps the bounds, sits in the shape of a cormorant on the tree of life, as the highest in the garden to look about him. The garden described; Satan's first sight of Adam and Eve; his wonder at their excellent form and happy state, but with resolution to work their fall; overhears their discourse, thence gathers that the tree of knowledge was forbidden them to eat of, under penalty of death; and thereon intends to found his temptation, by seducing them to transgress: then leaves them a while to know farther of their state by some other means. Mean while, Uriel descending on a sunbeam warns Gabriel, who had in charge the gate of Paradise, that some evil spirit had escaped the deep, and passed at noon by his sphere in the shape of a good angel down to Paradise, discovered after by his furious gestures in the mount. Gabriel promises to find him ere morning. Night coming on, Adam and Eve, discourse of going to their rest: their bower described; their evening worship. Gabriel drawing forth his bands of night-watch to walk the round of Paradise, appoints two strong angels to Adam's bower, lest the evil spirit should be there doing some harm to Adam or Eve sleeping; there they find him at the ear of Eve, tempting her in a dream, and bring him, though unwilling, to Gabriel; by whom questioned, he scornfully answers, prepares resistance, but hindered by a sign from heaven, flies out of Paradise.

Our introduction to Adam and Eve is set into a context elaborately prepared for. Paradise is presented to us by Satan, the character in the poem best known to us. We have watched him winging his way towards this goal, aware also of the contradictions and self-torment inherent in his attitude. The external tensions gone, we now watch the internal tensions boil over, as the moral contradictions of self-love and other-destruction come into inevitable play. Not only the proposals for his mission in Book II are remembered, but also God's rehearsal of the conditions of human felicity in Book III. We know, we have been told, that Satan will succeed, but within the condition of freedom, as it has been spelled out to us, every benevolent protective measure, short of infringing free will, will be taken. So we observe the busyness of Uriel and Gabriel around the human pair, with a sharper sense of *why* they have to act thus than of *what* their actions can achieve. Milton first offers us an unshadowed and wholly present picture of Adam and Eve, though coloured with a faint sense of the unrepeatability of the moment when

> So hand in hand they passed, the loveliest pair
> That ever since in love's embraces met,
> Adam the goodliest man of men since born
> His sons, the fairest of her daughters Eve.   (IV, 321–4)

But sharply set against this fairly free-standing response is the voyeur Satan's self-torturing ambivalence in prophecy:

> Ah gentle pair, ye little think how nigh
> Your change approaches, when all these delights
> Will vanish and deliver ye to woe,
> More woe, the more your taste is now of joy;
> Happy, but for so happy ill secured. . . .   (IV, 366–70)

The prophecy that those now joyful will shortly be in sorrow is common in epic. Achilles can hardly turn round without a horse or some other improbable informant telling him of the day he will fall under the arrow of Paris and Apollo. But Achilles is the victim of Necessity and knows he is so. Adam and Eve live under the aegis of Providence not of Necessity; and Satan's prophecy is only an expression of *his* pressure on the situation, the attitude he brings out of his past and experience, one (but only one) of the elements available for free choice. The tendency to read Satan's prophecy as an expression of his personality, his aim rather than his knowledge, is even clearer a few lines later, when his statement of love becomes more heavily ironic:

> League with you I seek,
> And mutual amity, so strait, so close,
> That I with you must dwell, or you with me
> Henceforth; My dwelling haply may not please
> . . . yet such

Accept your maker's work; he gave it me,
Which I as freely give; hell shall unfold,
To entertain you two, her widest gates. . . .　　　　　(375–82)

Here it is clear that the gloating prospect characterises an obsessed mind rather than an objective truth. We accept that this is really going to happen, but see that it will not happen because of this or any other pressure on the situation. Only the free choice of Adam and Eve will turn the accumulated pressure into event. And Providence extends an infinite patience to the choosing mind. At the end of Book IV Milton gives us one of his most obvious imitations of Homer. Satan, detected by the angelic squadron guarding Paradise, 'collecting all his might dilated stood'; and God, to avoid decision by mere battle, hangs out his golden scales in sign of what is determined. In a similar way Zeus hangs out golden scales in *Iliad*, VIII, 68–77, and XXII, 208–13, and Virgil has Jove do the same in *Aeneid*, XII, 725–7. The meaning of the scales in *Paradise Lost*, however, is and must be very different. In Homer and Virgil the tipping of the scales represents what will inescapably happen. Those who see the phenomenon understand their fates and must then proceed to fulfil them. But the necessity that the scales imply is potential only in *Paradise Lost*. Satan looks up and sees that he would be defeated if he were to fight. But the defeat is quite hypothetical here; he remains free to choose not to fight, and in fact does choose to flee. Like Malvolio's, his exit is threatening: 'I'll be revenged on the whole pack of you'; but by postponing necessity Milton has in fact removed its heroic power. The fight, when it comes, will be in very different terms.

The rejection of Necessity and the vesting of decision in the actual moment of freely choosing out of a complex of potentialities makes the movement towards climaxes a difficult matter in *Paradise Lost*. Given its resistance to the merely narrative, climaxes had, in fact, never been one of the strong points of the epic tradition. The Homeric method offers little that is complex in the way of accumulation. The climactic conflict between Hector and Achilles has been preparing, one might say, throughout the entire poem, but the 'preparation' consists largely in keeping the two heroes out of sight of one another till the climactic moment comes along (i.e. whenever the reciter decides it is time for it). And when the climactic conflict arrives Homer has no means at his disposal to express our sense of all that has led up to this moment. The pattern of conflict between two warriors (A throws a spear at B; B parries it and throws a spear at A) can be extended but hardly changed. Even in the *Aeneid*, when we come to the death of Turnus, we have to notice that the climactic nature of this battle and this death has to be expressed by the position it occupies in the poem rather than by anything said in the passage itself. What one can see in the *Aeneid* is the potential for accumulation which appears if one considers the state of mind in which the climactic deed is performed as at least as important as the deed itself. Achilles kills Hector to avenge Patroclus, but the motivation for the deed makes very little contribution to the actual description of the fight; there is no sense that Achilles would ever have 'forgiven' Hector. Aeneas likewise kills Turnus to avenge a friend (Pallas); but here the memory of Pallas makes the crucial difference between one kind of result and another, and it is carefully woven into our pattern of expectation. Aeneas hesitates over the prostrate Turnus; he (like us) is aware of the case to be made out for Turnus as a victim of circumstances. And then he sees the belt that Turnus had taken from Pallas when he killed him. It is this memory that drives his sword into Turnus' breast, so that (as Virgil says) it is actually Pallas himself who performs the revenge:

> Pallas te hoc vulnere, Pallas
> Immolat, et poenam scelerato ex sanguine sumit. (XII, 948-9)

(It is Pallas, Pallas, who kills you with this wound, imposes punishment on your criminal blood.)

In *Paradise Lost* the climactic exchange – between Satan and Eve, I suppose – is not simply a new and enlarged example of the conflicts we have met before, but a climax in the Biblical sense of a situation on which the weight of all our previous moral experience in the work exerts its full pressure, and which expresses and brings to fruition all that emotional weight. The different things we have seen in the course of the poem – Satan's view of man, God's view of man, the prophecy of Christ's intervention, the bad precedent of the Fall of the Angels – all these accumulate, not in the paratactic grammatical structure of Genesis or Homer – and . . . and . . . and – but with the complex subordination and internal relationship of Milton's hypotaxis – so . . . when . . . therefore is . . . what time . . . as if . . . so that. . . . We should note, of course, that the climax is one of understanding rather than of action. If one says that the interview between Eve and Satan is the climactic action in *Paradise Lost* (and the doubt itself is significant), and so comparable with the climactic duels of the *Iliad* and the *Aeneid*, one must go on to observe the complexity of such a judgement. The moral climax is clearly here set against a literal anticlimax. The 'heroic' promises of Satan, the intention to 'defeat' God are represented by an argument between a woman and a snake about eating an apple. The anticlimactic point is precisely the one Satan makes when he returns to Hell in Book X:

> Him by fraud I have seduced
> From his creator, and the more to increase
> Your wonder, with an apple; he thereat
> Offended, worth your laughter, hath given up
> Both his beloved man and all this world,
> To Sin and Death a prey, and so to us,
> Without our hazard, labour, or alarm. . . .   (X, 485–91)

But Milton accumulates towards the Bathos that Satan sees so as to make a point quite other than the bathetic one. The heroic gestures are made to accumulate towards an apple because Milton wishes to make clear to us (if not to Satan) the need the apple imposes on us to revise our notions of heroism or battle as appropriate to this complex world of spiritual conflict.

The conduct of the poem is thus a superimposed series of movements forward, but so superimposed on one another that no single sense of advance towards an end is endorsed. The death of Adam and Eve is announced as the consequence of eating the apple, just as death is announced as the consequence of Achilles' coming to Troy. But, for Achilles, death is a real end, an end of meaning, while for Adam and Eve 'death' turns out to be a thing problematical, still held open to choice inside Providence. In the formal terms of the poem, progression to an end can be as well (or better) viewed as an enlargement of understanding, an enlargement which has no end, and which accumulates centrifugally (like ripples in a pool) as we see more connections and parallels and parodies.

These connections can both operate in reinforcement of the poem's linear or chronological movement and also run counter to that dimension. Our attention is often drawn to the thematic or meaningful status of the events we see by the presentation of parallel patterns of words or things. This technique has been noted several times, but can bear some further exemplification. In Book II Satan so organises the 'great consult' that its climax will be the daring proposal that one person should venture out to test man's vulnerability, and God's weakness through man. The proposal produces (as expected) a gasp of dismay when the question takes the form *Who*?

> But first whom shall we send
> In search of this new world, whom shall we find
> Sufficient? Who shall tempt with wandering feet
> the dark unbottomed infinite abyss? . . .   (402–5)

The question asked, the audience sits on its hands:

> But all sat mute,
> Pondering the danger with deep thoughts; and each
> In other's countenance read his own dismay

Astonished.
    . . . till at last
Satan, whom now transcendent glory raised
Above his fellows, with monarchal pride
Conscious of highest worth, unmoved thus spake. . . .
                                                    (420–9)

The question, the silence and the answer have a resonance which is, as
so often with Milton, both Christian and classical. In Book VII of the
Iliad Hector challenges one of the Greeks to fight against him, single-
handed. At first no one is willing to take up the challenge:

He finished, and the Akhaians all sat hushed
Ashamed not to respond, afraid to do so
Until at length. . . .   (92–4) (Fitzgerald's trans.)

The form of the Satanic episode seems to be derived from Homer; the
meaning is, however, taken from theology, and is spelled out when the
episode reappears in Book III. There God forecasts the Fall and asks
who will undertake the Redemption:

Say heavenly powers, where shall we find such love,
Which of ye will be mortal to redeem
Man's mortal crime, and just the unjust to save,
Dwells in all heaven charity so dear?   (213–6)

And again, as in Hell:

He asked, but all the heavenly choir stood mute,
And silence was in heaven: on man's behalf
Patron or intercessor none appeared. . . .
And now without redemption all mankind
Must have been lost, adjudged to death and hell
By doom severe, had not the Son of God. . . .   (217–24)

The two passages are clearly designed to reflect on one another as well
as on the Homeric original; and I think it is equally clear that the second
one (Book III) gives us the true meaning, of which the diabolic version
is a parody. For one thing it is hard to conceive of Milton allowing
Christ to 'imitate' Satan; for another, the Son's intercession is close to
traditional doctrine, where Satan's proposal is Milton's own invention.
So we have to say we are given the parody before we are given the
truth it parodies, if *before* refers only to the explicit direction of the
poem. It may be, of course, that the material of the poem is never
separate from other relevant knowledge to this degree. Perhaps we should
notice, what Broadbent has pointed out, that Beelzebub's 'appeal for a

volunteer – "whom shall we send/In search of this new world" (II, 402) – is made effective before the divine parallel occurs in the poem by the reference to Isaiah's vision – "Also I heard the voice of the Lord, saying, whom shall I send, and who will go for us? And said I, Here am I; send me" (6:8)' (*Some Graver Subject*, 111). The Isaiah passage had long before this been seen as a type of the ministry of Christ (see the *Homiliae in Visiones Isaiae* of Origen). Part of the passage from Isaiah is, indeed, quoted by Christ as evidence for his own teaching, as reported in Matthew, 13:14 ff., and may have been reinforced in Milton's memory by the similarity of the opening lines of the chapter and the Book III vision of God enthroned (and correspondingly of Satan enthroned). If the passage from Isaiah is meant to be remembered as we hear the debate in Hell, then the sense of *before* and *after* in the poem is clearly limited in its relevance to the meaning of these moments. Satan is already seen to be a false Christ, a Mediator of destruction, when he makes his offer, and the driving home of the parallel when we reach Book III is not a matter of revaluing assumptions that the poem earlier imposed on us, but of reinforcing with further detail the assumptions which our grasp of theology and the Bible had already given to us.

In these terms it is not presumably an accident that the first complete action in *Paradise Lost* is a mock-creation – the creation of what seems to be a secular Greek city-state, the infernal city of Pandemonium. This creation is presented, first of all, as if free of judgement. It is only in the context of the whole poem that the status of the building becomes clear, as the meeting of Devils in Book X reflects back on the parliamentary debate in Book II. As we read through Books I and II in the natural order of reading we see much to admire, and I take it we were meant to see it. Does this mean that Milton is encouraging the reader to hold a 'wrong' view, of which he is not to be disabused till much later in the poem, when we learn the consequences of these secular and heroic 'virtues'? The assumption that the instructed Bible-reading audience will always judge the meaning by the known consequences is weaker here than in the previously cited example, for the creation of Pandemonium is a poetic invention with only vague doctrinal overtones. Certainly to rule out any positive response to the Devils' ingenuity and heroic persistence is to narrow the reader's freedom unduly. Stanley Fish has suggested, in a well-known argument, that we are indeed meant to hold 'wrong' views, so that we may be 'surprised by sin' (our own sin) when we find what is the consequence of such views. The argument as conducted seems too mechanical to be just, and too unresponsive to the variousness and complexity of the poetic medium. But it seems undoubtedly true that the shifting pattern of chronological and non-chronological information in the poem requires us constantly to be making cross-references and cross-judgements, correcting (without obliterating) what we formerly thought and anticipating fulfilments that need correction.

Another (and doctrinally simple) example of the way in which Milton builds up false types before he reveals true anti-types, so creating the context in which we have to understand the light and shading of the anti-type, appears at the end of Book II. In a poem less permeated by doctrine one might be tempted to think of Satan's adventurous flight from Hell as Homeric, episodic, haphazard, as in small part it is. But Milton has other aims in view as well. Satan (seeking 'deliverance for us all': II, 465) comes to the gate of the Underworld and meets there Sin, the Portress, and Death her son. The episode is one of the most powerful in the poem and powerful in a mode which is unusual if not unique in *Paradise Lost*. As I have noted above (p. 20) Milton avoids allegory on the whole: Deeds and Persons in the poem stand for themselves and require no deeper layer of meaning to support them. The point has been made by Rajan (*'Paradise Lost' and the Seventeenth Century Reader*, 163 ff.) that 'There is . . . only one simile which involves a literary allusion and only one place name, biblical or classical' occurring in Heaven. But Milton can appropriately break fast in Hell. Here is told the story of how Satan, conceiving his rebellion against God, had an immediate headache, out of which appeared (from the left side, of course) this shape or 'daughter', in whom Satan delighting engendered a second child, 'death'. The allegory is transparent and is meant to be so, simply reproducing James, 1:15: 'When lust hath conceived, it bringeth forth sin, and sin when it is finished, bringeth forth death.'

Milton avoids giving personalities, as against qualities, to Sin and Death (as he gives personalities to Belial or Moloch) because he wishes their meaning to loom larger than their existence. They are designed clearly to set up the *idea* of a dark parody or replica of the Trinity, in which the Father exalts the Son (or here the Daughter): 'Thou wilt bring me soon . . . among/The Gods who live at ease, where I shall reign/At thy right hand voluptuous' (866–9). Hell faces Heaven, not only as opposed to it, but also as parasitic upon it, not genuinely creative but only distortive of the true energies of Creation. True Creativeness, proceeding from love, aims at the freeing of the individual into the gift of his own Right Reason and the will that enacts it. The false creation does not liberate but enslaves: the lust and violence and hatred which bind together in a self-consuming knot the satanic or incestuous Trinity produces a ceaseless round of lust, generation, new lust, new generation, etc., in which each member preys on and exploits the other ('With terrors and with horrors compassed round/Of my own brood, that on my bowels feed': 862 ff.) So Satan comes to Eve, from beneath the garden, to deceive and exploit, to make man's race a part of the Satan-Sin-Death relationship. Raphael comes to Adam from above to liberate him by knowledge and to make him capable of freely refuting the Devil's arguments. The events *have* a chronological relationship which we cannot ignore, but also exist in a 'spatial' relationship to one another outside the time-sequence.

In a rather more pictorial and rather less narrative mode we can see the same technique being deployed in Book X when, the Father and the Son having meditated together on what can be done for fallen man, the Son comes down to earth to comfort and to prepare him. Suddenly and unsequentially the narrative switches ('Meanwhile ere thus') to Sin and Death, sitting 'In counterview within the Gates'. The word *counterview* used here may simply mean that they sat on either side of the gate and looked at one another (see line 235). But in the larger sense of the relationship established between the Divine and the Hellish sides of the human situation it is hard not to take it as showing Milton's consciousness of what he is doing: establishing by the *counterview* the force of the parody. Sin's opening words 'O Son . . .' can hardly be detached from the other Son–Father relationship we have just seen. And as the Son in Heaven is given 'All judgement whether in Heaven or earth or hell' (57) so here the Son feels 'new strength . . . and dominion given me large' (243–4). The ascent of these spirits to man is the means of establishing the middle role of man caught between the opposite effects his will and choice have released. Such parodic moments, which show us Evil in a non-narrative relationship to Good, illustrate the teeming fertility in mutation that Milton's cosmos contains, and the impossibility of making a simple diagram based on relationships of cause and effect. This makes for difficulty. In the interests of intellectual clarity readers often wish that Milton had endorsed a simplifying view of good as most truly itself when *enforced* on man by God; but these are simplicities which Milton clearly rejects. Instead, he shows us a dispersed universe centred on free-will, within which the argument for necessity can be seen to be, as he says, 'the tyrant's plea', locally effective but ultimately stultifying, a means of winning the battle but losing the war. This specious argument, that we understand the present by understanding the past, chaining events to one another in a necessary sequence, seems to be another Satanic misinterpretation of *Paradise Lost*. We must now turn to it to see how it affects our interpretation of the poem.

(iii) EPIC CAUSALITY

The epic poem, by its nature, is concerned with deeds so heroic that they have always had to be explained in terms of 'celestial interventions' or messages from Heaven. The formal opening of the epic is thus traditionally required not only to state a theme or subject ('the wrath of Achilles', 'the far journeys of the resourceful Odysseus', 'man's first disobedience') but also to relate the beginning of the sequence being told to the intention of a god who will explain and in some sense justify the scope of the events. In the *Iliad*, for example, Homer cannot describe the quarrel between Achilles and Agamemnon without first asking the question 'Which of the gods was it that made them quarrel?' Rather typically, Homer answers the question without seeming to raise any moral implication at all: 'It was Apollo, son of Zeus and Leto who started it, punishing the king of men for his discourtesy to his priest.' Homer presents to us the *cause* as a fact of nature, unquestioned and irresistible; it is presented without any apparent expectation of further questions; we are not invited to speculate further about motivation. Such bland objectivity or disinterest is not, however, to be emulated by later writers. Virgil shows his modernity by raising precisely the further question that Homer avoided. He tells us that it was Juno who caused the opening event, and then he goes on:

Tantaene animis caelestibus irae?   (I, 11)

– a line which Milton translates as 'Can envy dwell in heavenly breasts?' (IX, 729). Like Homer's Apollo, the Queen of Heaven provides an opening cause of the action; and like him she acts because she feels that her godhead has been slighted *(numine laeso)*, and for this reason she harried a good and pious man into a long course of suffering. Virgil, like Homer, puts human ethics and divine power on the opposite sides of the struggle; but having done so he then asks the un-Homeric question – can we really suppose that that is how it is? The framing of the question is, however, the limit of his modernity; he does not offer us a straight answer. He achieves an evasion, and does so chiefly through syntax. The question comes at the end of a verse paragraph. And when he starts his new paragraph we find that he is talking about history, not about ethics: 'An ancient city there was, Carthage by name. . . .' It might seem that the poet had forgotten the question he asked. But the movement of thought is not simply one of cancellation and renewal. The historical struggle between Rome and Carthage reflects the malice of Juno in a different dimension from the myth of Aeneas, but the reflection is there none the less. At the end of the introductory section Virgil remarks on the nature of the effort it took to found Rome *(tantae molis erat Romanam condere gentem* – I, 33). He sees history as a chronological expression of an ethical development. The barbarian irrationality that it is Rome's historical mission to control and defeat emerges again and again. One might suppose that only celestial malice could challenge the Roman spirit so continuously. The ethical terms in which the

question is asked are indeed given up; but the historical excursus gives
a parallel answer: human dignity and determination eventually overcome, in the course of history, the historically embodied irrationality
and disorder of Juno. Gods may indeed be malicious, but Roman con-
stancy can overcome that.

Given Milton's neo-classical assumptions it is inevitable that he should
pick up the convention and challenge that Homer and Virgil had
forwarded to him, and base the proposition to his poem on the same
pattern of statement of theme and inquiry into cause. The theme of
Milton's poem is the Fall of man; and so even less for Milton than
for Virgil can the events be viewed as arbitrary, proceeding from
undetermined causes like Homer's wrath of Apollo. The first form of
his question is like that of his predecessors: he asks his Muse (the
Holy Spirit) to

> say first what cause
> Moved our grand parents in that happy state,
> . . . to fall off
> From their creator, and transgress his will
> For one restraint, lords of the world besides?   (I, 28–32)

Already we are given a sense that the irrationality at work belongs to
the human beings themselves rather than to their divine prompters.
The next form of the question projects this human irrationality back
into the non-human world of the 'machines' (or supernatural beings)
and suggests a direct answer to the first question:

> Who first seduced them to that foul revolt?

The answer then comes back easily:

> The infernal serpent; he it was, whose guile
> Stirred up with envy and revenge, deceived
> The mother of mankind, what time his pride
> Had cast him out from heaven. . . .   (34–7)

And so we are already launched on the opening narrative sequence of
the poem, which will expose and explore the nature of this cause, both
in terms of what it causes and for its own sake, both as an explanation
of what happens to Man and as a parallel process in the separate world
of the angels.

In presenting his opening moves in this way Milton has both followed
and transformed his models. It is as clear as it is inevitable that he is
closer to Virgil than to Homer. The Virgilian question *(Tantaene
animis caelestibus irae?)* must be supposed to lie somewhere behind the

description of Satan's motives as *envy and revenge*. But bringing the two poets together shows how far apart they are. For Virgil the question retains something of the old Homeric openness. Juno is clearly a divine being and equally clearly the cause of misery to a good and deserving man. No comprehensive ethical system to reconcile these opposites is offered by the poem. Olympus still retains much of the Homeric quality of a quarrelling family in which the father's will may be final because (come to the push) he can knock down anyone who opposes him; but where the other members can still enjoy their local triumphs when father is prejudiced or tired or inattentive or absent; and where we see relations swing through an irrational arc of subterfuge, rebellion, threats, tale-telling, apologies, forgiveness. Virgil's reliance on history and the Roman ethic of success may keep this theological chaos from too much prominence, but cannot transform it. Milton's heaven, however, cannot be in the least like this : Satan cannot rebel or quarrel or defy and then be chastised or threatened or forgiven. Milton's is a world in which theological and ethical absolutes percolate down to the most local detail of thought or behaviour. The identification of Satan as the one responsible for the action of the poem thus imposes on us as readers a detailed attention to Satan that Juno does not require. At the beginning of the *Aeneid* Juno's malice stirs up the sea around the Trojan ships and drowns the company. But she manages to do this only because Neptune isn't looking. At soon as he notices, her ploy is at an end. She then must twist and turn to something else (Amata, Juturna, the women who burn the boats, Turnus). Her presence in the poem is sporadic and casual, not brooding and causal. In the opening of Book I, once the storm is over she disappears from view, and the reader forgets about her as the recuperative elements in the story take over. But in *Paradise Lost* Satan is not only the centre of our attention in the opening two books but also an inescapable presence thereafter. He may be warned off from Eve by the angelic policemen; but we know that this can be nothing more than an eddy in the forward current of destruction that nothing will check. Every move that he makes takes him eventually nearer to his declared goal. The cause for which he works is constantly in our knowledge even if not in his declared mind. The early scenes in Hell, it is true, show him casting around for a particular aim worthy of his general malice against God. But once the figure of man swims into view the quality of the Satanic homing device is never in question. The Virgilian question is almost too obvious to be asked : *celestial malice* is not simply a quality of Satan; it is the principle of his being. One might argue, indeed, that the whole poem is about the question: it creates a context within which the harrying of a good man can be seen to be eventually compatible with the divine.

I have noted already that the haphazard and irrational machinery of Homer's poem finds its natural expression in the episodic structure. In Milton's poem the Satanic bid for total causality is reflected by Satan's dominance in the narrative process. I have already mentioned the ways in which Milton sets meaning against narrative in the conduct of the poem and of the extent to which these formal characteristics reflect the doctrinal polarities of freedom and necessity. Satan is, of course, the agent and proponent of necessity, which he sees as heroic virtue, and we see as self-destruction; the fact that he is the agent of the narrative derives from this. The poem expresses its freedom in terms of the large narrative blocks which it sets against one another; but Satan is never, we should notice, actually stopped at any of these discontinuities or re-creations. He continually wriggles his way from one to the other; however the viewpoint around him changes shape, he does not change intention. From Book I through Book IV he is constantly in motion, adapting new contexts to what he wants them to be, preserving his aim by changing his appearance (now a soldier, now a politician, now a 'family man', now a cherub, now a cormorant, now a toad). Never stopped

> O'er bog or steep, through straight, rough, dense, or rare,
> With head, hands, wings or feet pursues his way,
> And swims or sinks, or wades, or creeps, or flies.   (II, 948-50)

The idea of something like an incurable virus with a virtually infinite capacity for mutation attaches to Satan in both his moral and narrative function. The continuity of his progress from Hell to Garden creates a narrative spine for *Paradise Lost* to which everything else can be seen as in some way or other comment or reaction. I have spoken above of the opening of Book III when we see Satan put in his place, judged and transformed in our view from overbearing hero to self-ignorant truant. I do not wish to deny the truth of this; but if we turn the axis from judgement to action we see a different picture. When all the splendours of heaven, praise and anathema, incense and thunder-cloud, have rolled away, we see far beneath us the same tiny dark condemned figure as was there before it all started, still moving, still on target. This effect of narrative purpose undismayed by heavenly interruption is probably most easily seen in the arguments to the books (for the arguments give us the bare bones of the story without the agonies and exaltation of the poetry). Thus in the argument to Book III (whose subject-matter we have already discussed) we read: 'The Son of God freely offers. . . . The Father accepts . . . commands all the angels to adore him; they obey, and hymning . . . celebrate the Father and the Son. Mean while Satan alights . . . finds . . . changes himself . . . pretending . . . inquires . . . alights.' In this bare summary, concentrating on the verbs that tell us what is doing, it is easy to see how separated is the circular self-referential mode of Heaven from the linear self-directing mode of Satan. It is difficult to imagine, even in formal terms, any compromise between them.

The great interruption of narrative continuity in *Paradise Lost* is, of course, Raphael's narrative in Books V–VIII. Satan does not appear in present time throughout this lengthy interlude. At the end of Book IV he 'fled murmuring'. He appears again in Book IX, line 53. The effect of his reappearance is something similar to that described above in terms of Book III. The first man and his angel guest have talked of everything under and over the sun; we, following them, have been witness to the greatest events of which the mind is capable of forming an impression. But after all this, when we look up, Satan is still there, a few days older but totally unchanged in purpose. Indeed, we find him

> now improved
> In meditated fraud and malice, bent
> On man's destruction, maugre what might hap
> Of heavier on himself, fearless returned.   (IX, 54–7)

Throughout the angelic disquisition he has been skulking round earth, spending 'the space of seven nights' in the shadow on the far side from the sun, like a wolf prowling round a sheep-cote. From a merely narrative point of view the four books of admonition, precept, and example are shown to be as nothing: the causal mainspring of the action is still pressing round; the Enemy is unaffected.

The presentation of Satan as the causal mainspring of the action of *Paradise Lost* allows us to perceive in the poem a structure in which everything happens by necessity or predestination. It is sometimes thought that Milton as Calvinist and predestinarian must have had a similar view. God in Book III certainly speaks as if the iron laws of necessity required man to use his freedom to choose wrongly. Satan

> shall pervert
> For man will hearken to his glozing lies,
> And easily transgress the sole command,
> Sole pledge of his obedience: so will fall,
> He and his faithless progeny: whose fault?
> Whose but his own? Ingrate, he had of me
> All he could have; I made him just and right,
> Sufficient to have stood, though free to fall.   (III, 92–9)

A study of Milton's theological statements shows, however, that by the time he wrote *Paradise Lost* he had come to accept the position of Jacob Arminius, as against Calvin, in the matter of Predestination. Arminianism suggests that God does not elect in the sense of decreeing the particular individuals who will be saved of necessity, whether they wish to be saved or not; but, rather, decrees the conditions within which the elect will be able to achieve their salvation. It thus offers a compromise position between the irremediably fallen and powerless man of Augustine and Calvin and the free man capable of deserving salvation described by Pelagius. In Arminianism God lightens man's darkness only enough to allow him to choose faith and obedience and in this narrow sense 'deserve' salvation. From a modern point of view Arminianism looks strongly like a means of having it both ways – both God and man are saddled with responsibility and the thinker or poet can shift the weight from one side to the other as it suits his purpose. It suits the purpose of the poet of *Paradise Lost* particularly well. The presumption of a causal chain by which man's Fall can be seen to be necessary is not abandoned as it would have to be under Pelagius. But necessity is interpreted as deriving from man himself and not from God. Once again Milton's God spells out the detail. Adam and Eve cannot

> justly accuse
> Their maker, or their making, or their fate,
> As if predestination overruled
> Their will, disposed by absolute decree
> Or high foreknowledge; they themselves decreed
> Their own revolt, not I: if I foreknew,
> Foreknowledge had no influence on their fault,
> Which had no less proved certain unforeknown.
> So without least impulse or shadow of fate,
> Or aught by me immutably foreseen,
> They trespass, authors to themselves in all
> Both what they judge and what they choose; for so
> I formed them free, and free they must remain,
> Till they enthrall themselves. . . .   (III, 112–25)

The freedom of Milton's characters is thus very different from that found in Homer and Virgil; yet it is also sufficient to free the poem from the domination of Satan's necessitarianism. The classical heroes are free in terms of externals; and this is precisely where Milton allows necessity. Hector is free to rebuke Paris or talk to Andromache, fight with Ajax, wound Teukros, kill Hipponoös, without in any of this either retarding or advancing the trajectory of his fate; but no action is possible in *Paradise Lost* except as part of a perceived step towards or away from the Fall. Nothing in Milton's poem is haphazard, and no one is ethically neutral or ambiguous – as many of Virgil's characters are ethically ambiguous. The freedom that Adam and Eve possess is the freedom of mind that attaches to their innocence. Living assured of perpetual benevolence they are without ulterior motives or the desire to explain by cause and effect. Thinking thus, their free acts must be a fulfilment of their creation and the intention of their creator. Their freedom is sufficient, we are told with doctrinal emphasis, to resist the chains of explanation that Satan offers as a way to heaven. The poem is thus poised, formally as well as doctrinally, between the search for causes and the perception that cause, history, progression àre temporal irrelevancies, as incapable of explaining freedom as time is of explaining eternity.

Milton's art, like that of other major authors, is an art of having it both ways. He offers us, as Arnold Stein has recently pointed out (*The Art of Presence* (1977)), a series of premonitions or rehearsals of the Fall which look, when seen from a fallen point of view, like causes. But the status of the unfallen world does not allow man's freedom to be so restricted; the preceding events remain innocent in themselves; though our natural interpretation of them sees their conditioning relation to the subsequent Fall, the relation is neither sufficient nor necessary to cause the Fall. The handling of Eve's dream in Book V provides an excellent example. Eve is shown in her dream a preview of the actual Fall; in dream she hears the forbidden fruit praised, smells its delicious smell, tastes it and flies towards heaven, experiences the desire to be like a god, greater than she is. She is given, as it were, all the emotional content of the act of disobedience, but none of the moral content, since the events were without her will; and as soon as she wakes and speaks to Adam the emotional content is also overcome by her actual innocence:

> suddenly
> My guide was gone, and I, me thought, sunk down,
> And fell asleep; but O how glad I waked
> To find this but a dream! (V, 90–3)

Eve is still unfallen, as Adam reassures her, and cannot be other:

> evil whence? In thee can harbour none,
> Created pure. (V, 99–100)

Yet we see her surrounded by evil, and the overlap between her innocent impulses and those that belong to Satan has been made clear. Adam's lecture on faculty psychology, which follows, is doctrinally impeccable: the elements in the mind may mismatch their information, so that 'mimic fancy' offers what looks like reason. 'Last evening's talk' of the prohibition against the fruit can be transferred in sleep into an apprehension of what it would be like to eat it, so that

> Evil into the mind of god or man
> May come and go, so unapproved, and leave
> No spot or blame behind. . . . (V, 117–19)

True, it *may*! But Milton has arranged it so that we know Adam's sermon to be disablingly beside the point, however true in the abstract. We have already seen, what Adam has not, the actual cause or source of the evil in Eve's mind. In Book IV we participated in the search for Satan and found him:

> Squat like a toad, close at the ear of Eve;
> Assaying by his devilish art to reach
> The organs of her fancy, and with them forge
> Illusions as he list, phantasms and dreams,
> Or if, inspiring venom, he might taint
> The animal spirits that from pure blood arise . . .
> Vain hopes, vain aims, inordinate desires
> Blown up with high conceits engendering pride.   (IV, 800–9)

As usual, Milton is powerfully reticent. He does not tell us how far Satan succeeded. Nor does he say that Satan's presence by Eve's ear makes Adam's moralising untrue. Several potentials converge on our attention. Adam offers us no more than the allowed capacity of the mind to mismatch its faculties. To the innocent such things do not matter. But in this context, given the close proximity of evil to good, the toad to Eve, the accident of mismatch seems to bring us perilously close to the 'accident' of pollution. We find it easier to follow the wisdom of nature and take it that Eve is somehow tainted than stay with the undoubted doctrine that there is no sin but willed sin. Eve soon recovers her balance: indeed, the dream ends with something of a let-down:

> suddenly
> My guide was gone, and I, me thought, sunk down,
> And fell asleep. . . .   (V, 90–2)

But once again the potential of what we have already seen filters into our apprehension of the doctrinal simplicities of the present. Satan, we remember, was interrupted as he sought to reach into the recesses of Eve's mind. Does the sense of sudden abandonment correspond to the moment of interruption, just as Satan was about to offer her new and more piercing sensations of 'heavenly' delight? We are bound to wonder, and are meant not to know. The idea that Eve was 'saved' when the spear of Ithuriel touched the toad is not one that the poem actually endorses, for the possibility of a fall (however mimic) being avoided by luck is doctrinally intolerable. But the possibility does arise in our minds, even if only as the first stage of rejection, and there in our minds it meets other premonitions of Eve's vulnerability. We gain a sense, unofficial but none the less *there*, that Eve is a natural victim, and that the interruptions and protections that have preserved her innocence so far will not be able to do so indefinitely. With apprehensions that have nothing to do with doctrine we begin to feel the necessity of the Fall.

Milton seems to be steering his poem between the necessitarian cause-and-effect pressures of the Satanic narrative (which after the Fall becomes the process of human history from any point of view) and the *ad hoc* freedom of individual and unfallen response. As I have indicated above, from a modern angle the handling of predestination looks like sleight of hand: now you see Responsibility, now you don't. But Milton's theological tightrope-walk enables him in fact to express his theme in terms which are deeply humane and natural. The anthropomorphism of the Old Testament, and Milton's acceptance of its literal truth, oblige him to translate cause into motive, as proceeding from a quasi-human intention, which is meaningful for us as an index of his mind as well as an impulse towards acts with consequences. Dryden's complaint that *Paradise Lost* is unbalanced because the machines are many and the human beings but two is counteracted in the actual poem by the psychology imputed to the supra-human beings. God seems to be seen as both responsible and not responsible, as human beings tend to be. Theological niceties apart, he can be said to be responsible because he allowed the Fall to happen. Actually the theological niceties clear God; but Milton does not try to persuade us by relying exclusively on these. Rather he seeks to convince us by showing us the alternative – God's positive regard for freedom, seen as the inevitable product of His aims and His 'temperament'. It is obvious in almost everything Milton wrote that he felt a deep need to assert the likeness of the divine and the human; he is happy to accept, if not go beyond, the anthropomorphism of Genesis. I have spoken above of this and of the need he clearly felt to limit the range of Biblical interpretation and the scope of 'accommodation' (pp. 29–31). He tells us that we must take what Genesis (for example) says about God's motives to be literally true. But we must not be simple-minded about it. He asks (*De Doctrina*: YM, VI, 134) if one can allow *anthropopathy* (the explanation of divine actions by the attribution of human emotions to God) and decides that there is no scope for the devout heart here. But the accent of Milton's temperament and religious preferences shows itself not only in such 'allowed' areas as the excursuses on angelic sex and angelic digestion but also in a general pressure on the question of God's motives, shown in the poem if not actually endorsed by it.

The question about *anthropopathy* is close to Virgil's question: can anger, and not only anger anger but unrelenting anger *(tantae . . . irae)*, be assumed to be 'in' celestial minds? The epic asks the question naturally; but in this case the author does not stay for an answer; the wrath of Juno is obvious enough from the action, and the doctrine need not be pursued. In classical poems asking why the gods do as they do tends always to produce reductive and irrelevant answers – this god was jealous of that god, or had this human favourite or that enemy. No modern poet would wish to be trapped in such dead-end psychology. But Milton cannot evade the question so easily. And the danger of such a trap is by no means absent from the Fall story as it appears in Genesis. The prosecution of cause in such a story seems only to lead to a stultifying regress. God asks Adam why he has sinned and 'the man said, The woman whom thou gavest to be with me, she [caused it]'. Eve is asked in her turn why she caused it, and she replies, 'The serpent beguiled me.' Genesis halts the slide by representing the malice of the serpent as a fact of nature not requiring further explanation. But Milton cannot stop here. It is not simply that his serpent is explicitly the Devil, but that his Devil has been given a psychological profile. He is obliged to ask in some form or other the third question that Genesis avoids – a question of the type of 'And the Lord God said unto the serpent, What is this that thou has done?' In the forensic speeches of Book I Milton makes it clear what his Satan would answer to such a question. God, it there appears (see I, 637–42), deceived Satan into his revolt, concealing His strength and making it look as if He could be overthrown. And so one can easily assume that the serpent when questioned by God could follow the rhetoric of the woman and say, 'God beguiled me'. Can there be malice in the mind of God? Milton has to abide the question that Virgil could avoid, and to face the obvious danger of a reductive answer, If God is to be cleared of the charge that He beguiled Satan and so 'caused' the Fall of man, we must be shown the positive aims that He has 'in mind'. Then we can distinguish between the benevolence of His intention and the distortion that appeared when others used the freedom He wanted for them so as to blame Him for alternatives they themselves had chosen. This positive defence of God is often ignored in readings of *Paradise Lost*. And in part this is Milton's fault.

As I have noted before, the chronological beginning of God's acts and the declaration of His purpose are given a strangely muted structural position in the poem (V, 577 ff.). Milton not only buries the Beginning inside Raphael's narrative but also presents it as part of an afterthought. The matter only appears at all, it seems, because there is a bit more time left after dinner, and

> sudden mind arose
> In Adam, not to let the occasion pass
> Given him by this great conference to know
> Of things above this world. . . .   (V, 452–5)

So there is a discussion of angelic digestion, followed by comments about *obedience,* in the course of which the Fall of the angels is mentioned, and from that mention arises Adam's further question about the occasion of such a Fall. Milton approaches the first Cause with what looks like a deliberate desultoriness. In part no doubt his wariness is due to his sense that the language of time and place is particularly inappropriate to an event that precedes time and space. Raphael's apologies measure Milton's self-consciousness in this matter. But more is involved than this. The quality of God's intention, the nature of the divine mind, which forms the circumference of all experience, must be seen to exist primarily out of time. Raphael's story takes a slice out of eternity and presents it to Adam as if it were time, and Satan actually converts his experience of eternity into a process in time. But Milton, miraculously enough, allows us to glimpse a manifestation of godhead which has not been reduced to sequence, a Dantesque vision of Cause without Effect. Once upon a non-time, we are given to understand, there was only God, a total, ineffable and perpetual Unity, expressing Himself not only in the centripetal force that draws all into Himself but also in the centrifugal force that throws out his radiance and love from the centre to the circumference. I call this vision 'Dantesque' for the great expression of this idea of godhead appears in Dante's poem; but the power of the concept in Dante is closely related to its impersonality, its radiant abstractness. The Love which in one direction 'moves the sun and the other stars', and which in the other direction calls the stone 'home' to the centre of the earth, is a force so generalised that we do not think of it as issuing from the will of a person. But Milton's Protestant sensibility required him to see man's inner experience as the model for the divine and God's love as centrally like human love. The love of God that exists before the begining (and for all time) is thus in part a self-sufficient system, without change and without movement, and in part a system of perpetual motion, outward and inward. The tendency of love (as it can be understood and described) is to desire another, a not-me that can respond in freedom to the desire for union that love implies. In these terms the 'parts' of God's unified being can be considered to be separate or free as well as joined together or unified. God offers separateness to the parts of his Being so that his love can be multiplied by the response of love from the separate free parts of the Unity. The situation that Milton seems to envisage is neatly explicated by Dante in the fifteenth canto of the *Purgatorio.* Virgil here explains to Dante the expansiveness of the love 'above' *(in suso)* which does not forbid sharing *(consorto divieto)* or cause envy, in the manner of human love, where sharing is taken to lessen the amount available and where we grow jealous of those who may steal our share. In the higher love *(l'amor della spera suprema)* 'the more there are who can say "ours" the more of the goods each individual possesses'. The situation is explicated by the image of a bright light and a set of mirrors. The more mirrors there are, the more intense the quality of the light. The light on one mirror is not diminished because it has to 'share' with another one; indeed, it might seem to be augmented. So the true love (from above) multiplies itself by increase in the number of lovers, who, deserving love by showing love, are loved the more: 'The further spiritual love *(carità)* extends, the more the power of the Eternal grows upon it; and the more people on high who love one another the more there is to love.' Dante's freedom from Scriptural language allows him these clarifications. The forms of expression are, of course, all analogies rather than truths, evocations of the existence of a Mystery rather than statements of what was there. In describing the scene before the beginning Milton naturally enough shows the attraction of the symbolic, the mode of Dante:

> Thus when in orbs
> Of circuit inexpressible they stood,
> Orb within orb, the Father infinite,
> By whom in bliss embosomed sat the Son,
> Amidst as from a flaming mount, whose top
> Brightness had made invisible. . . .   (V, 594-9)

The concentric circles leading the eye inward to the invisible point of ultimate brightness indicate the organic wholeness and indivisibility of the diagram. The Father and the Son are, however, two persons. Typically, Milton's language allows both their unity and their separateness. We can see him, in fact, worrying over the language the Scriptures had left him. Separateness and unity of the two Persons are both asserted and denied in Scripture. The opening verses of St John's Gospel tell us: 'In the beginning was the Word, and the Word was with God, and the Word was God. The same was in the beginning with God. All things were made by him; and without him was not any thing made that was made.' It seems to be the purpose of these words to assert that the Son was always both incorporate *(embosomed)* in God and different from Him. The opening section of the Epistle to the Hebrews, on the other hand, makes God say of the Son: 'This day have I begotten thee.' This, read straight, must be taken to mean that the Father begot the Son in a way analogous to the begetting of any son by any father. The immediate consequence, for our purpose, is that a time must be conceivable when the Father was alone without the Son, not yet having begotten him. The passage in the Epistle to the Hebrews is particularly troublesome for Milton, for it is the basis of the scene of the Beginning as he describes it in Book V. He worries over it in the *De Doctrina* and comes to the traditional conclusion that

Paul's *begotten* (*gegennêka*) means *exalted*. Technically this removes the contradiction between Paul and John: the Son was with the Father from the beginning, but not yet exalted; at a later point he was exalted. The trouble with this compromise is that it avoids the contradiction only at the cost of fatally weakening the organic identity between the Father and the Son and so strengthens the case that Satan wishes to make. Satan argues that the exaltation is an arbitrary, non-organic, unnecessary, political act. Milton finds it difficult, in the circumstances available to him, to argue the opposite, that it is a wholly natural and inevitable expansion of godhead. Milton tells us that the Son is 'in bliss embosomed' 'by' the Father. It seems probable that the word 'embosomed' is there because John, 1:18, reads: 'No man hath seen God at any time: the only begotten Son, which is in the bosom of the Father, he hath declared him.' The Son, that is, is embosomed in the Father 'in bliss', in a representation of the identity that John declares. But Milton not only implies '*in* the Father'; he also says '*by* the Father'. The natural word to use might seem to be the Scriptural word *with*, which John used in the opening sentence of his Gospel to describe the co-existence of the Son and the Father – 'the Word was with God' (*ho logos ên pros ton theon*). Milton is normally scrupulous in his following of Scripture. Why not here? I think one can see that *by* offers ambiguities useful to Milton's purpose that *with* does not. In the hierarchial picture that Milton paints, the Son does not simply accompany the Father; he is 'now . . . At my right hand'. But *by* does not only mean 'beside'; it also means 'through the agency of': it is because of the will of the Father that the Son sits embosomed in bliss. The Father's power and love go out of himself to the Son, who as a mirror reflects love back to its source and declares the brilliance of what is else invisible. From this point of view the exaltation or declaration of the Son in no way alters the organic structure of the infolded heavens:

> Under his great vicegerent reign abide
> United as one individual soul
> For ever happy: him who disobeys
> Me disobeys, breaks union, and that day
> . . . falls
> Into utter darkness. . . .   (V, 609–14)

The mystery of the Trinity allows that this exposure of the Son as a separable part 'of godhead does not 'break unity'. As yet, in God's speech, time has not begun. To establish a Beginning, a point of view is needed which denies the mystery of the circularity of Father and Son and angelic host, one that pries into the sequential logic of the Son's separateness and freedom. And this point of perception is, of course, provided by Satan. Satan is the first demythologiser of the Trinity; with characteristic reductiveness he sees the event in terms of time: if the Son wasn't the Son before this 'day', then we have witnessed an arbitrary innovation; if He existed in this form before, then there is no need for new orders. He sees the externalisation of God in the Son and also in the angels as a process not of expansion but of separation; and the freedom that exists to allow love to flow back to the source of love is detached from the end proposed. The freedom to reciprocate love must also be the freedom to reject love. From Satan's point of view the Son has this same freedom and simply (arbitrarily) declines to exercise it. It is not hard for him to understand why when he considers the rewards and honours the Father has given to Him. There is no coherent theological view which will allow the Son's rejection of the Father to be a possibility; but Satan's point of view is totally coherent in itself. If freedom is the opportunity to escape the imposed will of another, then nature can be logically construed as a contest between the weak and the strong. The exaltation of the Son (seen as an angelic princeling unfairly preferred) provides a test of virtue as self-respect and other-rejection: 'since you did that, I will do this, so that you will have to . . . and I will then . . .'. Satan's role in the poem as the commander of time and sequence is thus early established.

Satan sees God's interventions in the world outside Himself as a series of demands for obedience to arbitrary rule, demands necessarily unsuccessful since freedom breeds rejection. God failed with the angels (or some of them); he will fail with man (in the short run); that He cannot be seen to have failed with the Son must be due to the peculiar circumstances of that relationship. To see the opposite side one has, of course, to start with this 'exception'. The *causeless* love for his Father that is Christ's expression of His freedom provides a model of response for angel and for man, and this is the one that the poem finally comes to rest on: Christ will redeem man, we are told in Book III, not because man deserves it or has even the power to ask for it, because Grace is indeed arbitrary, and without cause,

> to all
> Comes unprevented, unimplored, unsought,
> Happy for man, so coming; he her aid
> Can never seek, once dead in sins and lost;
> Atonement for himself or offering meet,
> Indebted and undone, hath none to bring:
> Behold me then, me for him, life for life
> I offer. . . .   (III, 230–7)

The arbitrariness of the divine mode is one of the most difficult aspects of it for the modern sceptical mind: Grace is arbitrary, election is arbitrary, redemption is arbitrary and man's faith must be arbitrary likewise. Like Satan, we find this an argument against the divine. For Milton it clearly provides the dividing-line between belief and disbelief. What Satan learns is how to link part to part and justify the present because of the past. What Adam learns when he has 'attained the sum/Of wisdom' (XII, 575–6) is to recognise 'love . . . the soul of all the rest' and

> Acknowledge my redeemer ever blest   (XII, 573)

The prolonged narrative of human history which Michael retails to Adam in Books XI and XII shows us the Satanic mode at work. The fact that 'all this . . . evil turn to good', and that Adam sees Christ, is not the result of the historical sequence. The meaning of history is that history can be escaped from and life returned to the beginning. As Adam tells us, the power to find Christ in history is like that

> which by creation first brought forth
> Light out of darkness!   (XII, 472–3)

In other words, the intrusion of Christ into history is as much a *fiat*, an unprepared and unpreparable explosion of creativity, as was the Creation itself. Milton's poem operates of necessity in terms of preparation, expectation and fulfilment; but the values it endorses are arbitrary explosions from outside the system, reduced and known to be reduced by our 'explanation' of them.

CHAPTER 3

Paradise Lost as Drama

In what I have already said I have referred several times to the idea of Milton 'dramatising' his own attitudes or exploiting the dramatic tension found in the work between one generic implication and another. The derivatives of the word *drama* do not appear in such formulations by chance. One of the central problems of assimilating *Paradise Lost* to the epic tradition is the problem of finding an adequate epic vocabulary for its powerful dramatic effects. If we compare *Paradise Lost* with its greatest English predecessor, Spenser's *The Faerie Queene*, we can see clearly how Milton modifies the tradition he inherits, sharpening tensions, promoting differences, setting voices against one another. Looking at it the other way round we can see Spenser everywhere intertwining effects, so that we can no longer clearly separate them, finding meaning in overlap rather than in opposition, drowning the progression of the individual in the huge variety of his company.

I shall return to Spenser a little later. What I should like to point out first is the extent to which modern concentration on the doctrinal elements of *Paradise Lost* has narrowed our responsiveness to the drama of the poem – in terms at least of the responses that appear in formulated criticism. I am returning here to an earlier point, the danger of assuming that Milton's correction of one of his own poetically powerful descriptions is in fact a cancellation of that power. My argument is that the power of one is not cancelled by the co-existence of the other, but that the two powers continue to co-exist in an unresolved tension. Throughout this book I argue for the poem's structure as a system of checks and balances, setting one generic effect against another, holding aesthetic and moral forces in proportion, allowing (for example) that Adam's decision to fall with Eve has something of the mysterious power of a tragic act, magnetic and fascinating in this although clearly A Bad Thing from any doctrinal point of view. Such duality in persuasive power immediately relates the poem to the drama, for drama (and more specifically tragedy) is the genre which most powerfully energises the capacity of the Wrong to go on exerting its appeal to us even when known to be wicked or destructive. *Macbeth* is the Shakespeare play that seems to have had most influence on *Paradise Lost*; and Macbeth himself raises in a uniquely powerful form this whole question of the bad man who is yet allowed, identified with and sorrowed over.

Macbeth requires us to respond in ways which are only doctrinally tenable in terms of the largest assumptions about human life, requires us to assume that sinfulness is never the whole explanation of any fully perceived human being. We are always aware in reading or seeing *Macbeth* that every state we can define for him doctrinally is, at least up to the moment of his death, only a potential; so that definition or doctrine always runs simplifyingly ahead of dramatic experience, and is seen to do so. We know of Macbeth as a deeply guilty and deeply divided man, appalled by his own deeds and yearning for the virtues and the rewards he left behind him. But which is the real Macbeth – the object Macbeth looks at when he looks at himself, or the subject that looks? Clearly he is both; and the play draws its strength from our capacity to hold both the damned man and the free man, and the contradiction between them, inside a single viewpoint. From one angle the end of the play resolves the issue; but it does not dissolve that dimension within which the subject Macbeth remains free. We know the end (certainly do so for most of our acquaintance with the play), but this does not stop us hoping and fearing, wishing he wouldn't, regretting necessity while at the same time accepting it, seeing piognantly how much freedom remains and how easily it could all be different. Moral judgement and human sympathy affect us as continuously opposite and yet regularly complementary. If the tension between freedom and necessity is allowed to weaken, the play begins to collapse; it will then turn into a sentimental evasion or else become a tract for the times. It hardly need be argued that the same dramatic tension between narrative necessity and unfallen freedom sustains *Paradise Lost*.

A further dramatic example, even closer to *Paradise Lost*, appears in Marlowe's *Doctor Faustus*. Faustus' sin turns the screw of doctrine a little tighter than in *Macbeth*. Macbeth's sin is presented as part of his humanity, and therefore is as undefinable as human nature. But Faustus' sin is more objective, more impersonal, something chosen and sealed and quasi-legal. In its doctrinal clarity it is closer to Satan than to Macbeth. But the dramatic effect of the play seems hardly to take any account of this. As we watch Faustus we cling stubbornly to the possibility (or perhaps fantasy) that he can repent, that he is a man like us and not a demon (as the contract said he was). Indeed, if we did not believe that the possibility of salvation was an integral part of the play we could hardly follow the action, for the relation of present to future as cause to effect would lose the dramatic power that openness of potential allows it.

The action of *Paradise Lost* cannot be assimilated to these theatrical models in every respect. We know with much more oppressive clarity than is the case with Macbeth or Faustus that Satan will not repent, and are not long held in wonder if Adam will find grace. This is not

simply a point about our knowledge of the end of the story; it is rather
that the irrecoverable implications of a single crucial choice are everywhere made part of the experience we share with Adam and Eve. The
sense of unrealised potentials lurking round every corner is essential to
the freedom of life we detect every time we read Marlowe and
Shakespeare. But Milton's system is too closed to allow us to indulge
these freedoms. The actions of the characters are always being measured
for meaning in *Paradise Lost*; but drama depends on some feeling for
action as spontaneous. In terms of technique we can see the pressure on
Milton to render action into meaning as a pressure towards allegory.
Clearly he resists this pressure, and tends to present the free decision of
the individual as more a new beginning than a simple connection
between action and meaning. To the extent this tendency is realised,
Milton writes dramatically, even theatrically. The comparison with
Spenser, which I promised to return to, underscores this point. The
characters of *The Faerie Queene* offer no foothold for any resistance
to interpretation of action in terms of meaning. The brilliantly realised
evil characters – Duessa, Archimago, Busirane, Malegar, Despair – have
extraordinary functional strength, and are capable of stirring our
deepest sense of the malice hidden in ordinary experience; but clearly
they draw their sustenance from particular contexts and fade if our
imagination transfers them to another world. Take Lucifera out of her
pageant so that she can no longer operate as the focus of its energies and
she disappears from sight. Of course we recognise in the functioning of
these figures the moral characteristics we know from ourselves and our
neighbours: the puffed-up pride and disdain of Orgoglio, the tremulous
obsession of Malbecco, the hollow fanaticism of Malegar, all give
precision to our extra-literary experience. But their characteristics and
actions ring true only of the static qualities of our own lives, the
qualities we can perceive when held inside fixed frameworks of meaning. The movement from one such quality to another is as mysterious
as the pathways through the forests in Spenser's poem. Milton's Satan,
however, though he may momentarily assume this iconic power (as when
he lies on the burning lake, or leaps over the wall of Paradise, or, in
Book X, turns into the infernal serpent), operates more often and more
forcefully when he seems to be the independent creator of his own
meanings and the transformer of his own contexts. That in the end he is
not so is doctrinally explicit and exactly stated in the poem. When he
is still chained on the lake we are told that he rose up from there only
because God allowed it:

> . . . nor ever thence
> Had risen or heaved his head, but that the will
> And high permission of all-ruling heaven
> Left him at large to his own dark designs. . . .   (I, 210–13)

The ambiguity here exactly fits Milton's purpose. God *wills* the event, and in that sense Satan is his puppet. But the relationship can also be rendered as *high permission*: God merely withdraws, and the causative agent is Satan himself. Enough space is made available for Satan to 'hang himself' as we say. Though we acknowledge God's overall power to act thus, we do not, in our move-by-move reading of the poem, see divine hands fastening the rope around the infernal neck. In other words the moral impulses which in Spenser are refined and isolated to a chemical purity are here combined with enough impurities in the system, apparent spontaneities, to present wholly believable 'human natures' whose actions seem to be directed from within. They seem to achieve the total meaning that God requires only because there exists an inexplicit system of spontaneous convergence so large that it can be seen only in terms of results.

In these terms the drama of the particular can be seen to be eventually reconcilable with the doctrine and narrative of the whole. To argue too committedly for either dramatic freedom or narrative control is to distort the experience of reading the poem. Thus our allowance of Milton's dramatic power has to stop short of allowing his characters the full freedom of Macbeth or Faustus, even in the particular moments where their existence is most vivid. The apparent freedom of self-generation in the action is always held inside a series of perspectives which both permit it and criticise it. This duality, typical of the poem as I describe it, operates chiefly through the interventions of the narrator, the invention of what Mrs Ferry has called 'the epic voice'.

I have spoken above (pp. 8–11) of the effect and general purpose of the author's intrusions into the poem. It is my function here simply to note the relation of these passages to the balance between drama and doctrine. The debate with the self that such passages propose is not about doctrine; doctrine is (or should be) clear; but the requirement to express it personally involves the author in a sharp drama between self-doubt and triumph over the self. On the one hand the narrator is simply the vehicle for divine inspiration. The 'celestial patroness'

> deigns
> Her nightly visitation unimplored,
> And dictates to me slumbering, or inspires
> Easy my unpremeditated verse. . . .   (IX, 21–4)

But this certainty is set inside uncertainty. The celestial patroness is by no means to be relied on; the sure verse will only flow 'If answerable style I can obtain' (IX, 20). The author has had to struggle, 'long choosing and beginning late' (26), and even now success may be cancelled, if

> an age too late, or cold
> Climate, or years damp my intended wing
> Depressed. . . .   (44–6)

An interesting variant form of such drama, in which the narrator is
caught between the necessity of telling the truth and the awareness that
there are different ways of telling it, between simple believing and complex telling, appears in the thunderclap opening of Book IV:

> O for that warning voice, which he who saw
> The Apocalypse, heard cry in heaven aloud,
> Then when the dragon, put to second rout,
> Came furious down to be revenged on men,
> *Woe to the inhabitants on earth*! that now,
> While time was, our first parents had been warned
> The coming of their secret foe, and scaped
> Haply so scaped his mortal snare; For now
> Satan, now first inflamed with rage, came down. . . .   (IV, 1–9)

Here the drama of authorship presents not the tension between inspiration
and failure, but that between poetry and apocalypse (or revelation).
Even the most inspired poetry cannot alter *things*, and most especially
cannot alter the past; it can only describe it. Milton sets against that a
longed-for power to abolish time and affect events directly by imposing
the voice of Heaven on those who, having heard it, will change their
history. Natural sequence is thus violently dislocated. Milton in the
present takes on the voice of St John the Divine ('he who saw/The
Apocalypse') and cries out in his words 'Woe to the inhabitants on
earth' as if he could warn Adam and Eve in the same way as St John
warned his readers of the second coming-down of Satan at the end of
the world. The passage sets up a powerful dramatic separation of
Milton the mere narrator of the sequence of events from Milton the
Christian seer who knows last things as clearly as he knows the present,
and also from Milton the pained participant in the recurrent meanings of
these events. Milton endures with mankind the endlessly repeated failures
to defeat Satan, and longs for the verbal power to reveal to its inhabitants the meaning of the past as St John has revealed the future. But the
narrator can only narrate the truths that are complete. The *now* of line
5 reflects an extended present in which the voice of Milton rings in the
ears of Adam and Eve. But the *now* of line 8 separates the two,
narrator from narrated. It marks the disappointing return of mere
poetry, mere description of the past.

The drama of the author who poses himself for our attention between
the alternative possibilities (and impossibilities) of writing tends to
infringe the self-sufficiency of the subject-matter he writes about. The
attention he draws to his own writing seems to distance and explain

things which, to be fully dramatic, must appear to be spontaneous and unmediated. As I have noted above, the voice of the narrator is one of the principal means by which Milton limits the freedom and spontaneity of his characters. But we would be wrong to push this point too far. In a poem as long as *Paradise Lost* the local action has little difficulty in reasserting its independent and divergent ways. Thus the presence of Satan soon re-creates the dramatic present of Book IV. The sense of the narrator's control fades and has to be reinforced at various subsequent points in the Book, as I indicate below. The counterpoint between these two impulses in the poem is continuous. Sometimes the narrator's control draws back and allows those theatrical brilliances so characteristic of the style; but then it reasserts itself before the independent human interest of the dramatic present cuts free from the doctrinal perspective on which the didactic aim and power of the poem eventually depends. At such moments the past suddenly ceases to be merely past; for judgement made of action *then* is equally a true judgement *now*. So when Adam and Eve complete their evening hymn Milton speaks of them as

> other rites
> Observing none, but adoration pure
> Which God likes best. . . .   (IV, 736-8)

God's liking is, we are to understand, the same today as yesterday, and points to readers' practices as well as past events. The separation of audience from action which is essential to drama (whatever modern theorists say) is breached; the author requires us to superimpose the presentness of our lives on top of the pastness of the characters' lives and to think about our world rather than theirs.

The draft outlines of a tragedy on the subject of *Paradise Lost*, contained in Milton's notebook now in Trinity College Cambridge, shows how much of the epic material in the poem could be incorporated in a play. I have set out in tabular form a conspectus of what we can learn from the material in the manuscript, hoping by this means to make clear both what remained constant through the various revisions and what seems to have changed or evolved as Milton drafted and redrafted. The manuscript contains four drafts, the first three written on one page (fol. 33) and the fourth (headed 'Adam unparadized' and 'Adam's banishment') a few pages later. I refer to these as (1), (2), (3) and (4). The typographical devices I have used are intended to show what material in my synopsis is literal and what is conjectural. I have put quotation marks round Milton's own words, and placed square brackets around entries that are derived from analogy rather than direct quotation. I have added question marks to analogies with only uncertain support. I have not aimed to incorporate every word in the drafts; I have sought to uncover structure rather than to elaborate detail.

	Draft i	Draft ii	Draft iii	Draft iv
Prologos	Michael	Moses Justice Mercy Wisdom	Justice Mercy } debating what should Wisdom } become of man if he fall	'Gabriel . . . describes Paradise'
Parodos	Chorus of Angels	[sings the creation]	'sings a hymn of the creation'	Chorus 'showing the reason of his coming to keep his watch in Paradise after Lucifer's rebellion' 'a hymn of the creation'
Act II	Heavenly Love	Heavenly Love Hesperus	Heavenly Love Hesperus the evening star	Gabriel 'he relates what he knew of man as the creation of Eve with their love and marriage' Chorus }
Chorus II	[ ]	[ ]	'sing the marriage song and describe Paradise'	[marriage song]?
Act III	Lucifer Adam } with the Eve } serpent	Lucifer [Adam]? [Eve]?	Lucifer 'contriving Adam's ruin'	Lucifer 'appears after his overthrow, bemoans himself, seeks revenge on man' Chorus 'prepare resistance at his first approach' 'discourse of enmity on either side'
Chorus III	[ ]	[ ]	Chorus 'fears for Adam, relates Lucifer's rebellion and fall'	Chorus 'sings of the battle and victory in heaven'
Act IV	[Adam] [Eve] Conscience	[Adam] [Eve] Conscience	Adam } 'fallen' Eve } Conscience 'cites them to God's examination'	Lucifer 'insulting in what he had done to the destruction of man', Adam & Eve 'having by this time been seduced by the serpent, appears confusedly covered with leaves' Justice 'cites him to the place whither Jehova called for him' Conscience 'in a shape accuses'

Chorus IV	[bewails Adam's fall]?	[bewails Adam's fall]?	Chorus 'bewails and tells the good Adam hath lost'	Chorus '. . informed by some angel the manner of his fall . . bewails Adam's fall'
Act V	[Adam] [Eve] Death Labour Discontent Sickness Ignorance with Others } Mutes Faith Hope Charity	[Adam] [Eve] Labour Sickness Discontent Ignorance } Mutes Fear Death Faith Hope Charity	Adam Eve } 'driven out of Paradise' Angel 'presents' 'Mutes to whom he gives their names' { Labour, Grief, Hatred, Envy, War, Famine, Pestilence, Sickness, Discontent, Ignorance, Fear, Death 'likewise Winter, Heat, Tempest &c entered into the world' Faith Hope Charity } 'comfort him and instruct him'	Adam Eve } 'accuse one another, but especially Adam lays the blame to his wife, is stubborn in his offence' Justice 'appears, reason with him, convinces him' Chorus 'admonisheth Adam' Angel 'to banish them out of Paradise, but before causes to pass before his eyes in shapes a masque of all the evils of this life and world [Labour, Grief, Hatred, Envy, War, Famine, Pestilence, Sickness, Discontent, Ignorance, Fear Death] he is humbled, relents, despairs' Mercy 'comforts him, promises the Messiah' Faith Hope } 'instruct him; he repents' Charity
Exode	[ ]	[ ]	Chorus 'briefly concludes'	Chorus 'briefly concludes'

The date at which Milton wrote these drafts is not known, but it is likely that they belong to the late 'thirties or early 'forties. In 1641, in *Reason of Church Government* Milton describes his uncertainty whether to write in

> that epic form whereof the two poems of Homer and those other two of Virgil and Tasso are a diffuse and the book of Job a brief model . . . to lay the pattern of a Christian hero . . . or whether those dramatic constitutions wherein Sophocles and Euripides reign shall be found more doctrinal and exemplary to a nation. The scripture also affords us a divine pastoral drama in the Song of Solomon consisting of two persons and a double chorus . . . And the Apocalypse of Saint John is the majestic image of a high and stately tragedy, shutting up and intermingling her solemn scenes and acts with a sevenfold chorus of hallelujahs and harping symphonies.
>
> (*CM.* III, 237–8)

What seems relevant to the Paradise Lost tragedy in these latter remarks is the emphasis on the choruses. That such an emphasis (on commentary rather than action) was part of Milton's Paradise Lost plans from the beginning cannot be known. But the evidence of the drafts suggests that we can see Milton anticipating such a structure. Versions (1) and (2) are lists of *dramatis personae*, really variant forms of the same list, the first naming fourteen characters, the second naming nineteen. But the names chosen, and their order, suggest that the angle from which the material would be seen was already fixed. Version (3) is an act-by-act summary, based on the list of characters, but adding brief indications of the action – saying not only 'Lucifer' but 'Lucifer contriving Adam's ruin' etc. The fourth draft ('Adam Unparadized') is not only fuller than all the others but abandons their quasi-theatrical focus, telling the story as a continuous piece of prose. Milton remarks at the end of it: *Compare this with the former draft.* This I have taken as my justification for constructing a synoptic version which combines dramatic structure from (3) with narrative details from (4).

The setting-out of this material makes clear both the persistence of certain subject-matter and ways of organising it, and also the changes imposed when the story came into more detailed focus in Milton's mind. Both kinds of evidence are relevant to *Paradise Lost* and we must analyse the material from both points of view. The form contemplated in all four versions is that of a Greek tragedy, presumably of the strict kind represented in *Samson Agonistes* though divided into five acts in the neo-classical manner. One must suppose therefore that the unities are meant to be observed. The place is (technically speaking) Paradise throughout. The time seems to cover the period from just before the Fall until the Expulsion. A. D. S. Fowler (pages 443–4) has made the point that in *Paradise Lost* Milton seems to be calculating days in the Hebraic manner – from one sundown until the next. The presence of Hesperus the evening star in the earliest action of versions (ii) and (iii) suggests that the same measure of time was being employed in the tragedy also. It was traditional to suppose that Adam fell at noon (at the same time as Christ was crucified). If Milton used this assumption as part of his time-scheme (he allows it in *Paradise Lost*), then the fact that the Fall seems to occur in the middle of his tragedy – presumably during chorus 3 – may confirm an assumption that the total time employed runs from the evening of the day before the Fall until evening on the day of the Fall. The Unity that would seem to be most neglected in Milton's tragedy is the one that modern criticism thinks to be most important – unity of action. The action in Paradise is a mere pinhead, on which Milton dances a cosmic variety of anticipations and retrospections. The intellectual substance of the play is to be found in the context of Adam and Eve rather than their own performances, in the tissue of explanation, anticipation, debate, regret, retrospection, consequence that examines the meaning of what is happening instead of placing the central action before our eyes. The characters have been selected to give the widest range of reference rather than the most intense conflicts. The function of Michael in the prologue of version (i) is not clear; but in all probability he (like the other prologues Milton devised) expresses divine knowledge rather than human activity, as is common enough in the prologues of both classical and neo-classical tragedy. The propriety of Moses in this context is interesting for the study of *Paradise Lost*, though strange to the modern mind. Version (iii) well expresses this strangeness in a note it inserts opposite the name:

> Moses *prologizei* [speaks the prologue], recounting how he assumed his true body, that it corrupts not because of his [being] with God in the mount, declares the like of Enoch and Eliah, besides the purity of the pl[ace] that certain pure winds, dews, and clouds preserve it from corruption, whence he hastes to the sight of God, tells they cannot see Adam in this state of innocence by reason of their sin.

It is hard to imagine a comment less attuned to what we like to call the realities of drama. But it might also be argued that willingness to believe in what we see is of central theatrical as well as doctrinal importance. It is a measure of the seriousness of Milton's dramatic ambitions that he felt he had to have a doctrinal justification for presenting to his audience's eyes the corporal reality of a figure who was human and died. Classical and neo-classical drama abounded, of course, in prologuising ghosts; but clearly a mere literary example could not

remove from Milton's mind the doctrinal worry that such appearances
were either un-Christian or Popish (depending on the abhorred doctrine
of Purgatory) and in any case flatly contrary to Milton's apparent belief
in the physical totality of death (the heresy of mortalism). If Moses was
to be shewn on the stage as part of a true story, then a doctrinal defence
of the survival of Moses' body seemed to be necessary. But why, given
the difficulties, use Moses at all? The answer appears at the opening
of *Paradise Lost* where Moses is cited as

> That shepherd, who first taught the chosen seed,
> In the beginning how the heavens and earth
> Rose out of chaos. . . .   (I, 8–10)

Moses is the authorial vehicle through whom we know the truth of the
story of Adam's fall. As Prologue he justifies the action; he draws back
the curtain, as it were, giving scriptural warrant to what we subsequently
see. In the last version Moses gives way to the much more easily
justified Gabriel, who 'since this globe was created [had] his
frequency as much on earth as in heaven'. The change is cognate with
other changes, and I discuss the pattern below. What we should notice
now is that the interest in analysis of and abstraction from the physical
events is standard in all that we know about these plays. The most
startling evidence of this is the off-stage handling of the Fall itself.
It may be that there was a change of mind in this matter, but the
evidence for that is very thin. Certainly the third and fourth versions
omit both the temptation and the eating of the apple. At the beginning
of Act IV, version (iv) tells us that 'man next and Eve having by this
time been seduced by the serpent appears'. The note on Moses cited
above gives one doctrinal reason why the event had to be handled this
way: 'they [presumably the audience] cannot see Adam in this state
of innocence by reason of their sin'. Adam and Eve, therefore, can only
appear on the stage after they have fallen. One might suppose that the
point Moses makes in version (iii) he also would have made in version
(ii). In the first draft, however, Adam and Eve are said to appear
'with the serpent'. This suggests to me that in this version Adam and
Eve would have appeared before the Fall, in Act III, and that the
temptation (at the least) would have been dramatised. It is possible, of
course, that they only appeared 'with the serpent' in Act IV, and that in
this point the first version and the last coincided, both planning to show
'Lucifer insulting in what he had done to the destruction of man' and
'Adam and Eve . . . confusedly covered with leaves'. If this were so,
on the other hand it would be odd to call Lucifer 'the serpent', since
he assumed that guise only for the purpose of the temptation. That
Milton began with more obviously dramatic aims – for which he had

justification in one of the obvious models for his intended play – Grotius' *Adamus Exsul* (1601) – and then modified these under the pressure of doctrine is inherently probable but probably unprovable.

Another abstract and contextual element in the play, which was never modified in any of the drafts, in spite of its violation of neo-classical unities, is the 'masque of all the evils of this life and world' which the Angel shows to Adam in Act V. Presumably Milton thought some such forward glance at what the Fall was responsible for in the world of the play's spectators was a necessary part of a work contemplating meaning rather than enacting it. The same impulse justifies the survey of Biblical history in Books XI and XII of *Paradise Lost*; but, where Milton narrated personal stories in the epic, in the drama he seems to have contemplated only a dumb-show of abstract qualities, organised – so it would seem from the care with which he deleted and rearranged items in draft (ii) – to show the progress of a fallen life from *Labour* to *Death*. Within the sharp constraints of the dramatic form there is no space for particular histories; reference to lives outside those being dramatised has to be achieved at the level of Adam as Everyman. When the angel 'gives their names' (as version (iii) says) to these characteristic evils of mortality, the focus of our attention can hardly be shifted from the progression of attitudes in Adam to the elements outside himself that cause the progression. The function of the masque is to produce the stated effect on Adam: 'He is humbled, relents, despairs.' To this he must be brought before Mercy can 'comfort him, promise the Messiah'. The pattern of Act V is designed to enact a possible recovery from a Fall which is general enough to raise an echo in the breast of every reader. Similarly the early acts prepare us for a general pattern of bliss leading to pride leading to loss. Pressing so hard on the general, one can understand why the play found it difficult to rest the whole action on its crucial particular, the eating of the apple. Only when there is as much space as there is in an epic poem can particular histories be substituted for abstract analysis and the sharp edges of dramatic antithesis be softened enough to accommodate the indefiniteness and ambiguity of actual human behaviour.

The movement from draft to draft and from all the drafts to the printed version shows us Milton wrestling not with the subject-matter of *Paradise Lost*, nor with the general moral he wished to draw, but with shifts and modifications that might secure the right rhetorical effect, with problems of balance between dogmatic truth and vivid performance. The problem for Milton, as the earlier versions reveal it, was the problem of finding the most powerful blending of action and meaning, story and comment. The form of Greek tragedy as represented by the Athenian dramatists, by Buchanan and Grotius and by Milton's own *Samson Agonistes*, might seem at first glance to be ideally suited to a telling of Adam's Fall which was also a general interpretation of its significance. The Greek form offers in the main a process of retrospection and recovery, an understanding and valuation in the present of significant action in the past, leading to a resolution which finally answers the question posed by the action and joins up past and present. It is easy to see how the Fall can be handled in this way; but there is an obvious and central difficulty in the path of any such attempt – the role of Adam as protagonist. In *Samson Agonistes* the character of the hero is what gives continuity to the action and carries the past through the present and into the resolution. We understand the meaning of what is happening largely in terms of the hero's sense of his own developing meaning, even though that self is identified by doctrinal norms. But Adam's fall cannot be handled as a personal continuity of this kind. Samson's blinding and captivity, his betrayal of himself, his nation, his God is embodied in a personal history, even if the effects are national. Adam's sin is different not only in degree but also in kind, for his actions lack particularity, are significant because they reflect all men rather than one unique and attractive individual. Samson's recovery is apprehended first as a recovery of self and thereafter as a recovery of God. We apprehend a God who speaks, however mysteriously, through individual self-consciousness. But the movement from the sin of the first Adam to the redemption of the second Adam takes us far from any believable psychology. When Adam sees the Messiah, or when Eve knows the woman who will bruise the serpent's head, they are not represented as recovering their own lost or true selves. The history of the individual has been absorbed into the history of mankind. In *Samson Agonistes,* and in Greek tragedy in general, the buskin is on the other foot: the history of the race is absorbed into the history of its heroic representative. Lacking a tragic centre of this kind the tragic drafts of *Paradise Lost* drift from dialectic to flowing narrative. Some of the pressures on Milton, driving him in this direction, are visible. One of the duties laid on him was to render the particular events that appear in the literal Genesis story. At the same time an artistic form requires a unified judgement on the events he showed. He seems to have aimed to reconcile these two demands on his play by delaying action until the meaning of that action had been made clear to us. Thus in drafts (ii) and (iii) Justice, Mercy and Wisdom debate the Fall of Man before the story has ever begun. Presumably the action contemplated here corresponds to what now occurs in Book III of *Paradise Lost*. Justice (the Father) demands that death, the wages of sin, be exacted from the race of sinners. Mercy (the Son) offers redemption, and Wisdom (often equated with the Holy Ghost) offers a median position like that given again to the Father in *Paradise Lost*, III, 274 ff. One might guess that as long as the action on earth is represented in terms of the embattled alternatives of

Heaven and Hell, and commentary on that, as much as by the inter-action of Adam, Eve, Lucifer, Angel, so long the envisaged dramatic compromise between action and judgement may be expected to hold. But as soon as the individual voices take on the rhetorical power of self-justification (such as appears in Lucifer's soliloquy at the beginning of Book IV) the power of doctrinal correction available through chorus or abstractions becomes inadequate. The balance between the two aspects of Milton's genius, the didactic and the expressive, can only be restored by a more continuous intervention of the author than is possible in a play. The final draft version has, in a sense, already accepted this. It substitutes narrative for dialectic and joins up what was earlier left separate. We should remember that in the Trinity College manu-script of this draft the matter of the choruses is only present as an afterthought or an insertion. It seems as if Milton at some point thought that the story could be best told without the choral songs between the acts. The most obvious change in this last version is the substitution of Gabriel for the earlier prologue of Moses and the three daughters of God. The first four sections of the play are now unified by Gabriel and the chorus who, together or apart, occupy the stage for the whole of this period. If one omits the formal choral songs, the continuity by *liaison des scènes* becomes even more obvious, as Gabriel is joined by the chorus and then the chorus (now more integrated into the action) is joined by Lucifer. The matter is the same as earlier – the ever-nearer tragic fate of man – but now the crucial event is explained not by analysis of the divine decree but by discussing the history of man in Paradise. Likewise the change in Act III from 'Lucifer contriving Adam's ruin' to 'Lucifer appears after his overthrow, bemoans himself, seeks revenge on man' throws new emphasis (as far as the drafts are concerned, at any rate) on Lucifer's psychological state as against his diagrammatic relationship to Adam. As Milton fleshes out the reality of the individuals involved, the classical tragic form comes to seem an inadequate vehicle for their emotions. Two incompatible aesthetics compete with one another in the final draft; the sharpness and compression of a dramatic version of the story can only be preserved, it would seem, if the narrative particularities are held firmly in place by an analytic structure that makes clear to us what these events mean in terms of an overall diagram. But in version (iv) the personal lives of the characters are beginning to escape from the diagram. The fuller reliance on narrative in this version points forward to the epic form within which the incompatible impulses could be held together.

If we read the epic poem with this in mind, we can see how far Milton has been able to preserve the personal drama of a form more Elizabethan than Athenian, spontaneous self-expression and unprepared conflict (for example, the dispute about gardening in Book IX), and yet retain unbreached the total diagram of God's providence. Two elements already mentioned seem of greatest importance here: the controlling presence of the narrator and the great space the epic poem provides to allow both the action and the commentary their separate large-scale effects. It follows from this latter that collisions, when they occur, are collisions of completely realised value-systems not simply of kinds of persons. Satan's soliloquy at the beginning of Book IV is a powerful example of the way in which intensely dramatic material can both be given its head and yet remain harnessed to the purpose of the poem; he addresses the sun:

> O thou that with surpassing glory crowned,
> Look'st from thy sole dominion like the God
> Of this new world; at whose sight all the stars
> Hide their diminished heads; to thee I call,
> But with no friendly voice, and add thy name
> O sun, to tell thee how I hate thy beams
> That bring to my remembrance from what state
> I fell, how glorious once above thy sphere;
> Till pride and worse ambition threw me down
> Warring in heaven against heaven's matchless king: (32–41)

Edward Philips, Milton's nephew, told the antiquarian John Aubrey that 'about fifteen or sixteen years before ever his poem was thought of' he saw the passage I have just quoted (or at least 'about six verses' of it) 'which verses were intended for the beginning of a tragedy which he had designed'. W. R. Parker, *Milton: A Biography* (1968), II, 857, dates the sight of the verses to the years 1642–3. Philips's statement does not match with the evidence supplied from the Trinity College manuscript; there, as we have seen above, the opening of the play was to be concerned with a deal of heavenly information which the reader needed to understand the action which was to follow. But we have little alternative but to believe him; and, if we do so, we must assume that the *Paradise Lost* play passed through some further stages. We should notice that IV, 32–41, corresponds in function to the opening speech in Grotius' *Adamus Exsul*, which is introduced by Satan's statement of his own wickedness:

> Foe to the cruel thunderer, exiled from my heavenly home, I present myself in flight from the gloomy cave of Tartarus and the dark desert of eternal night. From those unlucky regions I have been drawn here by my hate for the good, turning over and over my criminal plans. I seek a crime which is terrifying, vile and awful, such as even I Satan tremble at.

This prolocutionary rhetoric comes from the plays of Seneca. The subtle indirection of Milton's style reflects rather the mode of the Elizabethan dramatic prologue. The obvious passage for comparison is in the prologue by Envy, set before Ben Jonson's *The Poetaster*:

> Light, I salute thee, but with wounded nerves,
> Wishing the golden splendour pitchy darkness.

In both Jonson's and Milton's prologues we find the same austere and unrelenting definition of self by the denial of all that an audience takes for granted. In both a force is exerted on us that we cannot deny, and yet whose purpose is to deny us. T. S. Eliot has finely said of the Jonson passage: 'It is not human life that informs Envy . . . but it is energy of which human life is only another variety.' As a dramatic prologue Satan's lines must have had the same negative force as Envy's (or Volpone's) opening lines, a challenge to the audience to take up a particular attitude to the show of life which follows. As embodied in the epic, however, the lines exert their force in a different relation to their context. They are not followed by anything like a slice of life. Paradoxically enough, if we take Philips's remark with complete literalness we must say that the epic goes on to enlarge the dramatic power of Satan's soliloquy. The direction of address turns from the external bearer of value, the sun, to the divided self;

> Ah wherefore! He deserved no such return
> From me, whom he created what I was
> In that bright eminence, and with his good
> Upbraided none. . . .
> Me miserable! Which way shall I fly
> Infinite wrath, and infinite despair?
> Which way I fly is hell; my self am hell;
> And in the lowest deep a lower deep
> Still threatening to devour me opens wide,
> To which the hell I suffer seems a Heaven.
> O then at last relent: is there no place
> Left for repentance, none for pardon left? (42–80)

This again is intensely dramatic and strongly reminds us of models in the Elizabethan drama, not merely of prologues but of fully dramatised soliloquies. The Act V soliloquy of Shakespeare's Richard III offers us the same terrifying paradox of the criminal who wishes to fly from criminality but cannot escape himself:

> Is there a murderer here? No – yes, I am.
> Then fly. What, from myself? Great reason why –
> Lest I revenge. What, myself upon myself!
> Alack, I love myself. Wherefore? For any good

That I myself have done unto myself?
O, no! Alas, I rather hate myself
For hateful deeds committed by myself!   (V, III, 184–90)

The final soliloquy of Dr Faustus provides another example of the same
mode, horror at damnation, desire to repent, inability to do so. The
Satan soliloquy differs, however, from both these (and probably from
any other possible theatrical example) in its relation to the explicit
doctrines which surround it. Satan expresses not only an awareness that
his wishes are self-frustrated (as Richard does also) but exhibits further
an exact knowledge of the doctrine he offends against. He 'understood
not', he tells us,

> that a grateful mind
> By owing owes not, but still pays, at once
> Indebted and discharged; what burden then?   (55–7)

Or again (closer still to Richard):

> Hadst thou the same free will and power to stand?
> Thou hadst: whom hast thou then or what to accuse,
> But heaven's free love dealt equally to all?   (66–8)

It is the last line here that takes us away from the world of Shakespearian
subjectivity and into the Miltonic world of patiently organised theological
standards and basic Christian data. The speech moves unrelentingly
through the specifics of Satan's theological development. A mere survey
of its key words will indicate the centrality of the Christian definition of
the individual in relation to God, the norm against which Satan here
defines himself and by which we are invited to define him: 'good . . .
service . . . afford . . . pay . . . due . . . good . . . ill . . . quit the
debt . . . paying . . . owe . . . owing owes not . . . fell . . . free will
and power to stand . . . free love . . . love . . . love . . . chose . . .
despair . . . repentance . . . pardon . . . fall . . . grace . . . relapse
. . . fall . . . hope excluded . . . outcast . . . hope . . . hope . . .
remorse . . . good . . . Evil . . . good'. Here the standard Christian
vocabulary – of a debt to God that requires redemption, but is
redeemed by free love, the only currency that does not cast the debtors
into evil and despair – is so strong and so continuous that our attention
is focused as much on the norm as on the person defying it. Compare
Macbeth:

> My way of life
> Is fall'n into the sere, the yellow leaf;
> And that which should accompany old age,

As honour, love, obedience, troops of friends,
I must not look to have; but in their stead
Curses not loud but deep, mouth-honour, breath,
Which the poor heart would fain deny, and dare not.

(V, II, 22–8)

The world that Macbeth has lost is defined for us by the poignant small change of human existence, and without doctrinal accuracy. The invitation to us is to identify our own experience with the emotion the protagonist expresses when he contemplates his own experience. The unstructured emotional power of the speech carries us into the sense of a man like us. But Satan's speech draws much of *its* power from the objective logic with which it exhausts the possibilities in Satan's position. We identify with the system so accurately described no less than with its victim.

Faustus, Richard III, Macbeth, as well as Satan, are all characters caught in the condition of despair. But the method by which the condition is conveyed to us is notably different in the epic and in the plays. The fully dramatic speeches I have referred to are all, of course, speeches of self-regard, but the situation of the self is in every case focused for us by the familiar objects which they see or hear and which we, in most cases, are made to feel present on the stage beside them. In *Macbeth*, the whey-faced servant and the emptily obedient Seyton reflect the isolation that the speech describes. In *Faustus*, the sense of the sun moving relentlessly, the vision of God in heaven, the ungaping rotundity of the earth – these allow the actor to animate the world around him as a reflector of himself, as part of his own emotional state. Similarly in Richard's soliloquy the light burning blue, the sweat of terror, the midnight silence, the scene of trial and condemnation that the rhetoric sets up – all these augment the central theatrical emotion of 'you are there'. Milton, on the other hand, gives us self-description rather than self-enactment. The externals that the dramatic characters use to project their emotions are given their values by the force of the protagonists' perceptions of them; we are aware that in a less heightened state the sun's motion is without moral meaning, that midnight is normally silent, that frightened persons often have white faces; but the force of the dramatic situation is such that these normalities are pushed aside and we are swept into the current of the protagonist's hallucination. But the values that Satan sees around him are really there. When he says

my self am hell;
And in the lowest deep a lower deep
Still threatening to devour me opens wide,   (75–7)

he uses words that could with little difficulty be spoken by Richard III.
But in Richard's mouth the *hell* must be heard as, in the main, the
creation of his own mind. When Satan says this he is, in fact, describing
an actual situation which the poem has already spelled out in some detail.

Another way of making the same point is to say that the force of
the theatrical characters depends on an intense presentness in which
the audience shares with the characters, and only a dim sense of the
limit to change or development allowed by the play. Even though
Faustus was born with pride and Richard with teeth, any sense of static
or limited quality in them is contradicted by our actual experience of
the variation that the plays characteristically allow. But Milton's
emphasis on doctrine means that limits are clearly defined and omni-
present. Some critics (for example, C. S. Lewis) speak of the 'progressive degradation' of Satan. Such a development may be intended; but
it is a 'development' along a single-track railway – the beginning
requires the destination. The possibility of true change is what Satan's
soliloquy specifically denies. One might suppose, he says, that things
would have turned out differently if circumstances had been different:

> O had his powerful destiny ordained
> Me some inferior angel, I had stood
> Then happy. . . .   (58–60)

But he quickly exposes the fallacy, as he must if the poem is to remain
true to itself. His outlook is not personal but the product of theological
absolutes, fixed in one direction:

> So farewell hope, and with hope farewell fear,
> Farewell remorse: all good to me is lost;
> Evil be thou my good. . . .   (108–10)

Such fixity raises its own problems, of course, for the story requires us
to believe that Satan *has* changed. So we ask, 'Was he wicked in heaven?'
and find no means of answering.

One of the most obvious changes between tragic and epic versions of
Paradise Lost is the showing in the epic of what had been carefully concealed in the drafts of the tragedy – the central events of the temptation
and the eating, now presented with documentary clarity and simplicity:

> So saying, her rash hand in evil hour
> Forth reaching to the fruit, she plucked, she ate:
> Earth felt the wound, and nature from her seat
> Sighing through all her works gave signs of woe,
> That all was lost. Back to the thicket slunk
> The guilty serpent. . . .   (IX, 780–5)

The epic telling of this crucial event makes it clear why Milton planned
to avoid it in the tragedy. Action and interpretation, event and meaning,

are woven here into a contrapuntal structure that depends for its effect
on the continuous control by the narrative voice, showing the event as
actually happening, but seeing it also from a later point of view that
reflects outside knowledge of the context. Grotius, in his play, does
show the eating; but with a degree of self-consciousness and self-
description that makes the character a mere mouthpiece. Here moral
debate, for which Latin rhetoric supplied a resonant vocabulary, controls
the form. Eve's eating is simply a point of transition between the debate
with Satan and the even longer debate with Adam. What the form
Milton was leaving did not seem to allow was a combination of vivid
humanity (which Elizabethan drama gave, but inside a vaguely defined
morality) together with contextual control and consistency. To see how
Milton achieved this combination in the epic one has to scan widely.
We should look at the whole sequence that leads up to the eating,
noticing how the dramatisable material is kept in place by authorial
manipulation. Book IX begins with the narrator both separating this
book from what precedes it and sharpening our focus on the choices
the writer has exercised in writing as he has done. I have already discussed this kind of section (see above, pp. 75–7). We enter the narrative
prepared for intense and extraordinary happenings. But first, as usual,
Milton sets time and place: night falls and Satan re-enters Paradise as
a watery mist, thus evading the check on the forward progression of
the story that was imposed at the end of Book IV. His soliloquy (lines
99–179) characterises the order of the God-given universe and places
the chaos of his own heart inside it. I have devoted some comment to the
power of self-projection that appears in such speeches (pp. 86–7). What I
have not spoken about is the way in which the internal emotional state
is immediately caught up in the essentially undramatisable description
that follows. 'Like a black mist low creeping' Satan squirms through the
thickets and finding the serpent asleep possesses him; the 'sacred light'
dawns over Paradise and the grateful earth sends up a steam of praise.
The irony of darkness amid light, hate amid love, chaos amid order, is
thus spread through the landscape in which Adam and Eve now begin
their ceremonious conversation (206–385). Their formality and elaboration is itself, of course, a part of order, based on the conversational
modes of epic heroes and gods. It is typical of Milton that he should
set the mode and the subject-matter against one another. We see a
husband and wife arguing whether they should garden together or apart.
Beneath the trivial domesticity of the situation there lurks, of course,
not only the waiting serpent but the largest decision that mankind can
make. The scene operates through the gap it creates between the surface
action and the eventual meaning. The value-bearing locutions with
which Adam and Eve address one another:

> Sole Eve, associate sole, to me beyond
> Compare above all living creatures dear,   (227–8)

or

> Offspring of heaven and earth, and all earth's lord,   (273)
>
> Daughter of God and man, immortal Eve,   (291)

– these mark the stance of those who believe themselves totally transparent, even though we, the fallen audience, recognise how close to our
kind of special pleading the arguments come. The mode of speech implies
that they occupy a stable and luminous world at the opposite polarity
from Satan. But perhaps they become more like him as the dialogue
progresses. At any rate his hidden but unforgotten presence provides us
with a bench mark to measure the adequacy of the sense of self that
appears in their talk. The complexity of judgement that is demanded
of us here – to be derived from style, speakers, content, context, visible
alternatives – points to the richness of detail with which Milton
surrounds the explicit drama of his speakers.

The end of this dialogue releases from Milton a flood of 'placing' and
'interpreting' descriptions, linking what is past and what to come and
preparing an appropriate frame of mind for the next dialogue, between
Satan and Eve, sharpening our ironic sense of its inevitable consequence. Thus the freedom and indeterminacy of the to-and-fro dialogue
(the freedom that Eve sought) is given the long-perspective framing of
our awareness of history already determined. The density and elaboration of the method (as of the garden) allows us to see Eve and Satan
circling round one another –

> now hid, now seen
> Among thick-woven arborets and flowers
> Embordered on each bank. . . .   (436–8)

– while Milton circles round both of them accumulating means of
reflecting the resonance of the event, picking up both ordinary experience
(the delight of the townsman in the country) and cultural precedents.
Nearly 250 lines have passed before the actual conversation begins, and
in this space the Oreads, the Dryads, Delia, Pomona, Pales, Ceres,
Adonis, Odysseus, Solomon, Sheba, Hermione, Cadmus, Esculapius,
Ammon, Scipio, Olympias and Circe have all lent their complicating
presences to the margins of our perception and expectation. To achieve
his purpose Milton has to make this interview both humanly convincing
in itself and a reminder of all such situations in human history, of which
it is the original model. Satan's opening speech must have the sharpness

of all other flatteries towards seduction ('I can't help looking at you; you're so beautiful', 'What's an angelic girl like you doing hidden away in a place like this?', 'You'd be queen of the ball if only you'd let yourself go'); while at the same time it remains free (unlike Dryden's version) of the social modes of its repetitions in later time. Eve's dialogue with Satan has the same formality as that with Adam, and, indeed, seems consciously contrived to remind us of that, replacing

> Daughter of God and man, immortal Eve,   (291)

with

> Empress of this fair world, resplendent Eve,   (568)

but transforming factual relationship into intoxicating fiction. This dialogue differs from the preceding one in the rhetorical mode employed – there dialectic, here persuasion. In the Adam–Eve exchange each speaker retains a single fixed and defensible position. Even if Eve may be suspected of special pleading we accept that there *is* a case, or we can understand at least that she supposes there is one. But in the Satan–Eve dialogue the relation of speaker to speaker changes constantly, since Satan's argument springs not from any supposed truth but from an intention to reach a particular end, by hook or by crook. We, the readers, can watch the artistry with which it is done, and perhaps we are meant to count down the stages. His flattering *proem* (549) leads to his specious *narratio* (571–612) and so to the *highth* (675) of his oration, the *impassioned* (678) confutatio of the threat of death (684–732). The rest of the standard classical oration, the confirmatio (that the plant is not only not evil but even actually good) and the conclusio (it should be eaten) can be left to Eve herself, no longer listening to the serpent, but self-deceiving, self-pleasing, self-absorbed, eaten away by the magical force of eloquence and now (like Satan) a skilful soliloquist on her own account. And so, 'Forth reaching to the fruit, she plucked, she ate'.

The drama of the Fall, our sense of participation in the central moment of the crucial act, is thus woven round with a skilfully created awareness of judgement and value, educed from every part of place or time. For the Garden is never a mere collection of plants and trees, neutral background to the significant human action. The actor may be allowed in drama proper to dominate the stage; but such self-confidence is seldom justified in *Paradise Lost*, where comment continually infringes or denies individual assertion. The rhetoric is, indeed, often that of the theatre. When Satan begins his soliloquy in Book IX we are told:

> Thus he resolved, but first from inward grief
> His bursting passion into plaints thus poured. . . .   (97–8)

The *bursting passion* turns out to be a description of the Garden, that is of the context which defines the need for passion rather than any enactment of the passion itself. The dramatic power of the situation is brilliantly allowed by Milton but no less brilliantly contained inside the doctrinal necessities of the epic.

In describing *Paradise Lost* in terms of the formal polarities of drama and epic it is easy to push things too far and think of these genres as inevitably separate and opposed. The major epics of the world in fact show us formal overlap as a recurrent characteristic. The special case of *Paradise Lost* arises from the pressure on its human or quasi-human drama from doctrinal as well as epic assumptions. The difference this makes may be seen in a quick comparison with the *Iliad*. One of the most powerful peripeteias in *Paradise Lost* is that moment where Adam awaits Eve, innocent of the knowledge that oppresses us, that she has already fallen. As she runs into his sights, flushed with guilt and self-justification, Adam stands rooted in the welcoming posture his ignorance had assumed, and hears her:

> while horror chill
> Ran through his veins, and all his joints relaxed;
> From his slack hand the garland wreathed for Eve
> Down dropped, and all the faded roses shed.   (IX, 890–3)

Martin Mueller, writing in *Comparative Literature Studies*, VI (1969), has pointed out the reminiscence here of Andromache waiting for the return of Hector in Book XXII of the *Iliad*, who then, seeing Hector dead

> let her shining headdress fall, her hood
> and diadem, her plaited band and veil
> that Aphrodite once had given her. . . .   (468–70)
> (Fitzgerald's trans.)

To deny that the adjective 'dramatic' is as justified of the Homeric scene as of the Miltonic one would be quite improper. But the placing of the dramatic vignette is quite different in the two poems. In Homer the peripeteia of Andromache, seated at her loom, watching the water heat for Hector's bath, hearing the wailing and then rushing to the tower to see him dragged behind Achilles' chariot – this transformation, and the recognition that goes with it –

> Both
> had this in store from birth – from yours in Troy,
> in Priam's palace, mine by wooded Plakos   (477–9)

– are held within the Homeric poem's characteristic perception that this is what life is necessarily like. Hector and Andromache as individuals are simply large-scale models of what we have seen again and again. But the relation of Adam and Eve to the rest of mankind is rather different. They are not only representative; they are also unique. Achilles' obsessive cruelty is simply a given of the world we are in; but Satan's malice, Eve's folly, Adam's misjudgement are not only that: they also represent a unique process which changes everything, once and for all. History in the *Iliad* is simply a sequence of repetitions. Hence we may say that the string of vignettes that comprises the *Iliad* (Achilles and Agamemnon, Odysseus and Thersites, Helen on the walls, the Doloneia) offers plenty of dramatic excitement but lacks the forward drive to establish continuous large-scale dramatic interest. The drift of the story and the fates of the individuals in the *Iliad* are so close to one another that there is little space for the dramatic excitement of wondering which of the large number of potentials the individual will choose, and which of the paths chosen will lead forward and which will come to dead ends. They all come to dead ends. Milton was the inheritor not only of un-Homeric assumptions about individual creative power, but also of an expressive rhetoric, refined especially in Elizabethan drama, for individual experience. This inherited language allowed Milton to focus our attention on the iridescent indeterminacy of the individual who chooses, while keeping the issues of choice sternly determinate. The nature of this language and the methods by which it is used are the topics to which we must next turn our attention.

CHAPTER 4

Style and Meaning

Milton was the inheritor of a linguistic organism which had come to fulfilment in the previous generation, particularly, it would seem, in response to a felt need to express the inner lives of characters who are caught in the awareness of their isolated selves. As a language of drama English poetry had obviously sharpened its potential in one direction rather than another, learning (for example) to evoke the sense of a man thinking even more powerfully than the sense of the things he thought about, developing the capacity to reveal the movement of the mind as a sifting through potentials rather than a march towards decision. The method by which the cloud of self-awareness resolves itself into the shape of action is always mysterious in Shakespeare and his contemporaries, but often triumphantly matches our own sense of the mysterious nature of thinking, feeling and deciding. Take an example:

> *Macbeth*: If it were done when 'tis done, then 'twere well
> It were done quickly. If the assassination
> Could trammel up the consequence, and catch,
> With his surcease, success; that but this blow
> Might be the be-all and the end-all here –
> But here upon this bank and shoal of time –
> We'd jump the life to come. But in these cases
> We still have judgment here, that we but teach
> Bloody instructions, which being taught return
> To plague th' inventor. This even-handed justice
> Commends th' ingredience of our poison'd chalice
> To our own lips. He's here in double trust:
> First, as I am his kinsman and his subject –
> Strong both against the deed; then as his host,
> Who should against his murderer shut the door,
> Not bear the knife myself. Besides, this Duncan
> Hath borne his faculties so meek, hath been
> So clear in his great office, that his virtues
> Will plead like angels, trumpet-tongu'd against
> The deep damnation of his taking-off;
> And pity like a naked new-born babe,
> Striding the blast, or heaven's cherubin hors'd
> Upon the sightless couriers of the air,
> Shall blow the horrid deed in every eye,

That tears shall drown the wind. I have no spur
To prick the sides of my intent, but only
Vaulting ambition, which o'erleaps itself,
And falls on th' other.   (*Macbeth*, I, VII, 1–28)

The way in which evidence and passion, logic and imagery, flow and
ebb throughout this speech, the speed with which argument becomes the
apprehension of an experience that the argument implies – all this
animates our sense that it is in the mysterious recesses of the mind that
men are most real and that the external witnesses of these states (in
action, for instance) are partial and unreliable.

What Milton needed for *Paradise Lost* was not exactly supplied by
this gift of tongues. The epic poem requires, for its over-all stability,
a style which is more constant than drama can properly endure, one
which tempers responsiveness to the iridescent moment with a larger
sense of the explicit recurrencies and continuities of a unified outlook on
the subject. Satan and Eve, Adam and Christ, must be made to sound
more like one another than Hamlet and Polonius, Ophelia, Gertrude and
Osric ever do. What is more, they must all remind us strongly of
Milton the narrator, whose stylistic norm provides the circumference or
Primum Mobile within which these other planets fly their turns. These
characteristics of the epic style, as against the dramatic style of the
Elizabethans, are often considered as straight poetic loss. To this
travesty I shall return at a later point. What I wish to talk about now
is the possibility of a positive rather than a negative relationship between
Elizabethan dramatic verse and the epic verse of *Paradise Lost*. Milton,
let me repeat, was not required by the task in hand to reject the vivid-
nesses of Elizabethan English, but only to absorb it, or (in other words)
to keep the individual responses in touch with the central assumptions
of the poem. To set against the Shakespearian example above, let us
take a Miltonic example – Adam's words when he sees the fallen Eve:

O fairest of creation, last and best
Of all God's works, creature in whom excelled
Whatever can to sight or thought be formed,
Holy, divine, good, amiable or sweet!
How art thou lost, how on a sudden lost,
Defaced, deflowered, and now to death devote?
Rather how hast thou yielded to transgress
The strict forbiddance, how to violate
The sacred fruit forbidden! Some cursed fraud
Of enemy hath beguiled thee, yet unknown,
And me with thee hath ruined, for with thee
Certain my resolution is to die;
How can I live without thee, how forgo

> Thy sweet converse and love so dearly joined
> To live again in these wild woods forlorn?
> Should God create another Eve, and I
> Another rib afford, yet loss of thee
> Would never from my heart; no no, I feel
> The link of nature draw me: flesh of flesh,
> Bone of my bone thou art, and from thy state
> Mine never shall be parted, bliss or woe.
>   So having said, as one from sad dismay
> Recomforted, and after thoughts disturbed
> Submitting to what seemed remediless,
> Thus in calm mood his words to Eve he turned. . . .
>   (IX, 896–920)

Adam's speech and Adam's emotions are inset in a narrative framework which requires them to operate within strictly defined limits. What
is most powerful in Adam's speech (spoken to himself, we are told, not
out aloud) is the combined weight given to personal emotion and to the
necessary and untouched external order which the emotion contradicts.
Macbeth's speech liberates him (and us) into a freewheeling universe
of his own creation. It seems as if his poetry and his sensibility could
go in any direction, conjure up any imaginary object. The real world
(Duncan and his situation) is presented to our attention, but is hardly
spoken of before it is transformed into a scenario of shapes that represent the perceiving mind in its self-exciting response to the thing
perceived. No image is too intense or lurid to be used, even if only for
indicating his (and our) perception of what he is going to do. Adam, by
comparison, merely reports how things are. He accepts the contradiction
between emotion and fact. He does not (even momentarily) transform it.
The fraught simplicity with which he expresses Eve's sweetness and his
own total commitment to her allows us to participate at every point in
the total truth of the poem – that wilful humanity and divine order
co-exist in their separate and contradictory freedoms throughout time.
Our sense of the totality of the poem presses, therefore, on every line
of the speech, and gives it a weight that Adam himself could not
contrive. The transition at the end moves from thought to action as from
like to like and known to known. In *Macbeth*, however, the only way by
which the phantasmagoria of imagination can be led back to the
common life is by disjunction and contradiction. The real world breaks
in on the 'rapt' soliloquist. The practical wife demands action, and the
dream world is sealed away in its incommensurate dimension.

The permeation of one world by the other in Milton's poem (the inner
by the outer and vice versa) means that the doubleness of effect, which I
have pointed at again and again, is explicitly a method of describing
life as it really is. We the readers are continually invited to see the para-

doxes as a means by which we may guess a further and inexpressible truth. In Shakespeare's tragedies, on the other hand, the paradox of inner–outer contradiction is left without any suggestion of an eventual compromise. Milton operates, it might seem, with a *both-this-and-that* model, Shakespeare with a *now-this-now-that* one. As I have noted above, the interpretation of the momentary and the permanent and the need to compromise individual effects in the light of external meaning have usually been seen in Milton's poem not as *both-and* but as straight historical loss, mere dilution of the Shakespearian complexity. The univocal poetry that remains can then be described as opposite to Shakespeare, not as parallel to him, as classic versus romantic, Latinate versus vernacular, grand versus subtle, artful versus natural. The opposition thus set up has, of course, been used in the main to belabour Milton (so simplified) with the superior excellence of Shakespeare. It is convenient to Romantic and post-Romantic sensibilities to suppose that the immensely talented Milton made a wrong turning in middle life and so failed to realise his potential power to bridge the gap between the Elizabethan and the Romantic modes. The dangers of classicism are thus highlighted. Forming his epic style, as Dr Johnson had remarked, 'upon a perverse and pedantic principle' Milton can be seen to have sacrificed his native idiom on the altar of Virgilian idolatry. The defence of Milton's style is in fact difficult to sustain if these distinctions are allowed to be fully descriptive, not simply the partial consequences of prior generic choice. Douglas Bush has made a bold attempt to defend Milton's 'classicism' as more than a retreat from Elizabethan excess, as in fact a truly alternative style, with its own independent range of excellencies. He says, 'Since Milton's art is of the ancient kind, the charges brought against him must be brought likewise against nearly all the Greek and Roman poets'; he then goes on to discuss the charge that 'classical art is cold and dead' because it seeks to 'render the normal and universal, not the peculiar' and because it is highly selective in the interest of order and severe simplicity (*'Paradise Lost' in Our Time* (1945), 91–3). As a defender of 'classicism' Professor Bush makes many good points; as a defender of Milton his position is more dubious. That Milton admired the classical poets is certain and that he wished to be read by their light is probable. But who are the classical poets? If we look at Milton's Latin poems we find an admiration for Ovid so complete that it involves an almost total take-over of the Latin poet's cadence and vocabulary. Is the defence of Milton then to be conducted in the same terms as a defence of Ovid? This does not seem to be what Professor Bush is aiming at. His conception of 'the classical' is not Milton's. It is that bequeathed to the modern world by Johann Joachim Winckelmann (1717–68), who rephrased earlier conceptions in terms of a standard he thought he saw in the 'best' Greek statuary –

a standard of serenity and repose which appears most famously in English in Matthew Arnold's conception of a Sophocles who 'saw life steadily and saw it whole' ('To a Friend'). For Professor Bush this is Milton's quality also: poise, restraint and simplicity. As an example he quotes Book III, lines 40–55, as 'one perfect example of classical writing'. It is worth pursuing this particular passage to see how far its quality corresponds in fact to 'the classical':

> Thus with the year
> Seasons return, but not to me returns
> Day, or the sweet approach of even or morn,
> Or sight of vernal bloom, or summer's rose,
> Or flocks, or herds, or human face divine;
> But cloud instead, and ever-during dark
> Surrounds me, from the cheerful ways of men
> Cut off, and for the book of knowledge fair
> Presented with a universal blank
> Of nature's works to me expunged and razed,
> And wisdom at one entrance quite shut out.
> So much the rather thou celestial Light
> Shine inward, and the mind through all her powers
> Irradiate, there plant eyes, all mist from thence
> Purge and disperse, that I may see and tell
> Of things invisible to mortal sight.   (III, 40–55)

One must begin by allowing that the images of this passage do, indeed, exhibit one of the characteristics of a 'classical' style as Professor Bush describes it: they do not 'number the streaks of the tulip', they seem to avoid the peculiar and even the particular. But is it true to say further that the generalisations are 'packed with emotion because they are merely registered with impersonal restraint as the commonplace phenomena of every day. We feel the reserve of power behind such quietness. We are compelled to realise for ourselves what deprivation means, and we can do so because Milton universalises his own feelings, the normal feelings of the cheerful human race to which he belongs' (94)? The model which Professor Bush gives us is of a simple, severe, restrained, generalised, 'classical' surface, behind which lie the powerful emotions of the particular individual. I do not quarrel with the description of the separate elements, but dispute the relationship we are supposed to register between them. I cannot read the surface of this passage as smoothly impersonal. It seems rather that the sharply personal 'me . . . me . . . me . . . I' is as much on the surface as the impersonal process of nature which alternates with it. I do not think it serves any purpose to say as Professor Bush does (following C. S. Lewis, *Preface to 'Paradise Lost'*, 58): 'He feels, to be sure, as John Milton, but he writes as "the blind poet" (*'Paradise Lost' in Our Time*, 94). No mere reader of the poem takes the personal pronoun as having other than a personal force; when the poem says 'I' we sophisticate intolerably if we spend our time asking 'Which "I" is this?' My contention is, then, that the surface is not smooth but broken up by the alternation of the intensely personal and the external and impersonal. This point seems even clearer if we begin the passage, not where Professor Bush does, but a few lines earlier:

> Yet not the more
> Cease I to wander . . .
> nor sometimes forget . .
> Blind Thamyris, and blind Mæonides . . .
> Then feed on thoughts, that voluntary move
> Harmonious numbers; as the wakeful bird
> Sings darkling, and in shadiest covert hid
> Tunes her nocturnal note. Thus. . . . (26–40)

The lines on the nightingale are powerful enough to have formed one of the starting-points of the most sharply Romantic and evocative stanzas in Keats's 'Ode to a Nightingale'; Keats's vision has imposed on him a trance-like blindness:

> I cannot see what flowers are at my feet
>   Nor what soft incense hangs upon the boughs,
> But in embalmed darkness guess each sweet
>   Wherewith the seasonable month endows. . . .

It is when his eyes are shut, like Milton's, that he hears the inner meaning of the nightingale:

> Darkling I listen; and for many a time
>   I have been half in love with easeful Death,
> Call'd him soft names in many a mused rhyme,
>   To take into the air my quiet breath;
> Now more than ever seems it rich to die,
>   To cease upon the midnight with no pain,
> While thou art pouring forth thy soul abroad. . . .

To both poets the nightingale offers the external correlative of a singer whose song is integrated into the impersonal cycle of nature. For Keats the contrast between poet and bird quickly modulates into the largest of all such alternations, that between being and non-being. The contrast is more explicitly complex in Milton. The *Thus* in line 40, which Professor Bush leaves dangling, is the hinge between a world of connections and one of isolation. The nightingale's song belongs to its environment as does Milton's *Nightly . . . visit* to the *warbling flow* of

Sion (29–32). In these terms the grateful vicissitude of night and day,
song and silence, and the seasonal cycle, offers a continuity between
subject and object, perceiver (Milton) and thing perceived. But the continuity is, as so often in Milton, also a discontinuity. *Thus* the cycle goes
on, but Milton is not on it. But this antithesis is by no means the whole
story. 'Not . . . vernal bloom, or summer's rose,/Or flocks, or herds, or
human face divine' seems to offer us a homogeneous set of items arranged
in a climactic order, the climax marked by the chiasmus of *human face
divine*. But the chiasmus marks, in fact, the instability of the whole
inner–outer arrangement. The *human face* is a very proper climactic item
in a list of things that Milton cannot see. But the *human face divine* is
an object whose importance derives from powers that cannot be seen
anyway – not, at least, with the eyes of sense. Is the blind poet deprived
or privileged? The rhetoric flips over on to its head at the merest touch.
Milton tells us that he is cut off from the *book of knowledge* and can
see only *a universal blank*. In fact he has just been itemising the elements
he cannot see, not only in their physical existence but also in their
relation to spiritual truth. He cannot see; but on the other hand he can
see, with new eyes planted in him by the *celestial Light*. The Book of
Nature is shut to him; but volume one, the Book of God (the Gospel),
is open to him as never before. With these new eyes he can see 'things
invisible to mortal sight'; but this does not create a simple disjunction
between the spiritual and the physical, inner and outer sight, for things
visible always remain (when rightly seen) the expression of things
invisible. The poet and the nightingale are parallel as well as opposite,
tuning their notes to a diapason that is beyond the senses.

A glance at the syntax of this passage reflects and confirms the
ambiguities and contradictions that I have been speaking about, suggesting a reading mode more Donnian than classical. Donald Davie has
remarked on the syntactical uncertainty between transitive and intransitive senses of *move* in line 37: 'This flicker of hesitation about whether
the thoughts move only themselves, or something else, makes us see
that the numbers aren't really "something else" but are the very
thoughts themselves, seen under a new aspect' ('Syntax and music in
Paradise Lost', in Kermode, *The Living Milton*, 73). We may see this
perception in another way if we ask the question: Are the verses inside
the poet's mind or outside? The syntax seems designed to evade such a
'fallen' question. In one reading (*move* is intransitive), the movement of
thought is itself the poetry. In the other reading (*move* is transitive) the
thoughts are the cause of something more visible and external, the verses.
The confusion of the borderline between inner and outer is a recurrent
Miltonic ambiguity. The 'flicker of hesitation' seems like a characteristic
tic at the end of many lines in this passage and elsewhere. In line 45
when we reach *dark* we think we have come to the end of the sentence,

'Not . . . Day . . . Or flocks . . . But cloud . . . and . . . dark'. But
when the eye travels back to the next line we discover that *cloud* and
dark are not tied to *returns* in line 41 but are the subjects of a new
verb *Surrounds* in line 46. Likewise when we get to *blank* in line 48 we
think we have reached a resounding and completed negative – instead
of the book, he has nothing. But then it turns out that this 'nothing'
needs to be qualified. We are told not simply that there is a blank but
what the blank is a blank of – "a universal blank/Of nature's works to
me expunged and razed'. Having given us an absolute, Milton then
requires us to consider it and modify it: only nature's works are
involved, and it is only for me that the deprivation exists, and even for
me there are more than compensating alternatives.

The complexity of the effects I am describing is far from what we
normally understand by the word 'classical'. But the *asprezza,* or harsh-
ness, that Milton (following Tasso) thought appropriate to epic (see
F. T. Prince, *The Italian Element in Milton's Verse* (1954), 38–43) is
classical enough, though from a baroque rather than a romantic viewpoint.
R. M. Adams has described with great brilliance and lucidity the use that
Milton actually made of his classical experience. He speaks of 'Milton's
use of alien grammars as devices for extending or delaying or, sometimes,
suspending the flow of an English sentence. Their most frequent controlling use is to render the verse slow and complex; they knot the thread
of assertion in loops. . . . The virtues of this extended style . . . are
not by any means the virtues of the long Latin period, that skilfully
braced fabric of complex yet precise interconnections. The style [of
Milton] is rather glancing and ejaculatory . . . [producing] mingled
textures, meanings arranged in depth, and subsurface controls slowly
rising to our awareness (*Ikon* (1955), 192–4).

The great advantage of Adams's method of handling Latin influences
on Milton's style is that he avoids the simple antithesis between English
spontaneity and Latin formalism (or English formlessness and Latin
grandeur), showing what extraordinary, unclassical and individual effects
Milton required of syntax, always the master and never the servant of the
various styles he had on call. But such patent complexity is hard to retain
amid the simplifications of literary history. The standard approach to
Milton's 'grandeur' in verse has been to think of it as remote, large-
scale, loud, generalised, full of long vowels and unusual words. Several
examples of eighteenth-century 'Miltonics' have such characteristics.
But probably the most telling expression of this view appears in the
octave of Tennyson's 'Alcaics':

> O mighty-mouth'd inventor of harmonies,
> O skill'd to sing of Time and Eternity,
>   God-gifted organ-voice of England,

Milton, a name to resound for ages
Whose Titan angels, Gabriel, Abdiel,
Starr'd from Jehovah's gorgeous armouries,
Tower, as the deep-domed empyrëan
Rings to the roar of an angel onset. . . .

This is a description of what may be called the 'bow-wow' (or even the 'oom-boom') sublime, appropriate to the Victorian religiosity of huge pipe-organs in neo-Gothic churches. The fact that Milton's religiosity was very different seems to have disappeared from sight as his poem itself became an English cathedral structure. 'Our language', says Addison, 'sunk under him.' If this is so, then the poem itself must be a remarkable essay in the Art of Sinking in Poetry, for clearly enough it stands on the language it can use. But the whole notion that Milton is characterised by mere weight of sonority is an error easily refuted every time we care to read the poem. On the other hand, the poem *is* an English monument and it is merely Quixotic to suppose that critical attitudes to *Paradise Lost* can avoid scribbling it over with the prejudices of later ages. Milton has often seemed something of an overbearing father to subsequent poets; and these have (as one would expect) used the myth rather than the reality of his epic to fashion their rejections, or their endorsements. The high Victorianism of Tennyson's Milton must be allowed to have played its part in the 'dislodgement' of Milton (as it was called) in the mid-twentieth century. But the relationship between Milton and Romantic poetry begins much earlier and can be most fruitfully studied in the Miltonism and anti-Miltonism of John Keats. I have already spoken of the positive use Keats made of Milton's poetry; the markings in the copy of Milton owned by Keats show the detailed nature of his attention to the earlier poet. But in the end Keats had to reject Milton as part of his effort to become himself. He gave up *Hyperion*, he said, because 'there were too many Miltonic inversions in it' and goes on: 'Miltonic verse can not be written but in an artful or rather artist's humour' (*Letters*, ed. Hyder Rollins (1958), II, 167). Later (II, 212) he enlarges on the point: 'I have but lately stood on my guard against Milton. Life to him would be death to me. Miltonic verse cannot be written but [in] the vein of art.' The opinion about Miltonic art which appears in both these contexts seems to be the crucial one. Milton's art stifles what Keats (II, 167) calls 'the true voice of feeling'. The effort to achieve a genuine sincerity of style is pulled out of true into mock grandeur or pastiche by the force of Milton's example. For *Hyperion* to succeed as more than a superb exercise in style, Keats needed to find a way of enlarging personal feeling and its associated patterns of perception into a vision 'beyond the size of dreaming', learn how to join together the poignant plangencies of individual experience and the context of a shared myth. Milton offered (and offers) the power of a mythic language, but not one expressing immediately the sharp intensities of the isolated individual. The world he created and offered was a world of experience validated by its intellectual as well as its emotional coherence, a world not of Keatsian word-magic but of words whose only magic is their meaning, their place in the total intellectual structure. Keats, lacking the knowledge that would sew together the separate intensities of Saturn, Hyperion and Apollo, could only hear in Milton's words the tinkling cymbal of art separated from understanding. In these circumstances he was no doubt right to reject them.

One Keats does not make a Hampstead; but the history of the nine-teenth-century literary tradition is in part a history of the movement of Keats's nervous individual sensibility into the centre of the picture. The second half of the Tennyson 'Alcaics' turns the booming organ-voice of England into a Tennysonian word-painter, pursuing sensuous detail for its own sake:

> Me rather all that bowery loneliness,
> The brooks of Eden mazily murmuring,
> And blooms profuse and cedar arches
> Charm, as a wanderer out in ocean,
> Where some refulgent sunset of India
> Streams o'er a rich ambrosial ocean isle,
> And crimson-hued the stately palm-woods
> Whisper in odorous heights of even.

What seems to be missing here is any sense of Milton's intelligence, the complement and source of his word-music. Why such a self-indulgent sensualist should be the God-gifted organ-voice of England is never made clear (though a split in Tennyson himself is probably highly relevant). But the two halves of this Milton remained powerful enough (even thus shakily connected) to sustain a dominant reputation until the end of the century. To Robert Bridges and Gerard Manley Hopkins, Milton's art retains a classic status even though its meaning was evaporating. Hopkins distinguishes between his own 'inscape' or 'distinctiveness' and what he calls the 'more balanced Miltonic style' (*Letters to Bridges*, ed. C. C. Abbott, 66); but it was to be 'inscape', individualism, isolated precision of visual detail, idiosyncrasy of character, indulged eccentricity that were to make Hopkins the morning star of twentieth-century poetry, not any feeling for the balance of public statement in Milton's verse. The modern poetry of private imagistic shock was almost certain to represent Milton as a windbag. T. S. Eliot's 'A note on the verse of John Milton', published in 1936 but adumbrated in other writings for at least fifteen years before this date, concentrates on verbal effects, the last bastion of Milton's reputation.

The booming imprecision of organ-music in vaulted buildings is now found to be a fair metaphor for Milton's insufficiency rather than his impressiveness. His sound-patterns are found to be divorced from sense, so that his verse is 'not poetry but a solemn game'. But it would be wrong to consider Mr Eliot's view of Milton without looking at the whole myth within which it is enshrined. The basis of this extraordinarily powerful myth is a set of largely concealed assumptions about life, speech and writing, including the assumption (common in innovative artists) that the world must have gone seriously astray in order to require the renovations of the writer and his colleagues. What is explicit is the idea that once there was a literary golden age when the quality of life was such that speech and communication from one individual to another led effortlessly towards the universal and the poetic. This 'organic community' energised something called 'living speech' (reminiscent of the equally impalpable 'living water' in the Bible), which can be glimpsed in Shakespeare and the Elizabethans. But then came a Fall, a 'dissociation of sensibility', not really capable of being dated, as is proper enough for mythic events, separating a 'healthy' situation from an 'unhealthy' one. Milton's fate is to be cast as the serpent who destroyed the linguistic Eden, substituting for 'living speech' a foreign idiom, an attention to sound rather than to image, and a departicularised vocabulary. Image, we should note, was thought capable of combining the sensual and the intellectual, sound was not. Milton's great power was thus acknowledged as, once again, the father's power to forbid. The organic life, the teeming and unbiddable variety of colloquial experience, was walled off from subsequent poets by 'the Chinese wall of Miltonic blank verse': soil-deep Englishmen had become stuffed mandarins.

F. R. Leavis's essay on 'Milton's verse' enlarges and in general coarsens these perceptions. The Good Thing, now called 'the expressive resources of English' or 'the essential spirit of the language', was sacrificed by Milton to the Bad Thing, called 'the Grand Style', seen as a 'laboured pedantic artifice . . . focusing rather upon words than upon perceptions or things' and so 'remote from speech' and 'incompatible with sharp concrete realization' (*Revaluation*, 49, 50, 56). Elsewhere, 'cultivating so complete and systematic a callousness to the intrinsic nature of English, Milton forfeits all possibility of subtle or delicate life in his verse' (53). It is hardly possible to deal with such comments except in respect of particular passages; and therefore it may be worth looking in some detail at a Miltonic passage that excites Dr Leavis to especial scorn:

> for God had thrown
> That mountain as his garden mould high raised
> Upon the rapid current, which through veins

Of porous earth with kindly thirst up drawn,
Rose a fresh fountain, and with many a rill
Watered the garden; thence united fell
Down the steep glade, and met the nether flood,
Which from his darksome passage now appears,
And now divided into four main streams,
Runs diverse, wandering many a famous realm
And country whereof here needs no account,
But rather to tell how, if art could tell,
How from that sapphire fount the crisped brooks,
Rolling on orient pearl and sands of gold,
With mazy error under pendant shades
Ran nectar, visiting each plant, and fed
Flowers worthy of Paradise which not nice art
In beds and curious knots, but nature boon
Poured forth profuse on hill and dale and plain,
Both where the morning sun first warmly smote
The open field, and where the unpierced shade
Embrowned the noontide bowers: thus was this place,
A happy rural seat of various view;
Groves whose rich trees wept odorous gums and balm,
Others whose fruit burnished with golden rind
Hung amiable, Hesperian fables true,
If true, here only, and of delicious taste:
Betwixt them lawns, or level downs, and flocks
Grazing the tender herb, were interposed,
Or palmy hillock, or the flowery lap
Of some irriguous valley spread her store,
Flowers of all hue, and without thorn the rose.   (IV, 225–56)

Of this passage Leavis has the following to say: 'As the laboured, pedantic artifice of the diction suggests, Milton seems here to be focusing rather upon words than upon perceptions, sensations, or things. "Sapphire", "orient pearl", "sands of gold", "odorous gums and balm", and so on, convey no doubt a vague sense of opulence, but this is not what we mean by "sensuous richness". . . . In the description of Eden, a little before the passage quoted, we have: "And all amid them stood the tree of life,/High eminent, blooming ambrosial fruit/Of vegetable gold" (lines 218–20). It would be of no use to try and argue with anyone who contended that "vegetable gold" exemplified the same kind of fusion as "green shops" [*Comus*, line 715] (49–50). Among the many points that may be raised here one may note particularly the strength of the response to epithets and the weakness in the awareness of syntax. It would be charitable to suppose that this is the reason why Leavis fails to register the hypothetical mood in which the whole description is couched. The key phrase in the passage is, of course, *if art could tell* in line 236. In the preceding lines Milton has indicated that one way of trying to talk about Eden would be to relate it geographically to other places, identifying its rivers by the places they subsequently pass through. This standard procedure appears in Grotius's *Adamus Exsul*, in Vondel's *Adam in Ballingschap*, and in du Bartas' *Divine Weeks and Works*. In *Paradise Lost*, however, 'here needs no account'. To depart from Paradise, to spend time cataloguing the places that the rivers eventually reach, is to substitute second-order facts for primary ones. Milton's concern is not with what happened to the rivers after they left Paradise but what they did inside Paradise. But can that be done? Certainly his business is to tell it if art can tell it; but Milton does not remove the question mark hanging over the capacity of art to tell such things. The excessive Latinity and stiff metallic splendour of the lines that follow exemplify the kind of *art* which might be used in an attempt to describe Paradise. Milton does not endorse this *art*; if we do not respond to the register of the diction in these lines, he helps us by indicating its status, once again, at the end of the artful passage. If you were to try to use *art*, he says at the beginning, you might write as follows; but you would be wrong in such a procedure, he says at the end, since 'not nice art . . . but nature boon/Poured forth profuse'. It was the quality of the Garden to be both precious and natural, both ordered and profuse, premeditated and spontaneous, simultaneously a Fabergé nightingale and a real bird. Any description is presumably required to stress one side of this antithesis or the other. Milton offers us both models, first one and then the other, but then cancels both sides of the antithesis as equally partial attempts to deal with a describable beyond all descriptions Leavis does not get beyond the first stage; but Milton is continuously augmenting the complexity of his presentation. The Garden is, as he says, characterised by its 'various view', and he then proceeds to play its variousnesses against one another. The trees seemed to show human emotions – they *wept* or *hung amiable;* if ever the Pathetic Fallacy was unpathetic, it was in the Garden of Eden, where man and nature lived uniquely interrelated lives; at least two trees had powers more than arboreal. But this is the kind of picture that fables paint; and pagan fables cannot be relied on to guide us towards Christian truth. They are in the poem, as I have noticed above (page 9) only to be rejected. Milton says of the bower of Adam and Eve:

> In shady bower
> More sacred and sequestered, though but feigned,
> Pan and Sylvanus never slept, nor nymph,
> Nor Faunus haunted.   (IV, 705–8)

The pagan deities bring their offering to the Christian scene and are then denied. The most famous of such comparisons comes towards the end of the description of Eden.

            Not that fair field
Of Enna, where Proserpine gathering flowers
Herself a fairer flower by gloomy Dis
Was gathered, which cost Ceres all that pain
To seek her through the world; nor that sweet grove
Of Daphne by Orontes, and the inspired
Castalian spring, might with this Paradise
Of Eden strive. . . .   (IV, 268–75)

The mass of commentary on this passage does not always allow the full force of its first word. Dr Richard Bentley, however, grasped the point with characteristic firmness: '*Not Enna*, says he, *not Daphne, nor fons Castalius, nor Mount Amara could compare with Paradise*. Why who, Sir, would suspect they could; though you had never told us it.' Bentley sees that the comparison is, in terms of immediate sense, completely redundant. No Christian reader could ever suppose that Eden was rivalled by any pagan garden, so why bother to tell us that it was not rivalled? The answer I wish to offer is that the simile is not present to give us a one-to-one comparison, but rather to show how comparison functions, what it can do and what it can not do when the matter is, as here, beyond compare.

Milton's poetic technique, like Milton's narrative technique, depends for its effect on a continuous shifting in the planes of our response. We are as readers continually challenged not only to feel but also to understand and to 'place' what we are feeling by noticing how we are being made to feel it. Dr Leavis responds to Milton's verse as if it all existed and was all meant to exist at a constant distance from the attention of the reader. When he tells us, in the course of the paragraph cited above, that 'It would be of no use to try and argue with any one who contended that "vegetable gold" exemplified the same kind of fusion as "green shops"' he seems to be assuming that the two different phrases can be subject to the same criterion, that the different contexts do not alter our expectations and the standards we find appropriate, inside a complex response that cannot be reduced to a hard and fast, good and bad, discrimination. 'Vegetable gold' is of course quite different from 'green shops', and there may, indeed, be little point in trying to argue with anyone who supposes that the difference between them can be expressed as a simple difference of valuation. The need, in reading *Paradise Lost*, is not only to notice what the passage is saying but also to notice what it is doing. One may return to Keats, and leave Dr Leavis in a more grateful posture. In a later essay, 'Mr Eliot and Milton', printed in *The Common Pursuit* (1952), Leavis compares the verse of Milton with that of Keats's 'Ode to Autumn', writing finely on the strength of Keats's imagery, of the way in which the analogical suggestions of the varied complex efforts and motions compelled on us as we pronounce and follow the words and hold them properly together (meaning, that is, has from first to last its inseparable and essential part in the effect of 'sound') enforce and enact the paraphrasable meaning. The action of the packed consonants in 'moss'd cottage-trees' is plain enough: there stand the trees, gnarled and sturdy in trunk and bough, their leafy entanglements thickly loaded. It is not fanciful, I think, to find that (the sense being what it is) the pronouncing of 'cottage-trees' suggests, too, the crisp bite and the flow of juice as the teeth close in the ripe apple.

It is easy to agree that Milton's imagery is not in the least like this. The excellency in Keats that Leavis points to arises from the power to realise the thingness of things in the verse which describes them. But Milton in describing the Garden of Eden (or anything else) has concerns quite other than the solidities of kitchen gardens. His aim is rather to express the mind, in which alone the realisation of a supernatural beauty can occur, the hue and texture of the perceiving rather than the perceived, the quality and meaning of responsiveness. Take an extreme example.

> To whom thus also the angel last replied:
> This having learned, thou hast attained the sum
> Of wisdom; hope no higher, though all the stars
> Thou knew'st by name, and all the ethereal powers,
> All secrets of the deep, all nature's works,
> Or works of God in heaven, air, earth, or sea,
> And all the riches of this world enjoyed'st. . . .   (XII, 574–80)

This is great poetry and, indeed, a touchstone of great poetry, but not for reasons that have anything to do with the 'Ode to Autumn'. In part, of course, we respond because it rises greatly to a great occasion. The quality of Adam's finally clarified vision of the meaning of Providence is given with a rapt simplicity which yet picks up and carries the accumulated weight of the poem. It is not simply that Adam and the reader can now look back on all that led them to this point and see now in its monosyllabic essentials what is meant by the command to put behind one all the glories of the world and all the pretensions of intellect. We participate not only in the understanding but also in the emotion that attaches to the understanding, the relief, the gratitude for having finally arrived and seen and been made part of the overarching patience of time redeemed. What these verses express is not the thingness of things but the quality of our shared humanity.

The other matter on which the traditional attack on Milton's poetry fastens is his syntax. Eliot and Leavis confess their distress when they find Milton's sentences requiring to be read more than once (a difficulty not wholly absent from their own sentences). The assumed root cause is once again Milton's Latinity: his long sentences and grammatical inversions are supposed to be copied from the Latin; they impose a 'departure from English order, structure and accentuation' that deadens the verse movement and prevents it from triggering a natural human response. More careful reading has shown, however, that the elaboration of Milton's syntax is quite un-Latinate in fact (see R. D. Emma, *Milton's Grammar*, ch. 8). Milton's paragraphs are not like Latin periods; they do not proceed by relentless subordination. They tend to be made up of long strings of appositional phrases linked by co-ordinating conjunctions. One particular stylistic effect of this is worth noticing. Let us look again at the description of Paradise in Book IV. The eye and the attention are invited to travel over this landscape, moving from one thing to another by a process of loose association: nor . . . but . . . and . . . or . . . others . . . another side . . . meanwhile. What is particularly interesting here is the use of the shortest of these words — *or* :

> Betwixt them lawns, or level downs, and flocks
> Grazing the tender herb, were interposed,
> Or palmy hillock, or the flowery lap
> Of some irriguous valley. . . .   (IV, 252–5)

Milton can hardly mean us to suppose that *or* . . . *or* here means *in one place* . . . *in another place*. Certainly to try to visualise it in these terms is to come to grief (though this may be taken only to point to the supposedly unvisual quality of Milton's verse). The phrases connected by *or* seem to refer, in fact, not to the alternations in the landscape but to the alternatives available to the reader: 'you might like to see it this way, or perhaps that' with the important Paradisal proviso, 'however you see it you will not be describing the thing itself but only the partial mind of the describer'. It is not, of course, a technique that is confined to Paradise. Let us return to the apostrophe to Light at the beginning of Book III: 'Hail, holy Light', etc. The opening phrase is hardly out of Milton's mouth before he has invited us to question it:

> Or of the eternal co-eternal beam
> May I express thee unblamed?   (III, 2–3)

The confident apostrophe of the first line is balanced by an alternative way of talking about the same thing:

> Or hear'st thou rather pure ethereal stream,
> Whose fountain who shall tell?   (III, 7–8)

– that is, 'Would you rather be called . . . ?' The description does not touch the thing described, for the meaning of the formula remains inaccessible ('who can tell'); but it expresses the desire of the human and fallen speaker to reach out towards what is assuredly there.

Such examples allow the gap between the explicitly present narrator and the eventually unattainable nature of the thing narrated to be focused for us by the appositional and loosely co-ordinated nature of the syntax. Elsewhere the ambiguity is attached to the dramatised speaker, who announces the way he sees things in terms which sound definite enough; but the loosely woven syntax leaves holes through which we observe, as it were, the larger purposes of the narration. The opening speeches of Satan are particularly rich in this kind of duplicity. Take the speech to Beelzebub describing their escape:

> But see the angry victor hath recalled
> His ministers of vengeance and pursuit
> Back to the gates of heaven: the sulphurous hail
> Shot after us in storm, o'erblown hath laid
> The fiery surge, that from the precipice
> Of heaven received us falling, and the thunder,
> Winged with red lightning and impetuous rage,
> Perhaps hath spent his shafts, and ceases now
> To bellow through the vast and boundless deep.
> Let us not slip the occasion, whether scorn,
> Or satiate fury yield it from our foe.
> Seest thou yon dreary plain, forlorn and wild,
> The seat of desolation, void of light,
> Save what the glimmering of these livid flames
> Casts pale and dreadful? Thither let us tend
> From off the tossing of these fiery waves,
> There rest, if any rest can harbour there,
> And reassembling our afflicted powers,
> Consult how we may henceforth most offend
> Our enemy, our own loss how repair,
> How overcome this dire calamity,
> What reinforcement we may gain from hope,
> If not what resolution from despair.   (I, 169–91)

The syntax here is in the main simple and idiomatic. Any attempt to paraphrase Satan's thoughts reveals, however, the care with which Milton keeps alternatives open. Take lines 171–4 ('the sulphurous hail . . . received us falling'). A prose version of this might read: 'The sulphurous hail which was shot after us overblew and has now laid flat the fiery surge which received us when we fell from heaven.' What this clarifies most obviously is the time relationship between the speaker's *now* and the Fall *then*. The secure present is an occasion for remember-

ing the insecure past. In Milton's version, the past is not so clearly
placed. The absolute use of the present participle *falling* in line 174
allows the continuity inherent in that form to join past and present. Is
the *falling* completed? We are not allowed to be sure. The past participle
o'erblown in line 172 has a similar effect. In its adjectival relationship
to *hail* it describes something the hail *is* rather than anything the hail
has done. The security of a real change is compromised by the possibility
of a real continuity.

We are fortunate here in having Dryden's version of the same speech
to cast some oblique light on the processes and effects of Milton's
syntax:

> But see the victor hath recalled, from far,
> The avenging storms, his Ministers of War:
> His shafts are spent, and his tired thunders sleep;
> Nor longer bellow through the boundless deep.
> Best take the occasion, and these waves forsake,
> While time is given. Ho, Asmoday, awake!
> (*The State of Innocence and Fall of Man*, I, i, 7–12)

What Dryden's Satan describes is an external situation held at a constant distance from speaker and reader. This is how it is out there;
and the decision to act comes as a natural consequence. The thunders
and (by implication) God are tired by the effort of pursuing and
bellowing; the logic of warfare tells us that this, then, is the proper
moment for a counter-move. In Milton, however, the natural phenomena
(hail . . . surge . . . thunder . . . lightning) are less clearly part of a
unified military expedition. The angelic soldiers return to heaven; but
the climatic powers may be a permanent part of the landscape. The
thunder 'ceases now/To bellow', but that does not mean it has gone
away. The hypothesis that God has gone back is kept insecure in
grammar as it is improbable in sense. When Satan tries to describe
what he sees, in the passage following, the hypothetical nature of his
perception is spelled out by the sprawling alternatives in the syntax –
'Perhaps . . . whether . . . or . . . Save what . . . if any . . . Consult
how . . . If not'. The strong assertiveness of the speaker is played against
the uncertainty whether there is anything he can properly assert; the
structures of the world observed float on a wide sea of conjecture. The
most famous statement of the power (or incapacity) of the mind that sees
just what it wants to see occurs in the slightly later speech which
Dryden placed at the beginning of his opera version:

> Is this the seat our conqueror hath given,
> And this the climate we must change for Heaven?

What Dryden does not represent is what lies at the centre of Milton's
presentation of Satan here:

> The mind is its own place, and in itself
> Can make a heaven of hell, a hell of heaven.   (I, 254–5)

Thus 'mournful gloom' can be made into 'celestial light', the 'horrors'
into 'happy fields', by the will that determines that they should seem so.
This is usually seen as heroic endeavour; Satan certainly sees it in this
way. But the inability of the will to face up to what the syntax has been
showing us all along – that the individual perception is unreliable and
incomplete – is as much a defeat as a triumph. The syntax allows us to
see, behind the energy of the speaker who drives meaning in one direction or another, the limiting conditions within which fallen meaning can
be asserted, the strictly hypothetical nature of human statement.

Milton's epic similes offer yet another instance of the ways in which the
stylistic organisation of the material shifts our attention from one plane
to another, using one level of reference not only to reinforce but also to
subvert what is being said simultaneously on another level. Much of this
is, of course, inherent in the nature of the simile and is especially
obvious in that extended form of the figure which Homeric and subsequent usage leads us to call 'epic'. The 'epic similes' of Homer, especially
in the *Iliad*, have a particular reason for their strong establishment of
difference, which they set beside their assertion of similarity. The war
before Troy shows us the terrible sameness of death; the world of Greek
and Trojan warriors is dominated by the battle. Even though the situation of the Trojans would allow domestic and social life to appear,
Homer takes small advantage of that potential. In this world of warrior
sameness the similes have a particular value; they remind us of the
world the warriors have left behind them and of the possibility of a
wholly different point of view – from a world of farming and hunting,
cattle-raising and threshing, and of inhuman objects, animals, stars,
birds. A parallel but wholly separate world is established here, if
nowhere else in the poem. Thus when the two sides are fighting over
the corpse of Sarpedon, Homer transports us to the countryside:

> Think of the sound of strokes
> woodcutters make in mountain glens, the echoes
> ringing for listeners far away: just so
> the battering din of those in combat rose
> from earth. . . .   (XVI, 633–5; Fitzgerald's trans.)

Or when we hear of Achilles pursuing Hector round the walls of Troy,
we discover not so much the contrast of two equivalent but separated

worlds as the capacity for one to be transformed into the other. Achilles *becomes* the hawk, and Hector's death moves from choice to natural necessity:

> when that most lightning-like of birds, a hawk
> bred on a mountain, swoops upon a dove,
> and the quarry dips in terror, but the hunter,
> screaming, dips behind and gains upon it,
> passionate for prey. Just so, Akhilleus
> murderously cleft the air.   (XXII, 139–43)

The epic similes of Virgil show a movement away from Homer and towards Milton, in terms of technique as well as of time. They do not come from a poem as powerfully restricted as the *Iliad*, and so do not serve the function of escape from one world into another. What they show new is a tendency to be less concerned with the pattern of action and to be more easily related to the mental condition of the hero. Thus, when Nisus rages through the Rutulian camp in Book IX –

> even as a starving lion, raging
> through crowded sheepfolds, urged by frenzied hunger,
> who tears and drags the feeble flock made mute
> by fear, and roars with bloody mouth . . .
>   (IX, 339–41; Mandelbaum's trans.)

– the simile is less powerful as a description of what happened than as an evocation of the irrational frenzy of the immature hero.

But neither of these 'sources' really prepares us for the use that is made of epic simile in *Paradise Lost*. The change is, of course, related to change of function in the whole poem, discussed above. The Homeric similes are episodic just as the poem is episodic. They exist as separate vignettes with their own interest and splendour, leaving the narrative behind them as they make their own way. Like other parts of the poem, the similes are detachable elements that can be fitted in at different points, for their illustration relates to general characteristics rather than to particular ones. The fact that one hero is compared to a lion, a horse or an eagle does not mean that the same comparison cannot be applied, just as well, to another hero. The *Aeneid* is less episodic than the *Iliad* and therefore the similes are less detachable. I have already spoken of a particular propriety between the headstrong Nisus and the foaming lion. The procession of wild beasts set up to describe Turnus does not relate to heroism in general; for Aeneas is described by similes of a very different content. But *Paradise Lost* is integrated to a degree that no earlier epic had been, and consequently its similes enjoy a complex relationship with the whole moral structure of the poem. Mr James

Whaler has dealt with Milton's epic similes in a series of well-argued articles – *PMLA*, XLVI (1931), *MP*, XXVIII (1931), *PMLA*, XLVII (1932), *JEGP*, XXX (1931) – and has pointed to what he calls 'exact homologation' as their principal characteristic. What he means by this phrase is that the pictorial level conforms to the literal level not at one point (the noise of blows in the first Homeric quotation above) but at many. Take as an example the simile in Book III, lines 430–40, which describes Satan's ominous walk on the periphery of the world:

> Here walked the fiend at large in spacious field.
> As when a vulture on Imaus bred,
> Whose snowy ridge the roving Tartar bounds,
> Dislodging from a region scarce of prey
> To gorge the flesh of lambs or yeanling kids
> On hills where flocks are fed, flies towards the springs
> Of Ganges or Hydaspes, Indian streams;
> But in his way lights on the barren plains
> Of Sericana, where Chineses drive
> With sails and wind their cany wagons light:
> So on this windy sea of land, the fiend
> Walked up and down alone bent on his prey. . . .

Milton's vulture behaves – like Homer's hawk – more or less as such an animal ought to behave; certainly we are not invited to question its reality. But Milton's eyes are fixed, beyond the bird, on a theological rather than an ornithological meaning. This vulture comes in from frozen wastes to a land of great fertility, with a promise of easy prey. I do not know that vultures actually do this, or actually carry off newborn lambs. Certainly the elaboration does not make the bird any more real. What is clear is that the pattern is wonderfully apt for Satan, who comes in from frozen chaos to the fertile land of Eden so that he can carry off and kill the innocent and new-born inhabitants. The Chineses, with their aberrant transportation, are less clearly derived from the literal story and are, perhaps, only a random piece of local colour; but it may be suggested that the confusion of elements that appears in their sailing ships on land appears also in the literal nature of Limbo, 'this windy sea of land'. Milton's methods encourage us to stretch a point in our search for correspondences; we do not easily accept that any of the details are there simply to enhance the picture. The configuration of the simile picks up the variety of meanings that are present in the narrative moment from which it takes its rise, drawing on our knowledge of the whole story, past and future. It is also clear that Milton intends us to bring our moral judgement to bear on the simile no less than on the poem. Homer's hawk is magnificently alive and quite free of our approval; but Milton's vulture is given a moral status as well as a physical action related to that of Satan. Very often this effect is procured by the deliberate introduction of a morally responsible figure who judges what we see and makes the picture shown into a discrimination between good and bad. Thus in Book XI the descending company of angels is compared to other angelic visitations, but these are described only as they were seen by particular observers, Jacob and Elisha, the latter returning us to Adam's moral situation where the glimpse of heaven is set in the context of sin and betrayal. In the simile in Book X, lines 304 ff., the moral discrimination is a pagan one, between the enslaving tyrant Xerxes and 'the liberties of Greece' as between Death and mankind. In the simile in Book IX, lines 1058 ff., the distinction is between 'Herculean Samson . . . the Danite strong' and the 'harlot lap' of Dalila.

One extended comparison may help to clarify the nature of the transformation that Milton wrought on the traditional epic simile. In the *Iliad*, Book XI, Ajax is seen being forced to withdraw to the ships:

> He stood stock-still
> and tossed his sevenfold shield over his shoulder,
> dazed and dread. With half-closed eyes
> he glared at the crowd, a wild thing brought to bay,
> turning a little, shifting knee past knee.
> So formidable in his fear he was –
> like a dun lion from a stable yard
> driven by hounds and farmhands: all night long
> they watch and will not let him take his prey,
> his chosen fat one. Prowling, craving meat,
> he cannot make a breakthrough. Volleying javelins
> are launched against him by strong arms, firebrands
> bring him to heel, for all his great élan,
> and heartsick he retreats at dawn. So Aias,
> heartsick before the Trojans, foot by foot
> retreated grudgingly for the ships' sake.
> An ass that plods along a field will be
> too much for attacking boys; on his dumb back
> stick after stick may break; still he will enter
> standing grain and crop it, even as boys
> are beating him – so puny is their strength,
> and barely will they drive him from the field
> when he is gorged on grain. In the same way
> the confident Trojans and their best allies
> continuously made the son of Telamon
> their target.   (545–65)

In Book IX of the *Aeneid* Turnus breaks into the Trojan stockade, but is forced to retreat towards the Tiber. Virgil's simile here is clearly based on the one just quoted:

the Teucrians push on more fiercely
shouting and massing, just as when a crowd
will press a cruel lion with hating spears.
In fear, yet bold and glaring, he gives ground;
his wrath and courage will not let him flee;
and yet, though this is what he wants, he cannot
charge against so many men and weapons.
And even so is Turnus.   (791–7)

In Homer's version, though it is clear enough that Ajax's valour has
the author's approval, the simile allows no moral space for judgement of
the lion or donkey. All the elements of the picture – the dogs, the men,
the lion, the boys, the donkey – performs what each has to do according
to the laws of his kind. The men and the boys defend the meat and the
grain because they neèd it; but so do the lion and the donkey, and Homer
declines to judge between them. In Virgil's version the pattern is no
longer that of competing needs; Turnus as lion dominates the simile as
Turnus the man dominates this section of the story. The simile enables
us to feel with the person because we are enabled to feel with the animal.
But in Homer neither lion nor donkey gives us an insight into the mind
of Ajax.

Milton gives a superficially similar comparison in Book IV of *Paradise
Lost* where Satan leaps over the wall of Eden:

            As when a prowling wolf,
Whom hunger drives to seek new haunt for prey,
Watching where shepherds pen their flocks at eve
In hurdled cotes amid the field secure,
Leaps o'er the fence with ease into the fold:
Or as a thief bent to unhoard the cash
Of some rich burgher, whose substantial doors,
Cross-barred and bolted fast, fear no assault,
In at the window climbs, or o'er the tiles;
So clomb this first grand thief into God's fold. . . . (183–92)

Milton's wolf is initially allowed his own Homer-like natural space.
He is one that 'hunger drives to seek new haunts for prey'. But Milton's
wolf is marked (like Satan) more by his contempt for his prey than by
his need to eat in order to survive. Pressure against moral judgement
does not allow us to relax the standards of the Christian story. In Homer
the unmoral lion is followed by the even more unmoral donkey. But in
Milton the wolf turns into the explicitly immoral thief. What is common
to the two parts of the simile in Homer is the animal's need to eat; what
is common in Milton is the sly, furtive, planned hostility. But the moral
standards in Milton apply not only to the wolf and the thief; the

'secure' shepherds ('security' being a theological fault) and the *rich burgher* also carry some measure of disapproval. The simile is thus at a double remove from Homer's: in his case neither defenders nor attackers can be blamed; in Milton we blame both.

The distinctions I have been illustrating here measure the maximum distance between Homer's similes and Milton's. In Homer the warriors and the woodmen, Achilles and the hawk, give us opposed interpretations of a single physical event; in Milton the same *moral* pattern appears on both sides of the simile so that the physical difference is one of illustration only. But it is a mistake to suppose that Milton's similes are always of this kind. It is one of my objections to Mr Whaler's elaborate analysis that he tries too hard to find moral patterns, when he can do so only at the cost of misreading or overinterpretation. Take that simile in Book IX (445–57) where Satan's pleasure in Eden is compared with that of

> one who long in populous city pent,
> Where houses thick and sewers annoy the air,
> Forth issuing on a summer's morn to breathe
> Among the pleasant villages and farms
> Adjoined, from each thing met conceives delight. . . .

The comparison of Hell to a city and Paradise to open country is clear, and conforms to our expectations; but the moral status of Satan does not seem to affect the townsman. Because Satan will debauch Eve, there is no reason to suppose (with Fowler, for example) that the townsman, when he sees 'with nymph-like step fair virgin pass' will 'take advantage of the country girl's innocence'. It is true that the simile begins with Satan's pleasure and ends with his malice, but there is no reason why we must find the same configuration throughout the simile.

The first (and probably most famous) set of similes in the poem illustrates neatly how Milton's comparisons may move in and out of moral patterning. Satan lies on the burning lake

> in bulk as huge
> As whom the fables name of monstrous size,
> Titanian, or Earth-born, that warred on Jove,
> Briareos or Typhon, whom the den
> By ancient Tarsus held, or that sea-beast
> Leviathan, which God of all his works
> Created hugest that swim the ocean stream:
> Him haply slumbering on the Norway foam
> The pilot of some small night-foundered skiff,
> Deeming some island, oft, as seamen tell,
> With fixed anchor in his scaly rind

Moors by his side under the lea, while night
Invests the sea, and wished morn delays:
So stretched out huge in length the arch-fiend lay. . . .

(I, 196–209)

The simile begins by a simple extension from the literal to the mythological. The titans who warred against Jove represent pagan versions of Satan rather than anything radically different, brought into comparison with him. The tension between similarity and difference that is central to all simile only appears when Leviathan (another mythological monster) modulates into the familiar whale, seen in the context of everyday life. The commentators assure us that the comic error of the *night-foundered pilot* is a traditional image of our liability to take evil for good, whales for islands. No doubt this is true and important. But such knowledge does not remove the familiar literal meaning of *whale* or *pilot* or *skiff*. Once again Milton is playing divergent senses against one another. In meaning, the whale is highly homologous, significant of the evil that Satan displays. But the picture makes him only comically impressive. When we get to the end of the simile and hear 'So stretched out huge in length the arch-fiend lay' (the length of the line mirroring the meaning) we have been made aware of a certain grotesque clumsiness in this idea of mere bulk. The wallowing helplessness of the monster, its dull unresponsiveness even when an anchor is dug into its side, especially when set against the busy resource-fulness of the ship's company, reduces Satan from dynamic to static, active to passive. In these terms he is no longer the commander of our attention but rather its object. The next similes, which compare the fallen angels to leaves, sedge and broken chariots (I, 300–13), show the same modulations, though in a different order. The leaves and sedge are non-moral; the comparison only becomes moralistic when Pharaoh is introduced to give the sedge a Biblical context. Picture and judgement are manipulated to give the multi-layered effect that is almost Milton's stylistic signature.

CHAPTER 5

Subjective and Objective Vision: Book VI

Paradise Lost sets out to define and celebrate a heroism which is opposite in almost every way to the kind of heroism that we associate naturally with 'epic' – the heroism of daring, action, enterprise, glory, warfare, personal achievement, success in destroying enemies and establishing kingdoms, imposing oneself on the world. Milton celebrates instead the glory of acknowledged weakness, of self-abnegation, of confessions of failure, of repentance and forgiveness. He has to do so, of course, with the language and presuppositions of the traditional position; and this often involves strange alternations of the point of view. Thus, in Book XII Adam's epic expectations are quickly dashed by a doctrinaire Michael; when he hears of Christ's glory Adam cries out:

> . . . Say where and when
> Their fight, what stroke shall bruise the victor's heel.
>   To whom thus Michael. Dream not of their fight,
> As of a duel, or the local wounds
> Of head or heel: not therefore joins the Son
> Manhood to Godhead. . . .   (XII, 384–9)

But when Michael comes to tell the outcome of this unepic combat his rhetoric is very different from his doctrine:

> Then to the heaven of heavens he shall ascend
> With victory, triumphing through the air
> Over his foes and thine; there shall surprise
> The serpent, prince of air, and drag in chains
> Through all his realm. . . .   (451–5)

Adam is clever enough to respond to the doctrine, however, rather than to the rhetoric, as is clear from his final summing-up of the lesson he has learned from Michael:

> Henceforth I learn, that to obey is best,
> And love with fear the only God, to walk
> As in his presence, ever to observe

His providence, and on him sole depend,
Merciful over all his works, with good
Still overcoming evil, and by small
Accomplishing great things, by things deemed weak
Subverting worldly strong, and worldly wise
By simply meek; that suffering for truth's sake
Is fortitude to highest victory. . . .   (561–70)

Of this general point, that Milton's subversion of epic has to be
conducted in the language of epic, enough is said elsewhere. What I
wish to examine here is the extent to which the landscapes and physical
movements of the poem have to be transvalued or reseen so that they can
be appropriate to the heroism of patience no less than to the heroism
of achievement. The traditional epic shows landscape as a field of action.
In the *Iliad*, for example, territory is (as in the natural world) the
symptom of success: pinned back against the beach and the boats the
Greeks are at their lowest ebb (so to speak). Their achievement is
measured by their advance over the plain towards the city. The *Odyssey*
offers us a map of a different sort. Travel from Ogygia to Ithaca is
movement from the circumference to the centre, finally to the bed,
on which the journey comes to rest. Again, heroic prowess is the conquest
of space and advance into the desired territory.

These are the epics of earthlings – and the *Aeneid* is no more, though
it points to movement as part of national destiny in a way that neither
Homeric epic does. But space in *Paradise Lost* is a different dimension.
This epic, too, is a pattern of spatial conjunctions and separations, but
the separation of Heaven and Hell, the transfer of earth from dependency
on Heaven to the state that John Webster calls 'the suburbs of hell'
(*The Duchess of Malfi*, I, III, 337) – these uses of place and space do
not point towards human endeavour or achievement. The activity which
moves creatures through space in *Paradise Lost* is primarily a mental
or spiritual activity, and the displacement that occurs is seen as a moral
displacement at the same time as it is represented physically. Heaven,
Earth, Hell, above, beneath, within – these concepts give us a diagram
of spiritual status, which expresses heroic achievement, but in terms of
judgement rather than of action, in the static terms of 'placing' rather
than the dynamic ones of journeying. The potential of journeying is
several times referred to in the poem, in the plan of the devils to attack
Heaven, in Eve's dream of flying upwards, in Raphael's report of a
journey to Hell gates, for example, but only Satan's journey from Hell
to Earth and the sight of Heaven is given any prominence as a deter-
mining factor in the progress of the poem. And the exception is, of
course, significant. From the devilish point of view Satan *is* an epic
hero of the old stripe, as I have said before, and from this point of view
his journey is one of heroic conquest. But from another point of view

his travelling is a mode of standing still. The end of his journey is to make Earth like Hell; Marlowe's Mephistophilis says of his appearance on Earth, 'Why this is Hell/Nor am I out of it', and the same sense of the devil carrying Hell around with him wherever he goes is strongly suggested for Milton's Satan. The tripartite spatial structure of Milton's universe remains more powerfully present than any displacement that can occur inside it.

The movement of battle, advance and retreat, victory and loss, is so central a part of the epic tradition that Milton could hardly avoid referring to it, as I have noted above. But he does more than refer. In the central book of the poem, Book VI, he might seem to be challenging Homer on his own ground, leaving behind him the static moral structure of the poem, and demanding our attention for the to and fro of quasi-human battles. This certainly is how Addison views the matter in his *Spectator* paper 333: 'In a word, Milton's genius which was so great in itself and so strengthened by all the helps of learning, appears in this Book every way equal to his subject, which was the most sublime that could enter into the thoughts of a poet.' Addison's central concern is with Milton's classical art – 'all the arts of affecting the mind', as he says in the same passage – and he pays no attention to the fundamentally different set of underlying assumptions that separates Milton's art from Homer's. Milton himself might be thought to have pointed up the difference rather than the similarity. This is the narrative to which Raphael attaches his statement of 'accommodation':

> what surmounts the reach
> Of human sense, I shall delineate so,
> By likening spiritual to corporeal forms,
> As may express them best. . . .   (V, 571–4)

Modern critics, on the whole, have preferred to follow Raphael rather than Addison, finding the literal level of the War in Heaven not to represent Addison's sublime in agitation, 'greatness in confusion', but rather an empty *fortissimo*, more reminiscent of film epics than of Homeric ones. Sonorous and grandiloquent gestures occupy the wide-screen space. A cast not of thousands but of millions sweeps from one side to the other; mountains (or rather ranges of mountains) are moved. The mind faints as the grandeur grinds on. And what is really happening? Nothing much, it would appear. Until the short period of extra time at the end, the War in Heaven is a draw, nil-nil. The combatant angels cannot be killed. They can only be inconvenienced temporarily by being trapped inside unnecessary armour or buried under mountains. If swords cut them in half 'airy substance soon unites again', as Pope remarks of sylphs cut by scissors – or, as Milton puts it: 'the ethereal

substance closed/Not long divisible' (330-1). The two teams, numerically equal, advance and retire, as in the *Iliad*, as if territorial advantage
were their aim; and, indeed, the combatants speak as if it were. But
when the ultimate weapon, 'the chariot of paternal deity', is wheeled
out of its silo it appears to express not only a different kind of warfare
but also a different meaning for the word *warfare*. The chariot (taken,
like Beatrice's car in Dante's *Purgatorio*, from Ezekiel's vision) is transparently symbolic. Its advent is not merely that of a more sophisticated
kind of weapon, but a means of altering our whole perception of what is
happening. When Christ rides down the rebels,

> they astonished all resistance lost,
> All courage; down their idle weapons dropt;
> O'er shields and helms, and helmed heads he rode
> Of thrones and mighty seraphim prostrate,
> That wished the mountains now might be again
> Thrown on them as a shelter from his ire.   (VI, 838-43)

Christ informs the combatants (and us) that the battle up till now has
in fact been no battle at all but a test of faithfulness for the good angels:

> Faithful hath been your warfare, and of God
> Accepted, fearless in his righteous cause,
> And as ye have received, so have ye done
> Invincibly; but of this cursed crew
> The punishment to other hand belongs. . . .   (VI, 803-7)

Victory turns out to mean *acceptance* (doing well) and *defeat* means
punishment, not as a consequence but as an interpretation. When Christ
drives away the wicked angels, now 'a herd of goats or timorous flock',
their retreat or flight is merely the formal expression of a separateness
of condition (goats, not sheep), which had existed throughout the revolt
as a psychological or spiritual state. The fall over the wall of Heaven
into Hell is thus the final physical or spatial expression of a separation
that we noted earlier (in the time-scale used to express things timeless)
in attitudes of mind.

This transformation of warfare into moral discrimination does not
make it easy for us to correct earlier indications that warfare is meant
to be taken as warfare. If the point of the mimic war is to test the faithfulness of the angels, why are responses encouraged and emotions engaged
in military details that turn out later to be unreal? This question has
driven most modern critics into an assumption that the military details
were always meant by Milton to seem unreal, driving us to look for
meaning in the very inadequacy of the telling. Is the War in Heaven,
then, to be read as an allegory? Clearly enough in the climactic episode

of Christ's victory, the physical war-machinery is transparently a way
of talking about the arms of the spirit. But elsewhere the situation is
more complex. In some places angelic psychology seems to be the issue.
The wicked angels are not only morally damaged but also rendered less
effective militarily by their sin. This is not to say that their military
prowess directly represents their damaged personalities. The situation is
more like that of real people. Their actions in respect of God (resistance,
insult, attack) are obvious extensions of their sense of themselves in
relation to God; the absurdity of the latter finds an obvious expression
in the grotesquerie of the former. But there is no simple or direct relation.
Indeed, Abdiel raises precisely this point. You might expect, he says,
that sin would be immediately indicated by a loss of prowess; but in
this, as in the 'real' world, correspondence is not so neat:

> O heaven! That such resemblance of the highest
> Should yet remain, where faith and realty
> Remain not; wherefore should not strength and might
> There fail where virtue fails, or weakest prove
> Where boldest; though to sight unconquerable?   (114–18)

Milton does not deny the connection. But he seems anxious not to make
too much of it. Among the many curious acts of God in Book VI is the
decision to prevent sin from having an immediate effect on the fallen
angels – presumably to keep the game more interesting by having the
sides equally balanced:

> to themselves I left them, and thou know'st,
> Equal in their creation they were formed,
> Save what sin hath impaired, which yet hath wrought
> Insensibly, for I suspend their doom;
> Whence in perpetual fight they needs must last
> Endless, and no solution will be found.   (689–94)

This is a typically Miltonic piece of navigation between two opposites
equally destructive of God's majesty. He says that sin has had some
effect (else sin were hardly worth noticing), but enough power remains
in the angels to make their choices seem their own. The idea of their
loss of brightness remains a recurrent idea throughout the poem; but
we are only given isolated references, never any sense of the process
itself. What is most noticeable is the power that remains. When we first
meet Satan we are told he is

> how changed
> From him, who in the happy realms of light
> Clothed with transcendent brightness didst outshine
> Myriads though bright. . . .   (I, 84–7)

Milton's first four words pick up the formulaic *quantum mutatus ab illo* from Virgil's description of the dead Hector (*Aeneid*, II, 274). Virgil goes out of his way to describe what the change had made of Hector; Milton, however, is content to leave the changed Satan undescribed. A little later in the same book he returns to the nature of the change:

> His form had yet not lost
> All her original brightness, nor appeared
> Less than archangel ruined, and the excess
> Of glory obscured. . . .
> . . . his face
> Deep scars of thunder had intrenched, and care
> Sat on his faded cheek, but under brows
> Of dauntless courage. . . .   (I, 591–603)

Milton seems to be telling us here what the fallen Satan had lost; but he does it in such a way that he still appears more powerful than damaged. It is only *the excess* that he has lost; and, in any normal situation, that is no loss at all. In the second half of the quotation the change is presented as one that generations of readers have responded to as an improvement. The Byronic glamour of the careworn hero is no unambiguous sign of degeneration under the influence of sin; a description of this kind might seem to allow Satan to impose the terms within which he shows his sin. Less ambiguous is the statement of Zephon in Book IV:

> Think not, revolted spirit, thy shape the same,
> Or undiminished brightness, to be known
> As when thou stood'st in heaven upright and pure;
> . . . thou resemblest now
> Thy sin and place of doom obscure and foul.   (IV, 835–40)

But Satan's response to this rebuke measures again Milton's unwillingness to allow the physical simply to represent the mental or spiritual. Against destiny Satan asserts will; and Milton to some extent endorses the glory of will. At least our primary impression of Satan continues to be one of undiminishing power rather than of gradual decay. It is characteristic of Milton's endorsement of freedom that the moment of degeneration that seems most telling is that in which Satan *chooses* to be seen as a serpent:

> O foul descent! that I who erst contended
> With gods to sit the highest, am now constrained
> Into a beast, and mixed with bestial slime,

> This essence to incarnate and imbrute,
> That to the highth of deity aspired;
> But what will not ambition and revenge
> Descend to?   (IX, 163-9)

Compared with this the imposition of snakiness on Satan and his peers
in Book X (lines 504 ff.) seems arbitrary and unreal. The description of
the metamorphosis of Satan has a brilliant Ovidian sharpness of detail:

> His visage drawn he felt to sharp and spare,
> His arms clung to his ribs, his legs entwining
> Each other, till supplanted down he fell
> A monstrous serpent on his belly prone,
> Reluctant, but in vain, a greater power
> Now ruled him. . . .   (X, 511-16)

For all its brilliance, this is a wholly external event, something which
happens to Satan's skin, leaving our sense of the 'real' person untouched.
God trips him up by joining his legs together, but the last lines quoted
give us, not any sense that this is the latest stage in a degenerative
sequence, but that it is an arbitrary occurrence and a temporary incom-
modity. And so it proves; it is only an 'annual humbling', not a real
change.

The force of this episode is heavily dependent on Satan's having
chosen a serpentine shape in the previous book. The allegory in Hell is
powerful largely because it is validated by our sense of the inner life
involved in the previous act of choice. And this relationship is characteristic of Milton's handling of potential allegory in his presentation of
the outer or the physical as a sign of the inner or the spiritual. He is
unwilling, it would seem, to go far outside the range of relationships
that real life seems to offer us. We do not expect to see our more
serpentine acquaintances slithering over the real grass. But we interpret
their glances, the glitter of their eyes, and their human movements as
expressive of what we suppose are their mental states. In real life we
accept such interpretation, but we balk at any suggestion of a system
which will require that one must always mean the other. Focusing
primarily on individual minds and the choices they make, Milton
generally avoids imposing systems on the freedom of the individual. And
this is true even in the War in Heaven, in spite of the justification for
allegory that 'accommodation' would have provided. Take, for example,
the invention of gunpowder, attributed here to the devils on the second
day of their fight. We can hardly suppose that Milton is telling us that
a real Satan in a real Heaven invented real gunpowder. But it is
equally unlikely that we should read allegorically and suppose that gunpowder means something else, not gunpowder. However, it is common

as well as true to say that gunpowder is 'devilish', and the sentence 'It must have been the devil who invented gunpowder' is one that anyone could say, and with total intelligibility.* It is on this popular and unsystematised level of association that Milton handles the relation between perception and understanding, action and meaning. In the episode of the invention of gunpowder it is easy to suppose that we are watching a world of real warfare. The tactics used are, we are told, accurate for seventeenth-century practice. But the comments of Satan and Belial seem designed to punch holes in the reality. With diabolical malice the two leaders scoff and pun about the 'terms of composition' that the cannons are sending to the enemy. The dramatic appropriateness of these devilish puns is often noticed; but there is more than the appropriateness to person to be said about them. They remind us that the cannonballs are, indeed, modes of communication that the devils have chosen in order to express their own sense of relationship. The

---

*Indeed there was a literary tradition, to which Milton was heir, saying just this. In Book I of *The Faerie Queene* Spenser compares the effect of the giant Orgoglio's blow with that of a gun:

> As when that devilish iron engine, wrought
> In deepest Hell and framed by Furies' skill,
> With windy nitre and quick sulphur fraught. . . .
>
>   (I, VII, 13)

Behind Spenser, as so often, stands Ariosto. In Canto IX of *Orlando Furioso* we hear how the King of Friesland possessed 'A weapon strange, before this seen but seld'. Sir John Harrington's 1591 translation pushes the moralisation beyond Ariosto:

> No doubt some fiend of Hell or devilish wight
> Devised it to do mankind a spite.
>
>   (IX, 25, equivalent to IX, 29, in the original)

But this is no distortion of Ariosto's judgement on the gun. Later in the canto Orlando kills the King and drops the gun into the deepest part of the sea:

> O cursed device found out by some foul fiend
> And framed below by Belzebub in Hell,
> Who by this mean did purpose and intend
> To ruin all that on the earth do dwell.
>
>   (IX, 84=IX, 91)

J. R. Hale, in his contribution to the Garrett Mattingly *Festschrift*, 'Gunpowder and the Renaissance', *From the Renaissance to the Counter-Reformation*, ed. C. H. Carter (1965), gives a fascinating account of the wide diffusion of this idea. But Milton's usage must be, of necessity, different from that of all the others. His devils are not introduced to explain his real gunpowder. Rather his gunpowder is introduced to explain his real devils. More accurately perhaps, each is present to express the other.

cannonballs derange and dehumanise the ranks of the angels (or rather de-quasi-humanise them). Their 'devilishness' consists precisely in their power to impose a sub-human force on human life, disvaluing any pretence to freedom. Death in any form does this, of course. But the Homeric single combats which appear on the first day of the war show us men rejoicing to choose their opponents and expressing some free individuality, even if it is a choice to 'die'. The cannons express the minds of Satan and Belial in more ways than they intend, and their punning speeches, 'ambiguous words', 'gamesome mood', remind us of this. Their contempt for their opponents, their equation between talk and shot, debate and destruction, human contact and the confrontation of ball with body, all make the cannon a logical mode of 'expression' for them. Where allegory offers us an object through which we see a meaning, Milton offers us instead an entirely reversible conjunction of event and meaning. The cannons express the devilish minds of Satan and Belial, but Satan and Belial in their turn serve to express the devilish nature of cannons.

This approach to allegory and eventual denial of it is characteristic of Milton, and many examples of it can be found in the War in Heaven. We may conveniently continue to deal with the episode of the cannons. Once invented, these machines are, in Heaven as in Earth, a horrid success. The possibility arises, logically absurd, but available to the reader as a temporary (though wrong) deduction, that the bad angels may win. Within the same framework of logical absurdity but narrative potential one may say that Michael and the good angels are forced to devise a counter-strategy or face defeat. They do survive, of course; they devise the strategy of throwing mountains at the cannons so burying them, and begin to gain the upper hand, until the bad angels (who might have thought of it before) see how effective this is and throw mountains back. *Jaculation dire* occurs, which is dangerous enough to drive God into cancelling the game altogether. Two very different levels of expression seem to be present here. Warfare with cannons was to Milton's readers, as to us, a 'real' experience. Warfare by throwing mountains, on the other hand, was a literary hyperbole then as now (at the moment of writing at least). The poetic skill with which Milton here showed forth 'the full majesty of Homer . . . improved by the imagination of Claudian, without its puerilities' was much admired by Addison. Clearly it is a very different mode of presenting the meaning of what is happening from that we have noted in the episode of the cannons. The extraordinary image of the devils seeing the undersides of the hills before they are dropped on them seems designed to imply (as Fowler indicates in his note – misnumbered 664–7) that we cannot hope to visualise this history. The status of the events in the two modes of warfare is sharply differentiated : the cannons require us to evaluate the

meaning of our contemporary experience; the *jaculation dire* demands
instead an *admiratio* or astonishment. When we move from one plane
to the other we experience a jolt that disorientates our sense of the
relation between expression and meaning. The set framework of relationship that allegory demands is disrupted again and again in the poem by
the demand that we look again (and again) at the same events, but from
divergent viewpoints.

The grotesque mismatching of the planes of perception in Milton's
handling of his fictions of Heavenly meaning is often nowadays referred
to as his gift for 'comedy'. Joseph Summers, for example (in *The Muse's
Method*, 1962), and Arnold Stein (in *Answerable Style*, 1953) speak of
Satan as a 'comic' figure who is placed in this role for us because of his
grotesque failure to match the divine comprehension of what is happening
in Heaven or in Hell. Certainly in Book V, lines 719 ff., God laughs
at him and his unrealistic pretensions to power and importance. It is
worth noting, however, that if the Son had not told us that his Father
was laughing we might not have known it. What the Son says is:

> Mighty Father, thou thy foes
> Justly hast in derision, and secure
> Laugh'st at their vain designs and tumults vain,
> Matter to me of glory, whom their hate
> Illustrates. . . .　　　　　　　　　　　　　　　　　　(V, 735–9)

Now here is what God said:

> Son . . .
> Nearly it now concerns us to be sure
> Of our omnipotence, and with what arms
> We mean to hold what anciently we claim
> Of deity or empire, such a foe
> Is rising, who intends to erect his throne
> Equal to ours, throughout the spacious north. . . .
> Let us advise, and to this hazard draw
> With speed what force is left, and all employ
> In our defence, lest unawares we lose
> This our high place, our sanctuary, our hill.　　　(719–32)

God seems to be having fun, pretending not to be omnipotent; and
all logic tells us that His statements are not literally true. But we should
notice that the rhetoric is more convincing as truth than as burlesque.
The notion that God can be overthrown, which animates the revolt in
Heaven, is indulged at length in the poem as a serious, though wrong,
proposition. The picture of God as a bandit chieftain, of dubious
legality and now of waning powers, is perfectly coherent (though

illogical) and has the whole weight of the classical theogony behind it.
Milton takes no great pains to render the assumption absurd beyond
cavil. Indeed, we are pushed towards an acceptance of Satan's argument
that he was tempted into revolution because God allowed himself to
appear vulnerable, ripe for replacement:

> as one secure
> Sat on his throne, upheld by old repute,
> Consent or custom, and his regal state
> Put forth at full, but still his strength concealed,
> Which tempted our attempt. . . .   (I, 638–42)

The reply of the Son in Book V tells us that these divine understate-
ments require logic as well as probability for their interpretation, and it
would take the confidence of a Bentley to say that the Son is wrong.
But we should notice that the invitation to laugh is one that we do not
easily pick up, and certainly we should be wary of detecting further
examples of Jehoviality. Milton's comedy is, I am suggesting, so threaded
through his serious purposes that the tendency to laugh is hardly ever
free of the fear that this is no laughing matter. It is very difficult to find
the self-confidence to laugh at Satan's grotesque mismatching of his
perceptions, even with God acting as collateral for our laughter. God
laughs; but it does not follow that we are meant to join in the merri-
ment. The coherence between Satan's fallen perceptions and our own
should, for one thing, choke back any of the sense of superiority on
which laughter depends.

Arnold Stein, in *Answerable Style*, chapter 2, has seen the whole
War in Heaven as a gigantic scherzo, instancing as particularly jocular
the scene of the wounding of Satan (320–53), that which describes the
effect of cannonballs on the good angel (590–607), and the final exit of
the wicked over the

> crystal wall of heaven, which opening wide,
> Rolled inward, and a spacious gap disclosed
> Into the wasteful deep; the monstrous sight
> Strook them with horror backward, but far worse
> Urged them behind. . . .   (VI, 860–4)

It is true that in the first and third of Stein's cases God is debasing his
enemies and rendering them ridiculous; in the second case gunpowder
has the same effect on the ranks of good angels. But I believe that the
attitude of the reader in the poem is no more simply aligned with God
than with gunpowder. Once again, to assume the posture of 'scornful
laughter' is to simplify the complex relation of the human reader to
pictures of sin and fallibility that we know too well from our own lives.
'He that is without sin among you, let him first cast a stone.' With

characteristic good sense Joseph Summers notes the problem: 'From the point of view of Hell, Satan, Sin and Death are heroic; from that of Heaven they are comic; from that of earth they may be the terrifying agents of tragedy' (*The Muse's Method*, 41). What is less clear is how one applies this wisdom to the reading of the individual passages. Is one meant to note the co-presence of these alternatives by drawing back from all of them? If that suggestion were to be followed literally we would, I suspect, be rendered incapable of responding to the poem at all. But there are half-way houses. It is surely true of the many speeches in *Paradise Lost* that they tend to persuade us to the speaker's point of view, while he is actually speaking. When he stops we may see that we have been deceived, in whole or in part. We read, in the main, by first accepting, and then modifying and taking into account the alternative viewpoints to which the speech is subject. Satan's misunderstandings may indeed seem comic from one point of view. But we err if we do not notice at the same time that his speeches to his followers in Heaven are no less magnificent (and no more fallacious) than his speeches in Hell. Eventually, of course, his misunderstandings recoil on his own head. But the local excitements of the poem are not to be reduced to the meaning they must eventually be given when all the action is concluded. Satan squatting toad-like beside Eve's ear is no doubt comically deflated from one point of view, but he is also frightening, as the eventually successful betrayer of man. The comic does not seem to be here, or in the War in Heaven, the primary effect that is aimed at. The hateful toad that explodes like 'a heap of nitrous powder' into 'the grisly king' provides a grotesque moment; but the controlling point of view is that of the guardian angels, wariness and contempt. The comedy that lies in suspension in the situation colours and complicates our response, as it does also in the grotesque discomfortures of Book VI. A story told, like *Paradise Lost*, from divergent points of view must have the comic perception of their contradiction as one of its potentials; but the full realisation of this potential involves closing the gap between the fallible reader and the infallible truth that the poem (if I am right) holds at the centre of its telling.

The only extended passage in the poem with a prime aim at comedy is the Limbo of Vanity, discovered to Satan in Book III (lines 440–97). Milton is here able to indulge his sardonic humour in a simple and straightforward way, for the constraints I have discussed above are absent. The episode is self-contained (Bentley thought it the interpolation of another author); it is not required by what precedes it and it has no effect on what follows it. More important still is the fact that this true scherzo relates not at all to the time of the action but to modern times, specifically to the absurd Poperies of modern times. The mode of action is one that we have noted before. If I quote the lines about

Cowls, hoods and habits with their wearers tossed
And fluttered into rags; then relics, beads,
Indulgences, dispenses, pardons, bulls,
The sport of winds . . .   (III, 490–3)

the reader may well be reminded of the good angels, blown away by
gunpowder in Book VI:

none on their feet might stand,
Though standing else as rocks, but down they fell
By thousands, angel on archangel rolled. . . .   (VI, 592–4)

In finding the first disruption actually comic and the second only
potentially so I rely on the criteria already discussed. A secure superiority allows us to laugh at the foolish Papists; but no such superiority
can secure us in the case of the angels or even of the devils. When the
subject-matter is the ephemera of our own day the process of reading
through revisions and alternatives that characterises our relations with
the main body of the poem is suspended. And the Limbo of Vanity is
not entirely unique. If we compare the passage with the more glancing
references to the modern world as these appear, especially in the similes,
we can see, I think, the way in which our sense of superiority in the
modern 'real' world is played against the more prismatic quality of the
timeless fiction. I have discussed above (pp. 118–19) the string of similes
used to describe Satan's contemptuous leap over the wall of Paradise
(IV, 179 ff.). What I have not described is the way in which the similes'
movement from the morally ambiguous (the wolf) to the explicit (the
'lewd hirelings') is also a movement from the timeless to the contemporary. In so far as the 'theft' is the tragic theft of human innocence, we
are too personally involved with the loss to isolate the pure emotion of
contempt for the thief. But when we get to

So since into his church lewd hirelings climb   (193)

the effect is different. In the world that this line refers to we know easily
enough how to separate ourselves from those we despise. I am not saying
that this line is comic, but that it is only in such a world that comedy
is possible. The objects described have a simple and direct reference;
they are, as it were, outsides without insides.

   In the main body of the poem the objects described are seldom without the ambiguity of external objects that have to be made internal
before they can have meaning. John Broadbent has written interestingly
on the Hell of Book I as an internal state as well as an external place
(see *Some Graver Subject*, 80–5). Certainly when we first meet Satan
in Hell we are not allowed certainty whether the things he sees are really
there, outside himself, in the form described:

> for now the thought
> Both of lost happiness and lasting pain
> Torments him; round he throws his baleful eyes
> That witnessed huge affliction and dismay
> Mixed with obdurate pride and steadfast hate:
> At once as far as angels' ken, he views
> The dismal situation waste and wild,
> A dungeon horrible, on all sides round
> As one great furnace flamed, yet from those flames
> No light, but rather darkness visible
> Served only to discover sights of woe,
> Regions of sorrow, doleful shades, where peace
> And rest can never dwell . . .
> but torture without end
> Still urges, and a fiery deluge, fed
> With ever-burning sulphur unconsumed.   (I, 54–69)

Notice particularly the *witnessed* in line 57, a master-stroke of ambiguity. The *baleful eyes* are witnesses or evidences of the *affliction and dismay* that Satan feels, so that in these terms Satan himself is part of the landscape, like Dante's Satan. But the *eyes* are also, of course, the witnessers, the means by which Satan witnesses the *affliction and dismay* outside himself. Likewise, at a later point, the *darkness visible . . . discovers . . . doleful shades where peace . . . can never dwell . . . but torture . . . urges.* What is never allowed to appear entirely certain here is whether the torments that are discovered belong to the mind of the beholder or to the bodies of the beheld. As it is, earlier, the *thought . . . of . . . pain* that *torments him*, rather than the fact, so again the qualities whose deprivation is tormenting – *Peace . . . rest . . . hope* – are mental rather than physical. The *utter darkness* of line 72 is seen by Satan as *darkness visible*, and in this paradoxical light it is not clear whether the things Satan sees are the hallucinations of the damned or objective truths. Milton does not intend it to be clear. The *angels' ken* seems to operate not only by a fusion of present and past (as I have noted above: p. 24) but also by a confusion of subject and object. Satan is the object of God's punishment and to this extent he suffers in a real physical objective Hell. But Satan is also the author of his own misfortunes, and therefore 'makes up' his own punishments. Milton allows a continual contradiction between the two aspects of what is happening. Thus from God's point of view Satan is

> Chained on the burning lake, nor ever thence
> Had risen or heaved his head, but that the will
> And high permission of all-ruling heaven
> Left him at large to his own dark designs,

> That with reiterated crimes he might
> Heap on himself damnation, while he sought
> Evil to others. . . .   (210-16)

When we see Satan and Beelzebub, immediately after, 'Both glorying' (boasting)

> to have scaped the Stygian flood
> As gods, and by their own recovered strength,
> Not by the sufferance of supernal power . . .   (239-41)

we are invited, it seems, to observe how wrong they are. We cannot, however, help but be impressed by Satan when he is the subject of his own activities, as for example when he lifts his bulk into the air, and when

> with expanded wings he steers his flight
> Aloft, incumbent on the dusky air
> That felt unusual weight. . . .   (225-7)

Logically we must believe that it is God who is allowing Satan to fly, but the majestic act of flight shows us Satan active, imposing himself on something else (the air); and when he expresses the congruity between his destiny and the landscape, not as a result of another's judgement but as the effect of his own choice, we are bound to be exhilarated by it:

> Be it so, since he
> Who now is sovereign can dispose and bid
> What shall be right. . . .
> Farewell happy fields
> Where joy for ever dwells: hail horrors, hail
> Infernal world, and thou profoundest hell
> Receive thy new possessor. . . .   (245-52)

The description of Hell is such that it is equally patient of both interpretations: it is both an objective limitation to Satan's powers and a malleable entity that Satan can make into what he wants.

A particular problem arises from the presence in Milton's poem of physical objects, intended not only as limitations but also as prohibitions, but which dissolve magically when confronted by sufficient force of will. The chains which attach Satan to the burning lake vanish miraculously when he chooses to rise. Why put them there at all? seems an appropriate question. The same might be said of the triple gate of Hell, massively impressive in description but wholly inadequate in function, or the guards, walls and gates of Paradise, only effective for the expulsion of the fallen pair. The point of such contradictions is not obvious, and yet one must suppose that they are intentional. One may hazard a guess that their presence marks God's loving care for man; while their weakness marks the true threat as other than physical violence, a threat not to the body but to the will. Adam and Eve are thus both protected and unprotected, as Satan is both captive in Hell and yet free to raise Hell, God holding all things inside his providence and yet allowing them to find their own level. Simultaneously we see the adequacy of the objects in physical terms, and note their inadequacy to a world where subjective freedom provides the dominant focus. If we assume a simple continuity between God's will and His achievements in the world, wishing him to impose his goodness on all creatures, we will find these contradictions unsatisfactory. Milton, however, would seem to be quite deliberate in his presentation of such continuity as complex and paradoxical. The reader may have noted some aspects of this already: linear continuity of narrative is never wholly adequate to carry the meaning; the planes and levels of the poem regularly meet but seldom match; the perceptions we are offered add up, but never quite reach the total declared.

CHAPTER 6

A Tale of Two Falls:
Books II and X

In *Paradise Lost* Milton offers us two accounts of Fall, one angelic and one human, presented at some points as causally related but at other points as related thematically – as separate illustrations of the same law. From the causal point of view man fell because tempted by Satan, who had himself already fallen and now sought revenge on God by securing new converts to his kingdom:

> Nor hope to be my self less miserable
> By what I seek, but others to make such
> As I. . . .   (IX, 126–8)

God made man when Satan fell, the other argument runs, to replace the fallen legions; having tried once (with the angels) and failed, he tried again (with man) and failed again, not so much because the first failure caused the second but because both failures derived from the same basic law – the law that individual freedom is created by escaping from the matrix, the condition of innocence, rejecting the Creator, the Father, his protectiveness and his hopes, and substituting self-interest for his love. Both Falls reflect this law; but they do so in different ways and to different degrees. There is a movement forward as well as a repetition. If it were not so, the story Milton has to tell us would offer no space for hope, for Christ or for resurrection; new creation would always be followed by new Fall.

It is typical of Milton that the most telling differences arise not so much from the external mechanisms as from the human (and quasi-human) reactions to the event, once it is past, to the consequential separation from God and the expression of divine anger. The reaction of Satan to his fall is the first thing we meet in the poem. The situation is one that draws out some of Milton's most famous lines. Books I and II, in which the Satanic reaction is exposed, are the most famous and most widely read sections of the poem. Hence it may we useful, in pursuit of a more balanced reading, to begin this chapter with Adam and Eve. The actual eating of the fruit in Book IX produces straight away, in both Adam and Eve, a number of unadmirable reactions –

sensual greed, a self-conscious pleasure taken in pleasure, a further access of pleasure at the thought of doing things forbidden. But, these mere solaces for sin having passed, the man and woman awake to shame, guilt, recrimination and eventually (lying beneath the others and finally revealed) despair:

> Love was not in their looks, either to God
> Or to each other, but apparent guilt,
> And shame, and perturbation, and despair,
> Anger, and obstinacy, and hate, and guile.   (X, 111–14)

Despair itself is, however, though a mortal sin, shown to derive from factors in themselves admirable – a natural love of posterity and an unevasive acceptance of all the blame:

> in me all
> Posterity stands cursed: fair patrimony
> That I must leave ye, sons; O were I able
> To waste it all my self, and leave ye none!
> So disinherited how would ye bless
> Me now your curse! Ah, why should all mankind
> For one man's fault thus guiltless be condemned,
> If guiltless? But from me what can proceed,
> But all corrupt, both mind and will depraved,
> Not to do only, but to will the same
> With me? How can they then acquitted stand
> In sight of God? Him after all disputes
> Forced I absolve: all my evasions vain,
> And reasonings, though through mazes, lead me still
> But to my own conviction: first and last
> On me, me only, as the source and spring
> Of all corruption, all the blame lights due.   (X, 817–33)

Adam stretched out on the cold ground, cursing his creation and crying out for death (850–4), offers an opposite as well as a parallel to the outstretched Satan of Book I, who rises from prone to upright, supported by disdain and self-justification. Satan rises to embrace separation from God as a permanent condition, learning to rely on himself rather than on anything outside himself. But Adam is raised by pity for another, who might seem to be in even worse case than himself – Eve. Her humility, fright, beseeching move Adam from rejection to acceptance. Her need for 'love . . . gentle looks . . . aid . . . counsel . . . peace . . . commiseration' (914–40) melts his anger and softens his heart. The interaction of the two makes despair seem a psychological condition rather than a doctrinal one, a temporary emotional phase to be passed through while searching for a way to endure the pain of separation and isolation. Eve's despair, her counsel of 'wilful barrenness' or else suicide has, like Adam's, a good cause behind it – pity for a condemned posterity. But she pushes the consequences in action even farther than he does. Suicide was regularly represented as the natural and damnable consequence of despair. By having the extension of Adam's attitude proposed by Eve, Milton holds up a mirror in which Adam can see the fruits of despair, at that point in his life where most he wishes to protect and comfort. Unlike the reinforcement that Beelzebub offers to Satan in the parallel situation in Book I, Eve's reinforcement of Adam's despair serves to break it. Moved by love and protectiveness Adam seeks to save her; and by believing in salvation saves himself. The comforts he finds for her are comforts for both of them:

> He will instruct us praying, and of grace
> Beseeching him, so as we need not fear
> To pass commodiously this life, sustained
> By him with many comforts, till we end
> In dust, our final rest and native home.   (X, 1081–5)

The forgiving of Eve has led us naturally towards the forgiving of Adam. Her weakness, contrition, cry for help, gesture towards despair, awake in the self-accusing Adam a sense of implication in and responsibility for another. The need to speak and act purposefully turns him naturally towards the powers above in whom alone human purpose can be found. He finds that he sees himself still as a man walking in the shadow of God. To know her weakness and dependency on him is to remember his own weakness and dependency on God. And this perception may be seen, in its turn, as the occasion for Christ's intervention and the influx of divine mercy. I am not saying, of course, that Adam's perception of his own power to forgive *causes* God's forgiveness of Adam. It is rather that man's act shows his heart ready to receive God's mercy and all that follows, Christ's promise and Michael's narrative.

In Book X Milton shows us the processes by which despair gives way before the mutuality of human love under God. In Book XI he looks at the same event from the other side and notes that the recovery has only been possible because

> Prevenient grace descending had removed
> The stony from their hearts, and made new flesh
> Regenerate grow instead, that sighs now breathed
> Unutterable, which the spirit of prayer
> Inspired. . . .   (XI, 3–7)

We now learn, at a more theological than psychological level, how sighs are changed to prayers, and prayers made acceptable to God, how despair is turned to contrition and barren self-accusation into fruitful repent-ance. In God alone rests the power of regeneration; but God's regenera-tive power operates only on minds that are open to it, where man freely chooses to humble himself, repents and asks for forgiveness. As in other passages I have discussed, Milton avoids too narrow a presen-tation of doctrine by repeating the episode and seeing it from different points of view. What God looks down and sees is undoubtedly true doctrine; but from the point of view of man the experience is different. God describes what he offers; man describes what his state of mind allows him to be aware of. God's is the larger view; but man's description speaks directly to the human heart. We should notice that doctrine as well as poetic strategy requires Milton to walk a tightrope here. His theology will not allow him to say that man deserves Grace or that Grace is a response to man's plea for it. Grace must be *ex gratia*, freely and even arbitrarily given to those who cannot deserve it. Man must be free, however, to accept or reject Grace. His state of mind is an essential part of the process of Regeneration. For if the power of God is able to override the freedom of the individual, God becomes responsible for both falls, since it would have been simple for him to have prevented them. The cause of Adam's and Eve's regeneration is thus complexly derived from both man's choice and God's bounty (as faith is said in the *De Doctrina* to be both 'a receiving of God and an approach to God': YM, VI, 475). Even after *prevenient grace* has removed the stone of despair from their hearts the human capacity for change makes regeneration still insecure, as God notes:

> He sorrows now, repents, and prays contrite,
> My motions in him, longer than they move,
> His heart I know, how variable and vain
> Self-left.   (XI, 90–3)

This is one of the most enigmatic pieces of divine syntax; but the general sense seems to imply that the variability and vanity of man's heart will outlast the motions of repentance that God has implanted in him. Michael, it follows, must be sent down to Eden to control by prohibition what man cannot control by choice. But because the stirrings of con-science are present (and are to be a recurrent part of human nature) Michael is not only to 'drive out the sinful pair'; he is also to strengthen their virtuous impulses by describing the long path of human history that will permit those who conquer their variable and vain hearts to pass beyond the physical impediment and 'regain the blissful seat', as Milton promised at the beginning of the poem.

It is hard to imagine a stronger contrast to the wavering and contra-dictory responses of Adam and Eve after the Fall, their pleasure, their tears, their unreliability, than what is reported to us of the rebel angels. We first meet Satan 'rolling in the fiery gulf', and we are told that he is tormented with the 'thought/Both of lost happiness and lasting pain'. But what we notice when we hear Satan speak is not a psychological state of torment but rather the leader's determination to suppress all feelings save those that will hold his followers in subordinate fascination – the 'study of revenge, immortal hate,/And courage never to submit or yield'. The famous first speech of Satan to Beelzebub is a powerful expression of the heroic refusal to admit defeat. But we should not forget what Milton adds:

> So spake the apostate angel, though in pain,
> Vaunting aloud, but racked with deep despair. . . .
>
> (I, 125–6)

What we learn here is that the speech is a calculated choice from a variety of alternatives. Satan is using what is available in the situation to secure a particular kind of effect. Satan's rhetoric is a triumph of the will: the determination 'never to submit or yield . . . bow and sue for grace/With suppliant knee' is splendidly heroic when set against Adam's tearful waverings. But our response to this 'hardness of heart' is meant to be moral as well as aesthetic. Satan's political purposes are meant to be as visible, I think, as the matter he gathers together to promote them. He alleges that to 'bow . . . with suppliant knee' would be to grant God a superiority he does not indisputably possess. Are we to suppose that Satan really believes this, or that it is the kind of convenient supposition a leader has to make if he is to keep his followers in heart? Milton's comment that Satan was 'vaunting aloud' suggests the latter. But the personal magnetism that the speech exudes invites the opposite response and drives us to suppose that such objections are petty spoiling. In this well-balanced dialectic the parallel with Adam's fall is particularly important. I have suggested above that Eve's sorrow, humility and plea for forgiveness play a crucial role in the movement of Adam's heart from despair to hope. Adam's love for Eve is both a cause of his undoing (he chooses to eat the apple rather than be parted from her) and a cause of his recovery. Human love ties together the members of the race in a way which offers both a reductive parody of divine love and a true reflection of it. Satan suffers neither the weakness that love imposes nor the capacity for forgiveness it allows. His political focus means that he remains unopen to all around him, successful, cold and manipulative. But relationships without love seem to be an essential part of Hell. There is, of course, a complete propriety in the fact that there are no lady angels, either in Heaven or in Hell. Milton, however, goes out of his way to indicate that something akin to sexual love exists in Heaven; Raphael tells Adam:

Whatever pure thou in the body enjoy'st
(And pure thou wert created) we enjoy
In eminence, and obstacle find none
Of membrane, joint, or limb, exclusive bars:
Easier than air with air, if spirits embrace,
Total they mix, union of pure with pure
Desiring; nor restrained conveyance need
As flesh to mix with flesh, or soul with soul.   (VIII, 622–9)

We see nothing of this in Hell, where, Satan tells us,

neither joy nor love, but fierce desire,
Among our other torments not the least,
Still unfulfilled with pain of longing pines;   (IV, 509–11)

When, after their political and military labours in Book II the fallen angels are bid to take their leisure, they behave like high-minded members of a men's college. Their recreations, like their architecture and their institutions are modelled on those of a Greek city-state: competitive sports, mimic battles, verse-readings, philosophic debates, walking tours of the region. Neither love nor desire appears to have any effect on them. The capacities that Raphael describes seems to have disappeared at the time of the expulsion. This fits perfectly with what we see. The fallen angels are without the emotional rawness of Adam and Eve, the see-saw of their feelings, their interdependence. The fallen angels seem to see themselves wholly as functionaries of a new order, related to one another not by emotional ties of love or pity or comfort or even resentment, but as parts of a necessary enterprise. One attitude, like death's 'mace petrific', pulls the separate members towards a single response – self-love and hatred for God. It is as one functionary to another that Satan addresses Beelzebub at the beginning of the poem:

If thou beest he . . .
who . . .
didst outshine
Myriads though bright: if he whom mutual league,
United thoughts and counsels . . .
Joined with me once, now misery hath joined
In equal ruin . . .
so much the stronger proved
He with his thunder. . . .   (I, 84–93)

The joining of Satan and Beelzebub in *mutual league* and so on does not, of course, imply an emotional dependence of one on the other, but rather a common political interest and expedient alliance. It is worth noticing the extent to which this speech turns on gradings and distinctions of lesser and greater: 'bright/brighter', 'equal hazard', 'the stronger', 'mightier', 'me preferring'. The view of life that underlies it is one which sees relationships as essentially unequal, involved in a perpetual rise-and-fall, up-and-down struggle, whether explicit or not. It is in this context that we should understand Satan's refusal to bend the knee. If God 'holds the tyranny of heaven', as Satan says, then the only attitudes available are, first, resentful self-denial ('forced halleluiahs') and, secondly, unrelenting struggle. And if these are the only two alternatives there is no doubt which is preferable. But we have only Satan's word for it that the possibilities are so limited, while everything else in the poem suggests the opposite. In particular we have the case-history of Adam to point up the function of love in the relationship to God. Milton gives us nothing like the Neo-Platonic vision of human love as a process leading naturally to God. But he allows that there is a connection, however broken-up and circuitous. Adam and Eve both expose their sense of the imperfection and incompleteness of self and their yearning for completion outside oneself – a yearning that can only finally be satisfied in the love of God. These emotions are, of course, cross-hatched by others more or less contradictory. Competitiveness is an important part of the relationship between Adam and Eve, and an important factor in the process leading to the Fall; but it, too, is written over by the love and need for one another that both feel. The mutuality of Adam and Eve is not, like the mutuality of Satan and Beelzebub, a temporary alliance set up to secure a particular end, but a natural and inevitable expression of their deepest humanity, an end in itself and not a means to a further end. Man's superiority to woman, like God's superiority to man (which it reflects), produces angry or guileful resistance; but where Satan's resistance to God's superiority is frozen in a blind rejection of all relationship, Eve's resistance, tearful, confused, contradictory, unstable, is so shot through with love and the desire for love that it cannot finally resist God's (and Adam's) support and correction. Satan's famous and magnificent words to Beelzebub mark the opposite to this female openness to love:

> Fallen cherub, to be weak is miserable
> Doing or suffering: but of this be sure,
> To do aught good never will be our task,
> But ever to do ill our sole delight,
> As being the contrary to his high will
> Whom we resist.   (I, 157–62)

It is worth noticing that Satan's expression of necessity in this speech moves ambiguously between God and himself. The *task*, he implies, is one set by God, which he is not allowed to vary. The responsibility for

what happens is thus laid at God's door. On the other hand he wants
also to claim the glory of making the choice to resist God. The necessity
is then of his own making. In neither case, of course, is there any
suggestion of a real alternative or of a movement of mind between contradictory desires. The same conflation (or confusion) of necessity ('the
tyrant's plea') and self-will appears at large in Satan's early speeches.
In line 244 he seems about to express the 'thought of lost happiness' that
Milton had ascribed to him· in line 54, a thought which (on the analogy
of Adam and Eve) could be the signal for repentance and a cry for help.
But such thoughts are quickly sealed off: the loss of Heaven is simply
another example of the necessity imposed by a tyrannical deity:

> Is this the region . . .
> this the seat
> That we must change for heaven, this mournful gloom
> For that celestial light? Be it so, since he
> Who now is sovereign can dispose and bid
> What shall be right. . . .
> Farewell happy fields
> Where joy for ever dwells: hail horrors, hail
> Infernal world, and thou profoundest hell
> Receive thy new possessor: one who brings
> A mind not to be changed by place or time.
> The mind is its own place, and in itself
> Can make a heaven of hell, a hell of heaven. . . .
> Better to reign in hell, than serve in heaven.   (I, 242–63)

The famous lines asserting the independence of mind are often read
without noticing the context. The Romantic view of them takes it that
the individual mind is in fact truly described as the source of all our
value judgements. Such a doctrine can hardly be attributed to Milton,
and the whole logic of the context denies it. The speech is marked by a
process of retreat: the search is for a place where one can impose one's
will on the environment, without the danger of come-back or response
or interference or the problems of mutuality. Since Heaven is not possible
in these terms, it must be thrown away. Hell is just as good as Heaven
if the mind succeeds in a total take-over of the usual commerce between
inner and outer. Satan secures his kingship by restricting his kingdom
to what he can permit himself to see. Hardness of mind, impermeability
of perception, is a less remarked characteristic of the damned than
hardness of heart, but the emotional cost of these determinations is
clearly enough spelled out in a later soliloquy, whose passion is derived
from an incautious glance out of the fortress of the hardened self into
the universe of light and love. At the beginning of Book IV Satan,
returned from imprisoning darkness, looks up at the sun and remembers

what has happened to him, alone and for the moment released from the distortions of political rhetoric. He now sees his progress not as wise tactical withdrawal to a safe place but as flight:

> which way shall I fly
> Infinite wrath, and infinite despair?
> Which way I fly is hell; my self am hell;
> And in the lowest deep a lower deep
> Still threatening to devour me opens wide. . . .
>   is there no place
> Left for repentance, none for pardon left?
> None left but by submission. . . .   (IV, 73–81)

As a commentary on 'the mind is its own place' this could hardly be bettered. The mind is, indeed, its own place, the later passage tells us; and what a terrible place it is! At a more psychological level Abdiel spells out the same process in his address to Satan at the beginning of the war in Book VI. It is not servitude, he says, to serve the worthier; it is the law of nature as well as the law of God. The unjustly rebellious in fact chooses, by that act, the real servitude:

> Thy self not free, but to thy self enthralled. . . .   (VI, 181)

Satan's assertion of independence is thus an assertion of the primacy of his own appetites – envy, pride, ambition – to which his reason must hereafter be in thrall, unless he can find that outside himself whose virtue compels reverence and love. Such a possibility exists for Adam and Eve, but Satan's willpower is all directed to make sure that it cannot happen to him.

Milton sets politics against mutuality as a mode of human relationship in which will excludes love. The fact that Satan is made a superb politician may be taken to indicate Milton's personal feeling about the political life he had known in the decades before *Paradise Lost*. But maybe not. The word *politician* had an unsavoury connotation in the language Milton inherited. Traditional ethics set the clever manipulator well down among the wicked. The ambiguity at least latent in the term was, of course, entirely to Milton's purpose; the depiction of Satan as a political opportunist allows him to invite our admiration for 'the prince of this world', the ruthless organiser of his own success, while at the same time we recognise that such success only serves to confirm spiritual failure. Satan's skills are well enough seen in his opening moves in Book I. The first words he addresses to 'the associates and copartners of our loss' show him already in command and already determined on the ends he seeks. First he rallies the fallen angels with a quasi-jocular sarcasm that draws on both their shame and their loyalty; he points to the burning lake, and asks:

> have ye chosen this place
> After the toil of battle to repose
> Your wearied virtue, for the ease you find
> To slumber here, as in the vales of heaven?
> Or in this abject posture have ye sworn
> To adore the conqueror, who now beholds
> Cherub and seraph rolling in the flood
> With scattered arms and ensigns. . . .   (I, 318–25)

When he has cajoled them into a vertical position he first feasts their emotions with sights and sounds that remind them of their own warrior status. He helps them to recover their past and therefore their own identities by replaying the context within which they once believed in themselves. There is nothing in all this of the future nor any revealed intention. First 'the warlike sound of trumpets', then 'from the glittering staff unfurled/The imperial ensign',

> all the while
> Sonorous metal blowing martial sounds:
> At which the universal host up sent
> A shout that tore hell's concave. . . .   (539–42)

The manipulated togetherness of Hell bears an unmistakable likeness to modern political rallies. The incessant music, the concentration of all eyes on spotlit symbols, 'ten thousand banners ris[ing] into the air', marching with mind-numbing regularity, learning to ignore and conquer external discomfort, and finally

> Awaiting what command their mighty chief
> Had to impose   (566–7)

– all this reminds us that political success is set not only against love but also against knowledge. To reach the ends proposed it is essential that they cannot be seen in advance. The contrast this creates with Heaven is an important part of the overall effect, and I will return to it later.

Satan only argues when he has brainwashed his followers into a receptive mood. He had spoken earlier, we are told, when 'with high words, that bore/Semblance of worth, not substance' he 'gently raised/Their fainting courage, and dispelled their fears' (528 ff.). But that was, it seems, merely hortatory. Now he takes up the central issue of what has happened to them and what they should do about it. His first speech is a masterpiece of political chicanery; and it offers us a model instance of that 'bad eminence' which so often characterises Satan. Like several classical heroes before him, and in accordance with the best canons of rhetoric, he shows that he can scarcely speak for the emotion he feels:

Thrice he essayed, and thrice in spite of scorn,
Tears, such as Angels weep, burst forth: at last
Words interwove with sighs found out their way. . . . (619–21)

The point is continued in the twists and turns of the broken syntax that
follows. 'What wonderful people you are' is a standard speechmaker's
beginning. Here Satan applies it with extraordinary boldness to the
defeated. What he tells them, of course, is that, though apparently
defeated, they are not really defeated; it is impossible to believe that the
present situation is more than a temporary setback; in any case it is not
anyone's fault (and especially not Satan's own), for God concealed his
strength and so 'caused' the revolt. 'In any case', he goes on, 'this
so-called defeat is, when properly looked at, really an advantage to us;
for now we know where we stand and can act realistically, not to be
aggressive against anyone but in order to defend ourselves against others.
God's so-called victory was simply a naked use of aggressive power, and
that gives us a moral advantage over him. The fact that he had to act
that way shows how morally bankrupt he has become; and now he is
so clearly in the wrong any action we take against him is justified. If we
cannot attack head-on, we can still move obliquely. Whatever is said, it is
a contradiction for *celestial spirits* to be confined in an *infernal pit*. We
will escape, and our action now must be to test the routes by which the
best escape and new assault can be effected. We must all think together
about that. Let us consult together and explore the question of
revenge; for who is so base as to wish to discuss any other possibility?
None of you, I know.'

Satan's speech anticipates and leads forward to the 'great consult' of
Book II, which shows us the democratic process as an element in
audience manipulation. Satan's opening speech to the assembly returns
to the points he wishes the 'debate' to circle round. What he develops in
more detail is the nature of his own position as leader (or *sultan*, as
Milton puts it). In an interesting mixture of democratic vocabulary and
tyrannic behaviour he describes his position and asks for it to be
approved. He was a leader first, he tells them, by *the fixed laws of
heaven*, though they also freely chose him as such, and were right to
do so, as his prowess in both politics and war has shown. Since the Fall
his primacy has been confirmed with even greater enthusiasm, in spite
of the recent disaster. We do not see any action which measures this
confirmation of Satan's power, but the skilled politician always takes
silence for consent. What Satan is after, of course, is the conclusion that
no other leadership is possible. He cuts off potential aspirants with the
reminder that this leadership

          exposes
Foremost to stand against the thunderer's aim

> Your bulwark, and condemns to greatest share
> Of endless pain?   (II, 27–30)

No one could possibly want such a job ('I'm doing you a favour by taking it', as they say). The hope that this is so is secured by the assertion that it must be so, and confirmed by the observation that willingness to rock the boat is treason to the whole cause. For this is their advantage over God, that in Hell there is total acceptance of the power structure, but Heaven (he implies) is full of complaints. This point of power once established, the debate can be 'thrown open'; but the positions that emerge in the following pages could be forecast by a practised political reader, and one must suppose that they had been foreseen by Satan (here offering a parody of God's foreknowledge). Moloc proposes violent retributive war, Belial suggests slothful acquiescence in defeat. Between these two come Mammon (consolidate our own empire) and finally Beelzebub, Satan's partner. Beelzebub first disposes of Moloc and Mammon: they can hope neither to win a war nor to be left alone to develop their own empire. He then turns to Belial's argument that God may eventually allow the devils to live their own kind of life. The only possible relationship between the devils and God is hatred and the wish to destroy; but they cannot dethrone God and therefore they must aim to vex him in 'some easier enterprise' (345). God's new toy, called Man, may be the means to do this. Let someone attempt Man's seduction, for

> This would surpass
> Common revenge, and interrupt his joy
> In our confusion, and our joy upraise
> In his disturbance. . . .   (370–3)

The debate thus ends at a point, Milton tells us, 'first devised/By Satan, and in part proposed' (379–80). The proposal that Satan thought of highly delights the infernal parliament. But the parliament itself cannot act on the proposal. The debaters are helpless to decide whether 'To second, or oppose, or undertake'. There is only one way of filling the gap: call in the strong man and give him full authority to act. Only Satan can occupy the space that Satan devised

> whom now transcendent glory raised
> Above his fellows, with monarchal pride
> Conscious of highest worth. . . .   (427–9)

But *monarchal pride* does not exclude political sharpness. Satan responds quickly, 'prudent', Milton tells us

>   lest . . .
>   Others among the chief might offer now
>   (Certain to be refused) what erst they feared;
>   And so refused might in opinion stand
>   His rivals, winning cheap the high repute
>   Which he through hazard huge must earn. But they
>   Dreaded not more the adventure than his voice
>   Forbidding. . . .   (468–75)

The elaborate civility of this great affair thus ends with a glint of the steel within the glove. The sharp advantage-taking of political life excludes all but the most ruthlessly devoted to self. The contrast to Adam and Eve could not be better established.

It would be improper to leave this contrast between the reactions of the humans and of the devils to the facts of their two falls without glancing, however briefly, at the Heaven they are reacting against. The move from the politics of Book II to the politics of Book III looks like a move from democracy to tyranny. This is certainly how the devils have taught us to anticipate it; and one can see why they describe it as they do. The use of the word *politics* for the goings-on in the Heaven of Book III almost requires us to think in that way. For there is no debate, no expression of contrary opinions, no wooing of voters in the heavenly assembly. The first two persons of the trinity exchange statements of what must happen, while the heavenly host is restricted to *wondering* (273), *adoring* (351) casting down crowns (352) and playing the harp (365 ff.). As a political process this certainly leaves much to be desired; and one can see why the sharp operators of Book II were so dissatisfied with it. There is, in fact, no space in Heaven for the power game of politics. And there cannot be, in any state where good is indubitably recognised and clearly embodied. The society of Heaven is more like that of the Garden than that of Hell. The conversation between the Father and the Son which occupies the business area of the heavenly scene is, if the word may pass, a *personal* affair. And it offers a model which Adam and Eve can aspire to, though Satan and Beelzebub cannot. The Father states the facts as they are, irrevocably; the Son draws out the implications of the fact; he asks questions where the Father makes statements. He does not do so to oppose or change. As the Father says:

>   All hast thou spoken as my thoughts are, all
>   As my eternal purpose hath decreed.   (III, 171–2)

He exposes a side of the Father's meaning which is not immediately clear from the Father's words, a side directed towards mercy and forgiveness, but which finds its necessary cue in the actual words of the Father.

It is only when the Father finishes his speech with 'But mercy first and last shall brightest shine' (134) that the Son begins to glow with the *divine compassion* which he then expresses in his own speech. The Father and the Son are of course a unity in a way that Adam and Eve cannot be. But the model of a marriage that the first two persons of the Trinity offer to us is one that we cannot wholly exclude from our contemplation of Adam and Eve. At their best moments, love makes their speeches chime with a harmonious sense both of one another and of the world outside themselves. Their sense of working together in relation to an outside order exactly complements what we see in Heaven. Emphasis on their difference rather than on their unity moves the rhetoric, however, from statement to persuasion. When Eve argues in favour of gardening alone, our attention is directed towards the ends sought rather than the facts stated. We are moving here into the world of politics and manipulation which, the long narrative of Books XI and XII is to show us, is the substance of human history. But history, whatever its methods, is a record of change; that is the cause of its hope (and its weakness). Hell, however, presents an unchanging present; that is its strength (and its hopelessness).

CHAPTER 7

Human History: Books XI and XII

Discussing the symmetries of *Paradise Lost* I have suggested that the two-book sequence at the end of the poem (XI and XII) balances the two-book sequence at its opening (I and II). In Books I and II we see the establishment of the Kingdom of Hell and the education of its inhabitants in the nature of their fallen state – its possibilities, its resources, its government and its national destiny. In XI and XII we see, correspondingly, the establishment of the kingdoms of this world as it had to be between the Fall and the Incarnation (with its completion in the Second Coming) and the education of Adam and Eve in the nature and consequences of their fallen state. In the preceding chapter I have discussed the likeness and unlikeness of Satan and Adam in their response to the Fall. The basic difference, expressed in terms of psychology or personality, concerns attitudes to God. But from these two opposite points spread explanations of everything that is. The 'everlasting Nay' of Hell creates a national identity based on the hardened pride of never changing from the fixed will to oppose God ('And what is else not to be overcome'). The kingdom of fallen man is rather founded on an Everlasting Maybe. Man's softened heart (see XI, 110), his openness to Grace, are virtues, one of whose consequences is the instability of human experience, its struggle and failure, its inherent and continuous capacity for change. The presentation of this capacity for change, with an account of the opportunity for redemption it eventually offers, is the principal business of that long section of Books XI and XII in which Michael reveals to Adam what will happen to mankind. This long narrative is probably the least liked part of *Paradise Lost*. Addison wrote: 'If Milton's poem flags any where, it is in this narration, where in some places the author has been so attentive to his divinity that he has neglected his poetry' (*Spectator* 369). Thomas Newton says that 'the last two books fall short of the sublimity and majesty of the others [as does the *Iliad*], which must be attributed to the alteration in the subject . . . the subject of these last two books of the *Paradise Lost* is history rather than poetry' (*Milton's Poetical Works*, ed. Newton (1770), II, 455). Modern critics have tended to be more direct and even less complimentary. C. S. Lewis calls the narration 'an untransmuted lump

of futurity' (*Preface to 'Paradise Lost'*, 125). John Broadbent says that
'in Book XII the more factual history is so intractable anyway – as the
shift from vision to narration admits – that the verse becomes arthritic'
(*Some Graver Subject*, 279). One must admit that these books do not
offer much splendour or resonance. But the demand that they should do
so takes us back to Milton the organ-voice once again. If we judge
Milton's effects in relation to his purposes in these books, and the whole
poem, we can see that a gorgeous representation of the penitential life
of man on earth would be quite inappropriate. Here speech is deprived
of the vast echo-chambers that Heaven and Hell provide earlier in the
poem; and properly so, for Heaven and Hell now draw back from the
life of man. Milton's low-profile poetry in these Books does not simply
mark his disengagement or his exhaustion. Our careful reading soon
exposes careful variation in the level of pressure he puts on his verse.
When there is a point in rising the verse rises. Take the passage at the
end of Book XI dealing with the Noetic flood:

> No sooner he with them of man and beast
> Select for life shall in the ark be lodged,
> And sheltered round, but all the cataracts
> Of heaven set open on the earth shall pour
> Rain day and night, all fountains of the deep
> Broke up, shall heave the ocean to usurp
> Beyond all bounds, till inundation rise
> Above the highest hills: then shall this mount
> Of Paradise by might of waves be moved
> Out of his place, pushed by the horned flood,
> With all his verdure spoiled, and trees adrift
> Down the great river to the opening gulf,
> And there take root an island salt and bare,
> The haunt of seals and orcs, and sea-mews' clang. . . .
>
> (XI, 822–35)

The opening is, like the passages which precede it, dry and bare. The
matter is seen as bounded by narrow factuality; it takes an effort to see
meaning beyond the particular statement. But when *this mount*, the
here and now of the narration, provides an immediate link between the
glamorous present and that denuded future something of the glamour
of the present begins to infect the verse. The power and beauty of
Paradise casts a glow over the featureless world of waters that destroys it.
The classical memory in *horned flood*, the sense of sweep and majesty
in 'Down the great river to the opening gulf' and, above all, the
wonderful last line quoted give deprivation an unusual power, a negative
image, but one through which we can see again the richness of the
positive it has replaced. But such moments must be, by their nature,

extremely rare. They must be so if Milton's purpose – to 'justify the ways of God to men' – is to be fully expressed. The *men* to whom God's ways are justified must, of course, be fallen men. How do you justify the ways of God to men whose defining characteristic is their having fallen away from the ways of God? Only, I suggest, by relating their state, in the middle of human history, to the two meaningful ends of the story, the Fall and the Second Coming. The narrative of Books XI and XII, covering the gap between these two, tries to define human existence in its relation to both of these. The appropriate emotion in such a state must lie between joy and sorrow and be most accurately expressed as a waiting, an attention to the events that surround one, an effort to detect meaning in a world in which neither God nor the Devil is an overt presence. Michael's story is also misliked because it seems disjoined and even haphazard. No continuous sweep of narrative carries us forward from the Expulsion to the Incarnation; but a series of self-contained miniature moments and dry summaries encapsulate highlights from Biblical history. Broadbent thinks 'the whole thing had been better done by du Bartas' (280) and bemoans the lack of epic similes, of any sense of scope or even of dramatic immediacy (278). The complaints point to true facts; what I want to dispute is whether these facts are meant to be simply elements in the landscape of the poem or whether we are meant to see them through Adam's consciousness, watching the vivid contrasts in his feelings rather than the external elements he is feeling about. As we see him, our representative, tossed from pillar to post by reactions to history, are we not being invited to participate in a process of humanisation, immensely speeded up, of course (like a film of a flower's opening), and offered a perception of the whole range of human variability. With Adam we learn to see the haphazardness of history inside the fixed framework of eschatology.

The narration begins, it is not always noticed (Summers, once again, is the exception), from Adam's complaint that the expulsion from the Garden is an expulsion from God, certainly from His manifestation in geography and human time:

> This most afflicts me, that departing hence,
> As from his face I shall be hid, deprived
> His blessed countenance; here I could frequent,
> With worship, place by place where he vouchsafed
> Presence divine, and to my sons relate;
> On this mount he appeared; under this tree
> Stood visible, among these pines his voice
> I heard, here with him at this fountain talked . . .
> In yonder nether world where shall I seek
> His bright appearances, or footstep trace? (XI, 315–29)

Michael's answer to this is that God is everywhere:

> surmise not then
> His presence to these narrow bounds confined
> Of Paradise or Eden . . .
> . . . doubt not but in valley and in plain
> God is as here, and will be found alike
> Present, and of his presence many a sign
> Still following thee, still compassing thee round
> With goodness and paternal love . . .
> Which that thou mayst believe, and be confirmed
> Ere thou from hence depart, know I am sent
> To shew thee what shall come in future days
> To thee and to thy offspring. . . .
> thereby to learn
> True patience. . . . (340–61)

The historical conspectus thus teaches *true patience* by showing the need to search for God's presence in the fallen world, where He cannot be forecast or looked for, and where a sense of the future can only be grasped as a tiny shining thread running through the complexity of experience. The experience, says Michael, is designed also to teach 'By moderation either state to bear,/Prosperous or adverse' (363–4). The relation between *patience* and *moderation* has, I think, sometimes been misunderstood. The later phrase might, indeed, suggest a Stoic detachment from joy or sorrow. But Milton elsewhere sets up a fierce antithesis between Stoical and Christian patience (*Paradise Regained*, IV, 300 ff.; *De Doctrina*, II, x: YM, VI, 740) and there is every sign that he does so here as well. The detachment from the issues of the world that Michael holds out before Adam is sustained not by 'philosophic pride' (as Christ calls it in *Paradise Regained*) but by faith and hope. As the *De Doctrina* says in another place: 'Patience is the virtue which shows itself when we peacefully accept God's promises, supported by confidence in the divine providence, power and goodness: also when we bear any evils that we have to bear calmly, as things which our supreme Father has sent for our good' (II, III: YM, VI, 662). This is what we seem to see in the history of Adam's reactions. At no point in the story is Adam shown as capable of Stoicism or detachment. When eventually he sees the meaning of the promise, he is sustained by a joy which makes all other emotions fall away from him; but there is no suggestion that he was wrong to feel these other emotions. Indeed, it is hard to see how Adam could have reached his Christian exaltation without his intense involvement in his wonder at sinfulness. With the naïvety of one newly emerged from the simplicities of the Garden he picks up every cue to joy or sorrow and rushes into immediate judgement.

His education consists of a series of wrong responses, which then have to be corrected and reformulated by Michael. One may say that it is the function of these disjointed little episodes to provoke such responses. And Adam is a wonderful pupil. Education works effectively only for those who wish to be educated, who invest in terms of enthusiasm what they want to take out as understanding. Adam's movement from stage to stage arises from error, but from open and productive error. As each situation is presented to him he responds to it with the absorbed seriousness of one who thinks that the whole story is now clear to him. And this provides the occasion for correction and so for movement forward. The minds of the devils are, on the other hand, closed to change and so ineducable. They exercise their intelligence on basic questions:

> Of good and evil much they argued then,
> Of happiness and final misery,
> Passion and apathy, and glory and shame,
> Vain wisdom all, and false philosophy: (II, 562–5)

Their arguments go in circles because their minds are already made up. The qualities of experience that they discuss cannot be more than intellectual playing-cards if they are not prepared to surrender to the mystery of such experience. Adam does not understand what is going to happen to himself or his race; but he is prepared to surrender control in order to expect understanding, in other words to rest on Faith. He has been given a promise which is also a mystery – the so-called Protevangelium or first gospel, in which God says to the serpent:

> Between thee and the woman I will put
> Enmity, and between thine and her seed;
> Her seed shall bruise thy head, thou bruise his heel.
> (X, 179–80)

The promise that man will be able to beat back the power of Satan is the bead of light at the end of the tunnel which sustains the recovery of Adam and Eve from despair, makes Adam grasp at the movement forward that Michael offers him, and that causes him to break out towards the end of the narrative:

> O prophet of glad tidings, finisher
> Of utmost hope! Now clear I understand. . . .
>   so God with man unites.
> Needs must the serpent now his capital bruise
> Expect with mortal pain. (XII, 375–84)

Adam is drawn through Books XI and XII as our representative, gladly embracing the reprehension and instruction that Michael deals out, sustained by faith in an eventual revelation, which he continually expects and continually has to postpone. In this sense his experience prefigures that of all Christians. He has to learn to wait in patience, to take things as they are, to hope and to show his hope by encouragement of the good and reprehension of wickedness. But at the same time as we see this inner process, which is endlessly repeated in human time, we see external Biblical history passing through time, apparently unrepeatable. Of course, this is not entirely true as a statement about Biblical history. The opening of the Epistle to the Hebrews gives a good indication of the way in which the history of the Jews can be seen as the development of faith:

> God, who at sundry times and in divers manners
> spake in time past unto the fathers by the prophets,
> Hath in these last days spoken unto us by his Son, whom
> he hath appointed heir of all things, by whom also
> he made the worlds.

The knowledge of Christ is a gradual discovery through time of what was always there, through a necessary sequence, each stage of which was required in order to produce the misunderstanding that followed it:

> So law appears imperfect, and but given
> With purpose to resign them in full time
> Up to a better Covenant, disciplined
> From shadowy types to truth, from flesh to spirit. . . .
> (XII, 300-3)

History is in this reading of it a spiritual discipline in which the *types* of the Old Testament are responded to but not understood until the antitype in the life of Christ is revealed. But we are wrong if we think that typology will explain the whole movement of Adam's attention through the scenes of Jewish history. The earlier episodes in particular show the search for understanding through material that has very little inherent development. The vignettes of men without faith, before the giving of the Covenant to Noah and then to Abraham, seem designed to indicate a progression without progress, a circuit of hope and fear whose meaning exists only in Adam's response to it, the *discipline* that this perception of fallen mankind imposes on him.

Seen in these terms the visions of Book XI fall into a fairly simple pattern, by which Adam is tempted through his responses to death, to secular peace and to power. The first vision is of Cain and Abel. This is a savage introduction to human history, but (Augustine and others thought) a wholly representative one. Milton makes nothing of the blood relationship between the actors and the spectator. Adam has to be told that these are his children; and makes no response when he is told. The function of the episode is to state truths about human life not about family pieties. The centre of the vision is not the identity of murderer or victim but the presence of much announced but hitherto concealed Death:

> But have I now seen death? . . .
> O sight
> Of terror, foul and ugly to behold,
> Horrid to think, how horrible to feel!   (XI, 462–5)

The centrality of the emotional tone rather than the historical fact is entirely in keeping with Michael's purpose. And, like the good teacher he is, he seizes on Adam's emotional state and drives into its open softness a hard reinforcing message: 'If you think this death's horrible, wait till you've seen these other ones.' The vision that follows is didactic only and quite unhistorical. The 'lazar-house' that erects itself before Adam's eyes is non-Biblical and indeed out of time altogether. The sonorous list of diseases:

> Convulsions, epilepsies, fierce catarrhs,
> Intestine stone and ulcer, colic pangs,
> Demoniac frenzy, moping melancholy
> And moon-struck madness, pining atrophy,
> Marasmus, and wide-wasting pestilence,
> Dropsies, and asthmas, and joint-racking rheums.
>
> (XI, 483–8)

reflects for the inside of man the same doom as is reflected for the outside of his life by the list of tyrannic citadels (XI, 385 ff.) – Peking, Samarkand, Ispahan, Moscow, Byzantium, Rome, Mexico, Angola (the list is extraordinarily modern). Both lists offer a conspectus of the kind of life fallen man will have to endure – enslavement both to nature and to other men. The picture of death, being the first lesson he is given, is the first one that Adam has to digest and he does so immediately:

> Henceforth I fly not death, nor would prolong
> Life much, bent rather how I may be quit
> Fairest and easiest of this cumbrous charge,
> Which I must keep till my appointed day
> Of rendering up, and patiently attend
> My dissolution.   (547–52)

But death is not the only or the most insidious of the new parameters. The second vision (556 ff.) attacks Adam (and us) from the other side.

We see what looks like peace, prosperity, plenty, the ethical goods of a secular society. Tubalcain and Jubal represent the technological and artistic advances available to fallen men, not overemphasised as alternatives to religion, for these

> Just men . . . seemed, and all their study bent
> To worship God aright, and know his works
> Not hid, nor those things last which might preserve
> Freedom and peace to men.   (577–80)

Perhaps we (with our literary sophistication) begin to have doubts when we see these sturdy artificers pushing their secular delights in the inevitable direction of dancing, feasting, and love with beautiful and complaisant women. But Adam preserves a more basic human response to

> Such happy interview and fair event
> Of love and youth not lost, songs, garlands, flowers,
> And charming symphonies. . . .   (593–5)

He is charmed by what he sees and hears, and relaxes in responsive pleasure to the change from hate and death: 'Here nature seems fulfilled in all her ends' (602). I have called this a vision of peace. Of course it is more than that. Its essential function is to offer Adam the temptation to accept the pleasures of ordinary unaggressive life as proper ends in themselves, ends to which the knowledge of God can be accommodated. The moral Michael wishes to impose is that such appearances must always be deceptive and unreliable. 'Man's effeminate slackness' leads him to 'swim in joy . . . and laugh' (625–6); the appetite for pleasure make him the victim of women (like Adam himself); he yields up his 'nobler end/Holy and pure', the knowledge of God, to immediate gratification, and so betrays the future.

The whole length of Michael's visionary history is built up on contrasts of seemingly unendurable ill, promoting despair, and seemingly pleasant idylls, encouraging complacency (as secret police interrogators are said to alternate between the brutally degrading and the brotherly and comforting). The third block of visions (638 ff.) begins with a return to death. But death which, in the Cain and Abel episode, is the private misfortune of individuals is now the principle of social organisation. Civilisation grows through the power of man's aggression. Cities are built (as in Hell), horses are tamed, the meek are harried, the 'fittest' survive. It is no accident that Milton moves closest here not only to Hell but also to the heroic world of the secular epic. That there is a relationship here between the vignettes of Michael's narrative and the panels on the shield of Achilles (*Iliad*, XVIII, 478 ff.) has often been noticed – for example in Pope's notes to his Homer and in Newton's commentary on Milton. I suspect that the rhetoric of Michael's visions is derived in general from the shield; but the particular closeness at this point seems accounted for by the overlap in their visions of the world of aggressive power:

> For in those days might only shall be admired,
> And valour and heroic virtue called;
> To overcome in battle, and subdue
> Nations, and bring home spoils with infinite
> Manslaughter, shall be held the highest pitch
> Of human glory. . . .   (689–94)

Adam's commentary on the vision is also, I would suppose, Milton's commentary on the Homeric subject-matter:

> O what are these,
> Death's ministers, not men, who thus deal death
> Inhumanly to men, and multiply
> Ten thousand fold the sin of him who slew
> His brother. . . .   (675–9)

Even the vision of Enoch's translation out of danger by means of a cloud seems to come from Homer (or Virgil) rather than from Scripture. There is no cloud in the Enoch story; and even the suggestion that the detail comes from Elijah (2 Kings, 2:11) does not serve, for not even a chariot of fire is a cloud. But the pagan epics are full of examples of this situation where a sorely beset hero had been 'seized with violent hands', as Milton says, had not a god or goddess provided nebulous intervention (see, for example, *Iliad*, III, 382).

The heroic world of the giants is followed by the vision of Sodom and Gomorrah, where 'All now was turned to jollity and game' (714). One may regard this as the second 'peace' temptation as the giants were the second 'death' temptation. In terms of the effect on Adam this seems right. The two 'death' episodes invite Adam to dissociate himself from his descendants; he has to learn to abhor himself for what his sin will visit on his inheritors. On the other hand the two 'peace' temptations invite him to identify with his descendants and to feel the pain of their destruction, which also must be accepted, 'For now I see/Peace to corrupt no less than war to waste' (783–4). The third and fourth temptations are, however, connected by continuity as well as by antithesis. Michael explains the cycle that leads from one to the other. The warrior race

> having spilt much blood, and done much waste
> Subduing nations, and achieved thereby
> Fame in the world, high titles, and rich prey,

> Shall change their course to pleasure, ease, and sloth,
> Surfeit, and lust, till wantonness and pride
> Raise out of friendship hostile deeds in peace.
> The conquered also, and enslaved by war
> Shall with their freedom lost all virtue lose. . . .   (791–8)

The cycle of death and jollity is thus inherent in the dynamics of history as also in the process of Adam's education. So the 'good man' is equally ineffective in war (Enoch) or in peace (Noah). We should note that Milton has emphasised the similarity of these two by saying that the latter 'oft/Frequented their assemblies' (721–2) as Enoch earlier had done (664 ff.). The detail is, of course, quite unscriptural. So when the climactic Flood comes it is an answer not simply to one phase of human corruption but to the whole cycle of human capacity for evil, both that phase deriving from aggressive self-justification and that based on 'effeminate slackness' or inattention.

The Flood is obviously the centre of Michael's story. As the angel tells Adam:

> Thus thou hast seen one world begin and end;
> And man as from a second stock proceed.   (XII, 6–7)

As the poem stands now, the climactic position is marked by the ending of one book and the beginning of another. We should not forget, however, that the original ten-book version gave it no such privilege. But the fact of climax does not vanish, even though the structural underlining does. One kind of relationship between Adam and Michael, as between Man and God, comes to an end, and a new set of relations is set up. In Book XI Adam is shown visions; he makes responses to them and learns by recognising his mistakes in interpretation. Michael introduces a new mode at the beginning of Book XII:

> Much thou hast yet to see, but I perceive
> Thy mortal sight to fail. . . .
> Henceforth what is to come I will relate,
> Thou therefore give due audience, and attend.   (8–12)

The success of the vignettes – tiny genre pictures, presenting social behaviour in a way designed to elicit an immediate moral response – ends with Noah. One can see why. 'The world destroyed and world renewed' (XII, 3) are radically separated by the coming of the Covenant, which given, Book XI comes to rest. The point is unequivocally made that this is no new temporary expedient but a central part of all experience in all time to come 'till fire purge all things new,/Both heaven and earth, wherein the just shall dwell' (900–1). In the vignettes of Book XI we have seen the alternating terrors of destruction and corruption, where the mystery of God's presence in the fallen world is elucidated only in the odd case of a good man taken out of the mêlée (Enoch or Noah). There is no sense of God having a continuous purpose in such a world. After the Flood, however, the Covenant provides an explicit thread of continuity: pictures are now less appropriate than narrative, for it is the relatedness of things rather than the vividness of separate experiences that matters. The need to have interruptions by Adam and corrections by Michael also disappears at this point.* The forward energy of the story of the Covenant, of the saving remnant with whom the Covenant can remain, through Abraham and Moses, fixes our eyes on the distant horizon when the Covenant becomes the Law and the Law is fulfilled in the Gospel. And so it is only at these points that Adam is allowed to intervene, not now with moral outrage but with questions about the outcome and with exclamations of joy when the outcome is in sight. The fallen world is still a world of sin; Michael tells Adam in his merciless way:

> Doubt not but that sin
> Will reign among them, as of thee begot. . . .   (285–6)

But the cycle of sin and punishment can be felt now to be rolling forward through the long history of deprivation and wandering and penance towards the sweetness and restitution of Christ.

One cannot wholly dispose of the charge that these aims imposed on Milton's poetic power a weight it could not expect to carry. The passage

*This is not literally true; and the fact that it is not points to a complexity in the pattern I have been describing, a blurring of the clear outline I have indicated above. I have referred to the coming of the Flood as the climax of the pattern and the point where one kind of treatment of Biblical history gives way to another. Not only the placing of the break between Books XI and XII at this point but also the language used to describe the transition indicates Milton's intention that we should respond as I have described. But the first episode of Book XII (Nimrod and the building of the Tower of Babel) does not entirely support the idea of a new dispensation. Though this episode is a narrative and not a vision, it has many of the qualities of the Book XI visions. Its image of sin and punishment (with no mention of the Covenant) calls forth the moral comments of Adam, as in Book XI. There is one mark, however, of a transitional status. Michael no longer condemns Adam's response; but he did not condemn him, either, in the last episode of Book XI. After the destruction of the Tower of Babel God, once again 'Wearied with their iniquities', decides 'thenceforth/To leave them to their own polluted ways' (109–10). We may feel that this 'new beginning' is one we have visited before and that the 'new world' is extraordinarily like the old. It seems to me wholly typical of Milton that he should offer us at once a clear-cut antithesis and a process of continuity effecting change only by tiny and unforecastable modifications.

that seems particularly indefensible is that compressed summary of the exodus which runs from line 80 to line 269. For the whole of this time Adam never speaks, and Michael hardly takes breath as he rushes us, in periods of extraordinary length – with an average of twenty lines between full stops – through Egypt, Sinai and Edom. An enthusiast for the theory of imitative form might argue that the Israelites' forty years in the desert are aptly represented by the long passage of the readers through this dry material. It is probably more to the point to notice that Milton is aiming at the establishment of the Law, but cannot reach Mount Sinai or Canaan without passing through the desert. The variation of his interest from that of Biblical paraphrasts like du Bartas is very obvious here. His statements are present only as foundation for his doctrine: it is the movement *through* Jewish history that matters to him, not the nature of the events themselves. The circumstances of the giving of the Law on Mount Sinai must be mentioned, it is clear; but the meaning of the Law is what he is aiming for:

> God from the mount of Sinai, whose grey top
> Shall tremble, he descending, will himself
> In thunder lightning and loud trumpets' sound
> Ordain them laws; part such as appertain
> To civil justice, part religious rites
> Of sacrifice, informing them, by types
> And shadows, of that destined seed to bruise
> The serpent, by what means he shall achieve
> Mankind's deliverance . . .
> they . . .
> Instructed that to God is no access
> Without mediator, whose high office now
> Moses in figure bears, to introduce
> One greater. . . .   (227–42)

Du Bartas takes some 140 lines to tell this story, lavishing his art on the various aspects which bring the separate event close to us – continual comparison to other occasions, apostrophe, self-consicous rhetoric, reference to the present, personal prayer to the Deity. The result is charming though wayward, perhaps even directionless. Here is some of his opening description:

> From Rephidim, along the desert coast
> Now to Mount Sina marcheth all the host;
> Where the everlasting God, in glorious wonder,
> With dreadful voice his fearful law doth thunder. . . .
> Redoubled lightnings dazzle the Hebrews' eyes;
> Cloud-sundering thunder roars through earth and skies,
> Louder and louder in careers and cracks,

And stately Sina's massy centre shakes,
And turneth round, and on his sacred top
A whirling flame round like a ball doth wrap:
Under his rocky ribs, in coombs below,
Rough-blustering Boreas, nurst with Riphean snow,
And blub-cheeked Auster, puffed with fumes before,
Met in the midst, justling, for room to roar:
A cloak of clouds, all thorough-lined with thunder,
Muffles the mountain both. aloft and under ı
On Pharan now no shining Pharus shows.
A heavenly trump a shrill tantara blows,
The winged winds, the lightning's nimble flash,
The smoking storms, the whirl-fire's crackling clash
And deafening thunders with the same do sing
(O wondrous comfort!) the everlasting king,
His glorious wisdom who doth give the law
To the heavenly troops, and keeps them all in awe.

Du Bartas assumes the inevitable unity of the Biblical story, and makes no effort to prove it. The relationship between the Law and the Gospel is clearly enough in the poet's mind as he writes about Sinai; but he does not organise his description around it. Instead he invites us to stay and luxuriate in one fact after another. This is the opposite to Milton, who sees the story as a seaman sees a chart, as a way of moving to the point beyond the horizon where the meaning of the route (rather than the fact of it) can be declared. In his haste to move he does not mind leaving a few ends quite loose. When Adam is finally able to interpose his comments on the long narrative, he picks up two points, the beginning and the end of the story, Michael has been telling, Abraham and the Law, ignoring all that comes between them. Abraham's role as the type of Christ has been adequately prepared for; but the comments on the Law do not arise from anything he has been told (in our hearing). He wonders, he says,

> So many and so various laws are given;
> So many laws argue so many sins
> Among them; how can God with such reside?   (282–4)

The variety of ritual laws is assumed by Milton, and we may be grateful that he was willing to foreshorten the perspective in this way, rather than spell them all out in narrative. What Milton is interested in is what Michael immediately takes up:

> So law appears imperfect, and but given
> With purpose to resign them in full time
> Up to a better Covenant, disciplined

From shadowy types to truth, from flesh to spirit,
From imposition of strict laws, to free
Acceptance of large grace, from servile fear
To filial, works of law to works of faith.   (300–6)

The movement of the verse here, the way in which it accelerates out of argument into the impassioned iteration of change and release in the Gospel shows us the true impetus that Milton relies on to draw us through the story of Book XII. If we compare the potted history of Joshua (307–14) with that of Isaac and Jacob (151–64), we can see that the emotional force which separates the former from the latter derives almost entirely from the presence of Jesus in Joshua's actions. The resonance of his historical role in crossing the Jordan and reaching Canaan comes from the meaning that the life of Jesus gives to these actions:

But Joshua whom the gentiles Jesus call,
. . . shall quell
The adversary serpent, and bring back
Through the world's wilderness long wandered Man
Safe to eternal paradise of rest.   (310–14)

The *rest* that is so powerfully evoked here is not only and not even primarily that of the Israelites, but rather the *rest* of the Christian soul.

The tension between Milton–Michael's need to note the milestones that measure the route and the desire to reach the climax is nicely illustrated in the story of David. Having reached David, Milton is clearly within doctrinal sight of his goal in Christ:

Of David (so I name this king) shall rise
A son, the woman's seed to thee foretold. . . .   (326–7)

Foretold . . . foretold . . . foretold . . . quickens the verse towards its climax in 'of his reign shall be no end'. But the end is not yet. Milton has to return to his history ('But first a long succession must ensue'). He has to tell us something of the exile,

that the true
Anointed king Messiah might be born
Barred of his right.   (358–60)

The process of history has a penitential aspect for the teller as well as for the told. The human mind, perhaps because it is fallen, perhaps only because it is human, is imprisoned by the need to grasp at understanding through the sequential process which leads through error to revelation of truth. I have spoken already of Adam's final error in which he sees the fulfilment of the Protevangelium in terms of a heroic combat. Michael has to issue his final correction:

> Dream not of their fight,
> As of a duel, or the local wounds
> Of head or heel: not therefore joins the Son
> Manhood to Godhead . . .
> nor so is overcome
> Satan. . . .
> Nor can this be,
> But by fulfilling that which thou didst want,
> Obedience to the law of God. . . .   (386–97)

It is not accidental that the error of epic thinking persists to the end of the epic. It is hard to read epic poetry or history except in terms of triumphs and defeats, survivors and victims, seen in physical shapes. But redeemed history, like the redeemed epic, leads towards a point where such vocabulary evaporates, revealing behind the 'local wounds' the larger pattern of providence

> That all this good of evil shall produce,
> And evil turn to good. . . .   (470–1)

The function of the pursuit of history is, as I have noted above (p. 71), the escape from history.

CHAPTER 8

The Creation: Books VII and VIII

Paradise Lost raises an obvious question about God's purpose in the Creation of man, and the creation of the world to contain man: since He foreknew the Fall of man, why did God proceed with the Creation at all? One answer, perfectly correct in theological terms, is that the ways of the Lord are unsearchable, Amen. But Milton's poem can hardly rest in such an Amen. Phrased as it is in intellectual and psychological terms, what is theologically correct easily comes to seem a deliberate evasion. The interrelation of parts, the laborious prosecution of cause, would make a pious blank at this point in the story seem more frustrating than humble. And Milton himself, very explicitly, calls our attention to the problem when, at the beginning of his account of the Creation, he repeats the *cause* question he had asked at the beginning of the poem. There he asked the Holy Spirit to tell what caused the Fall; now Adam asks Raphael to *relate*

> How first began this heaven which we behold
> Distant so high. . . .
> what cause
> Moved the creator in his holy rest
> Through all eternity so late to build
> In Chaos, and the work begun, how soon
> Absolved. . . .   (VII, 86–94)

Alastair Fowler in his note on lines 90–2 remarks: 'It is curious that Milton should put Adam's question so absurdly – as if he were to ask, like a child, what moved the prime mover.' The situation, however, demands what seems an absurdity, especially when contemplated from the point of view of Newtonian or post-Newtonian physics. Adam presumably seeks the reasurance of God's love; but by asking *How* (twice) he seems to be more concerned with process than with motivation. And it is certaintly the *process* of creation that Raphael takes up in his reply. The syntactic confusion of Adam's question may be thought to deserve the evasiveness of Raphael's answer. But perhaps we should credit Milton with an intention beyond this. The confusion between *How* and *what cause* questions may well be a deliberate presentation by Milton of the problem involved in trying to see motivation through process. Certainly he seems to be deliberate in his unwillingness to take a clear hold of the explanation of God's motives that lay to his hand, and that many distinguished theologians had assented to – that the Creation of man and his world was caused by God's desire to repopulate his empire, reduced by the departure of the wicked angels. Milton puts the two events together in God's mouth: 'Far the greater part have kept their station', He announces,

> sufficient to possess her realms
> Though wide. . . .
> But lest his heart exalt him in the harm
> Already done, to have dispeopled heaven
> My damage fondly deemed, I can repair
> That detriment, if such it be to lose
> Self-lost, and in a moment will create
> Another world, out of one man a race
> Of men innumerable. . . .   (147–56)

The *and* in line 154 misses causality by a hair's breadth, as it has to if Milton is to clear God of the imputation that he could be moved by forces outside his own will. 'I can repair the so-called damage', God says, 'if I choose to do so; and in fact, out of my own mere will I have now decided to create. . . .' Milton tells us elsewhere (I, 651 ff.; II, 345 ff.) that the Creation of man was a project discussed in Heaven before the revolt of the angels occurred. What seems to be clear is that he wishes to avoid both the exclusively causal relationship of the revolt and the Creation and the complete separation of the two. He wishes to avoid the exclusively causal, for that commits him to the hellish argument that Satan was the cause of man. But he also wishes to avoid complete separation of the two events, for that would remove the animating image of God's love overcoming hatred, unceasingly creative and resourceful, unshakably committed to 'One kingdom, joy and union without end' (161).

Without some such sense of an animating divine motive it is hard to keep the mere mechanics of the process of creation from occupying the centre of our attention, and much modern commentary speaks as if this was the line of interest that guided us through the action. Milton's connections with seventeenth-century science, the variation between Copernican and Ptolemaic models of the heavens, the nature of the material out of which God made the world – all this is often treated as if it was the end of Milton's writing rather than the means by which he conveys something else. These elements are, of course, important. But it may be proper to begin by noting the ways in which Milton plays down the physical facts of the Creation in order to play up the spirituality of the intention. The hymn of the angels, which follows the announcement of God's intention, deals exclusively with the benignity of God's will rather than the wonder of His acts. They sing

> to him
> Glory and praise, whose wisdom had ordained
> Good out of evil to create, in stead
> Of spirits malign a better race to bring
> Into their vacant room, and thence diffuse
> His good to worlds and ages infinite.   (186–91)

The narrative account of the Creation cannot escape from fact to purpose quite so easily. Raphael, of course, specifically tells that these 'facts' are not real facts, that

> Immediate are the acts of God, more swift
> Than time or motion, but to human ears
> Cannot without process of speech be told,
> So told as earthly notion can receive.   (176–9)

The reference to 'accommodation' saves the vocabulary from claiming truth; but it does not allow us to give other meanings to the words used. We have noticed elsewhere that Milton's hostility to allegory and his attachment to material events force him into a great deal of double speaking. I have suggested above that *how* and *what cause* questions have been allowed to cross one another to sustain our sense that fact and meaning in the Creation co-exist without any simple sense of subordination. Perhaps our post-Newtonian sense of words like *rest*, *movement, speed, distance*, and of the purely mathematical relationship between them, gives such meanings an undue prominence and distorts Milton's intention. But the difficulty is at the very least one that Milton has made room for. In reading Dante (for example) we do not face this problem, for it is clear throughout the *Divine Comedy* that space, time and movement are only present as ways of talking about spiritual truth. The speed of the Primum Mobile (or of the stone falling to the earth) expresses love and desire and purpose rather more than any simple or computable change of position. God (we are told) created this universe to express his love, and its movement answers to its creation by doing just that. The question *how* the universe works (repeatedly raised) is answered entirely inside the larger question *why* God made it to work that way. But in Milton's creation story, as so often in his poem, the two ways of looking at the material are present in dramatic dialogue rather than narrative subordination, so that both views have dialectical emphasis. In the conversation on astronomy at the beginning of Book VIII, Adam tells Raphael that the orbs move on their 'sumless journey' (36) at 'incorporeal speed' (37), 'Speed, to describe whose swiftness number fails' (38). Is this extraordinary sequence of denials given us in order to make the point that all numbers are irrelevant to such movements? Or does it simply express Adam's hyperbole about the unbelievably high numbers involved? Both possibilities are present. Raphael stresses the latter: numbers cannot tell you anything about God. But the central description of the Son wielding his golden compasses 'to circumscribe/This universe, and all created things' (226–7) hardly encourages us to discount arithmetic. In Dante's poem the complexities of number are absorbed into the mystery of the deity; and mathematical and scientific experiments are assumed to lead towards the apprehension of God. In *Paradise Lost*, however, simple denial of number keeps it in mind as part of a dialectic, silenced but not forgotten. Adam easily allows that his fascination with number and magnitude measures his wandering from the centre of human blessedness, that mutual commerce of understandings that Eve values and for which she abandons abstract astronomy at VIII, 40 ff. The doctrine in the poem places all its weight here. Thoughts of the earth as 'a spot, a grain,/An atom' (17–18), and 'sedentary' (32) into the bargain, arise from the heresy of placing abstraction above experience. For the most impressive part of creation is not the incomputable magnitude of the sun but the mind of the man who experiences through it the glory of God:

> And for the heaven's wide circuit, let it speak
> The maker's high magnificence, who built
> So spacious, and his line stretched out so far. . . .   (100–2)

The 'language' of the universe invites man to respond with joy, not measurement. It is worth noting that Raphael, at the end of his abstruse excursus on possible planetary motions, returns again to the sun and moon as poetic objects, making direct claims on the emotions:

> Whether the sun predominant in heaven
> Rise on the earth, or earth rise on the sun,
> He from the east his flaming road begin,
> Or she from west her silent course advance
> With inoffensive pace that spinning sleeps
> On her soft axle, while she paces even,
> And bears thee soft with the smooth air along,
> Solicit not thy thoughts with matters hid. . . .   (160–7)

This is not a simple prohibition. The language of beauty, power and attractiveness spells out the meaning of creation for those who were its designated objects.

The man-centred nature of the process is clear enough in the steps taken by the Creator. Out of clashing chaos the Omnific Word creates order and system (space and time) to protect man and give his divine reason matter for advancement. God's 'vital warmth' breaks up the inertia of matter, its physical hostility to change. Out of the meaninglessness, 'loud misrule' of 'chaos', 'The black tartareous cold infernal dregs/Adverse of life' (VII, 238 ff.), He creates the intelligible, 'conglobed/Like things to like'. The universe, the world, the garden, the animals, the wall are all designed to make man feel 'at home' as part of a coherent and benevolent system within his comprehension, keyed into a further system that may be glimpsed but not immediately understood, leading eventually to that end-point of rest or peace when earth will be 'changed to heaven, and heaven to earth,/One kingdom, joy and union without end' (160–1). When we look at the process in these terms we seem to move again from Newton to Dante. The *joy* which is the end of man's existence, the 'joy and shout' with which the angels greet the appearance of light, the 'Birthday of heaven and earth' (256), even the 'glad precipitance' with which the waters rush to their appointed place (291) – all these express motion and change not as computables but as glad fulfilment of divine purpose. The Creation seems to be less concerned with construction than with pleasure; and God's movement from 'holy rest' to building spree looks less like a series of successive states of divine being than an explosion of creative power which is both infinitely stable (it remains itself for ever) and infinitely dynamic (in an instant it changes everything).

The energy that reaches out to joy, in the Creation as Milton tells it, is by no means an energy imposed on passive objects by the active Deity. The poetry shows us the world as we know it seeming to create itself by its desire to exist:

> Forth flourished thick the clustering vine, forth crept
> The swelling gourd, up stood the corny reed
> Embattled in her field: and the humble shrub,
> And bush with frizzled hair implicit: last
> Rose as in dance the stately trees, and spread
> Their branches hung with copious fruit; or gemmed
> Their blossoms.   (320–6)

As so often in Milton, it is the verbs that carry the force of the poetry here. The recurrent inversion of verb and subject gives us a strong sense of the primacy of energy rather than form. The observer cannot tell what is going to appear till the vital reaching up to the light declares itself in a new noun, a new shape. Both the plants and the reader are given a sense of joyous participation in the rich variety of potential that is present. Much has been made from time to time of the idea that

Milton gives the devil the best tunes, and that particularly in *Comus*
the demon is given a full sense of nature's joy, while his pious opponent,
the Lady, only conveys virtue's chilling prohibitions. Those who argue in
this way (see above, p. 107) should reread Book VII of *Paradise Lost*.
But we should also note some other differences between Comus and
God. Comus's delight in 'mutual and partaken bliss', in the warm
overflowing plenty of nature, in the 'millions of spinning worms/That in
their green shops weave the smooth-haired silk' makes the vegetative
and vital elements simply reflect one another's delight in the accumulation of sensuous details. But in Book VII the sensuous exhilaration of the
particulars spreads out all the time towards a larger sense of general
meaning. The trees in the quotation above not only *rose* but 'Rose
as in dance . . . and spread/Their branches hung with copious fruit;
or gemmed/Their blossoms'. In the context of the hymning and dancing
hierarchies who appear in Heaven just before this, it is hard not to put
together the joy of nature in its creation and the joy of the angels who
welcome its 'birthday'. The sensuous energy of nature is here (though
not in *Comus*) wholly caught up in the pleasure of participating in a
completely meaningful universe, fulfilling itself in movement towards
light and spirituality. The stars, too, dance, expressing both joy and
order. The sun is

> jocund to run
> His longitude through heaven's high road: the grey
> Dawn, and the Pleiades before him danced
> Shedding sweet influence: less bright the moon,
> But opposite in levelled west was set
> His mirror, with full face borrowing her light
> From him, for other light she needed none. . . .   (372–8)

The mathematical order of the heavens is conveyed to us as not only
a dance of joy but also an expression of love, inside the tension of similarity and difference. The relation of sun to moon clearly reflects that
of Adam to Eve; and love shows itself here no less than there in the
balancing of distance and closeness (which we now think of, more
abstractly, as centrifugal and centripetal forces). The moon borrows light
from the sun, as noted above, but she also

> still that distance keeps
> Till night, then in the east her turn she shines,
> Revolved on heaven's great axle, and her reign
> With thousand lesser lights dividual holds,
> With thousand thousand stars, that then appeared
> Spangling the hemisphere.   (379–84)

The joy of separation, of difference, as well as the joy of likeness, of belonging, is an essential complementary part of the experience of order, self-realisation within the harmonious context of God's will. Modern desire for rank-ordering and single systems of judgement often conceals this. The moon has her own sphere and was created to provide such alternation. At the beginning of Book VIII, Eve gives up astronomy. She

> Rose, and went forth among her fruits and flowers,
> To visit how they prospered, bud and bloom. . . .
> Yet went she not, as not with such discourse
> Delighted, or not capable her ear
> Of what was high. . . .
> With goddess-like demeanour forth she went;
> Not unattended, for on her as queen
> A pomp of winning graces waited still. . . .   (VIII, 44–61)

Modern worry about whether Eve is as 'important' as Adam tends to ignore the point that Adam, too, is only important in so far as he fulfils his function inside the system that relies on joy in one another no less than joy in oneself. The Creation story, as Milton tells it, not only relates the delight of things created in their own existence, but also conveys powerfully the Creator's delight in his creation. When 'God saw that it was good' he is not shown simply as approving doctrinal propriety, in obedience to his commands. He is also shown, with extraordinary vividness, rejoicing in the sensuous particularity, the richness and generative energy ('Be fruitful, multiply') of the things that he has made, or (as more often seems) released from the generative matrix of his own Being:

> God said. . . .
> The earth obeyed, and straight
> Opening her fertile womb teemed at a birth
> Innumerous living creatures, perfect forms,
> Limbed and full grown: out of the ground up rose
> As from his lair the wild beast. . . .
> The grassy clods now calved, now half appeared
> The tawny lion, pawing to get free
> His hinder parts, then springs as broke from bonds,
> And rampant shakes his brindled mane; the ounce,
> The libbard, and the tiger, as the mole
> Rising, the crumbled earth above them threw
> In hillocks.   (VII, 450–69)

The sense here is not of God setting out the livestock as a child might set out cardboard figures from a *Make Your Own Garden of Eden* set. It is rather that there is a sudden lightning-release of energy which appears simultaneously in the Creator and the created. The gourds stretch into their maturity as in a speeded-up film, or perhaps rather a slowed-down explosion, a process inside time superimposed on an event outside time. The tawny lion leaps from non-being into being with a liberating power that reflects God's (in this like Blake's tiger), and the celebration of achieved freedom when he stands on his hind legs ('rampant') and shakes his mane is an emblem of what is happening everywhere at this moment when Heaven and Earth rejoice together. The interpenetration of all parts by the same divine energy is nicely expressed by the extraordinary and usually unremarked conceit: 'fleeced the flocks and bleating rose,/As plants' (472-3). What is meant is clear enough: the sheep rose out of the ground as plants do; they were already fully mature, fleecy and bleating. What is extraordinary is Milton's choice of a Crashawesque mode of expression, as if, for once, he was more interested in giddying the mind than clarifying the issue. One can see why he should be. The rhetoric of creation is designed to stress what all created objects share, not what separates one form from another. But this impression can only be achieved, inside a fallen language that exists by separating forms, by a kind of *trompe l'œil* effect, offering us temporary false relationships: that it is the *bleating* that *rose*; that the *rose* belongs with the *plants* rather than the *flocks*. As the articulated structure of syntax collapses we catch a glimpse of another dimension behind it. A few lines later Milton strains his rhetoric in a different direction, but to procure a similar effect. In the *carmen correlativum* at the end of the creation of the animals he sums up what we have seen:

> earth in her rich attire
> Consummate lovely smiled; air, water, earth,
> By fowl, fish, beast, was flown, was swam, was walked
> Frequent. . . .   (501-4)

Each form of life has its own separate element and its own mode; and yet, the rhetoric playfully insists, they belong together as variants on a single form, almost interchangeable.

The climax of the Creation is, of course, Man (and so Woman), a creature whose upward energy is not, like the lion's, a temporary expression of joy but a permanent state, appropriately erect, both for looking down on nature and for looking up to God. But man's sense of his existence is not primarily expressed by physical posture or movement but by the God-given power of speech. It is clear that Milton presents control, knowledge and naming as interrelated aspects of man's power. Raphael says of the beasts, 'thou their natures know'st, and gavest them names' (493); and later, speaking of man's destiny to rule and colonise every part of the earth, he points out that 'no place/Is yet distinct by name' (535-6), recording the undoubted truth that naming, knowing and ruling will come together. But we misinterpret the unfallen relationship of man and nature if we think of intellect and language as instruments of conquest or imperialism. They are more fittingly seen in the morning hymn with which Adam and Eve anticipate Psalm 19 and the Anglican Prayer Book. The *Benedicite omnia opera* in Book V (153–208) shows human language as the effective expression of all the created world, which else is tongueless. Man is the voice of nature and interprets its natural beauties as thanksgiving witness 'Made vocal by my song, and taught his praise' (204). More guide than king, he presents their joy to their Maker and beseeches bounty on behalf of all of them. But man's aspiration to God through the medium of language is not confined to praise; human energy and joy in self show themselves most characteristically in the desire to know, to use words for questions and answers. We approach here, of course, a more dangerous aspect of human joy in self, which can easily turn into self-regard. The difference is often seen in terms of a prohibition. Raphael certainly asserts that there are

> Things not revealed, which the invisible king,
> Only omniscient, hath suppressed in night,
> To none communicable in earth or heaven.   (VII, 122–4)

And Adam confirms the idea that the human mind needs to be forbidden for its own good:

> But apt the mind or fancy is to rove
> Unchecked, and of her roving is no end;
> Till warned, or by experience taught, she learn. . . .
>   (VIII, 188–90)

What is not always noticed is that the mind is not conceived to move naturally against these limits. Proper human joy in the capacity to understand and organise experience has to transform itself before it can challenge the unknowable. The image that Milton repeatedly uses to express this situation is that of food. Raphael, immediately after the assertion of secret knowledge (quoted above), goes on to point to man as a vessel with limited capacity:

> But knowledge is as food, and needs no less
> Her temperance over appetite, to know
> In measure what the mind may well contain,
> Oppresses else with surfeit, and soon turns
> Wisdom to folly, as nourishment to wind.   (VII, 126–30)

The same view of man's limitation rather than God's prohibition appears in Adam's description of human wisdom at the end of the poem:

> Greatly instructed I shall hence depart,
> Greatly in peace of thought, and have my fill
> Of knowledge, what this vessel can contain;
> Beyond which was my folly to aspire.   (XII, 557–60)

There is no suggestion here of God censoring man's knowledge, though there is in the poem a clear allowance that some knowledge is more important than some other. What is primary is the knowledge that leads to salvation, and beyond that a proper understanding of the things that God has placed within reach:

> That which before us lies in daily life,
> Is the prime wisdom, what is more, is fume,
> Or emptiness, or fond impertinence,
> And renders us in things that most concern
> Unpractised, unprepared, and still to seek.   (VIII, 193–7)

The vessel is full with this necessary and appropriate knowledge; to go on filling it, to gorge on sweet or strong victuals, is to risk an intellectual flatulence like Eve's presumption that she could fly to Heaven. But in the fallen world, and in those shadowings of the fallen world that lie across the poem, it is clear that Milton is strongly affected by the awareness that joy and knowledge tend to pull apart, that aspiration and arrogance are twins, one blessed one damnable. Once again the comparison with Dante shows how different ways of judging transform identical material. Dante's poem is full of mathematics, and expositions of contemporary science. But there is little or no sense that this knowledge will condemn unless handled with extremely devout attention. In Canto II of the *Paradiso* Dante is carried up to the sphere of the moon. He is restlessly curious about what is happening to him, and raises particularly the puzzle about the dark patches on the moon's surface. Beatrice invites him to state his own (scientific) explanation. This is inadequate; and it is inadequate in precisely the same way as the astronomical conjectures dismissed by Raphael in Book VIII of *Paradise Lost*. For Milton–Raphael such theories are contemptible:

> if they list to try
> Conjecture, he his fabric of the heavens
> Hath left to their disputes, perhaps to move
> His laughter at their quaint opinions wide
> Hereafter, when they come to model heaven
> And calculate the stars. . . .   (VIII, 75–80)

Dante, like the astronomers, errs in trying to explain heavenly phenomena in terms of physical rather than spiritual laws. But the error is allowed as an inevitable part of the process of ascent. Though himself part of fallen nature, Dante appears capable of almost infinite glorification, as if the physical world provided only the thinnest of impediments to spiritual truth, and as if physical observation provided a perfectly natural basis for theological vision. One might say that Dante's poem shows a sublime confidence that mathematical hypotheses and physical experiments necessarily converge on the basic and animating truths about God. Milton's sense of the relationship between the physical and spiritual explanations is more dialectical. When Raphael asserts the primacy of spiritual meanings he does so in terms which betray uneasiness. The doctrine is, of course, Dantean and traditional:

> The swiftness of those circles attribute,
> Though numberless, to his omnipotence,
> That to corporeal substances could add
> Speed almost spiritual.   (VIII, 107–10)

But the words imply possibilities that are not in Dante. Take *add* and *almost* in the last sentence. The implication is, I take it, that God makes an addition to something that is already there – a corporeal substance – and so speeds it up to a rate that one is *almost* forced to call spiritual. In Dante the physical operation of the spheres is a way of observing or talking about their truly spiritual existence: the physical simply dissolves before the light of the godhead. But in *Paradise Lost*, though Adam, like Dante the pilgrim, embraces correction, Milton continues to give physical objects a stubborn indissolubility. The physical and the spiritual come to seem more like two competing systems, sometimes in accord, sometimes in contradiction, but always separate. Dante managed to absorb his scientific interests into his spiritual aspiration. In Milton's poem scientific or mechanistic explanations are in tension and threatening to break out of the spiritual matrix. This is often spoken of in historical terms: seventeenth-century science was in such a position. What is more interesting than the assumption that Milton was confined by the cosmogony of his own age, however, is the perception that he was able to make something universal out of that confinement. It is part of Adam's freedom that enumeration and abstraction come naturally to his mouth. He asks Raphael for a *solution* to his problem about the stars: when he tries to *compute* the *magnitude* of the firmament, 'and all her *numbered* stars' (VIII, 19), he gets a number that is too large to be believed, 'for such/Their distance argues and their swift return/ Diurnal' (20–2). He is unable to accept this solution as God's since he is able himself to think of a more efficient or (as mathematicians say) elegant alternative, whereby the earth 'better might with far less compass move' (33). The Newtonian vocabulary has nothing in it of infidelity or revolt; as noted above, Adam immediately accepts Raphael's alternative view that this is frivolous knowledge, unnecessary to salvation. But the vocabulary remains unabsorbed, like the apple itself in the middle of the blessed garden, and our fallen response is continually aware of its power as a suppressed alternative articulation of the facts. The main thrust of Book VII — the representation of God's handiwork as an explosion of creative joy — is not in any way neutralised by the presence of this shadow. Given the centrality of the idea of freedom in the poem, joy, like other emotions, is bound to point in at least two directions. The pleasure in creation, in naming, in understanding, in exploring what is known, leads inevitably, by the lower route, to the tempting apple of good and evil. It does not require that man eat of it; but it does seem to require that the possibility has occurred to him. The liberation into free creativity that we are made witness to is also a liberation into danger, pleasure and danger being closely associated, as when the apple is made the climax of the Garden.

I began this chapter with a question: Why did God proceed with the Creation, knowing man destined to fall? I am not under any illusion that I have answered this question, or even that I can answer it. What I have tried to do is to indicate the status of such a question inside the actual picture of Creation that Milton gives us. I trust that it has become apparent that the question arises more from the general idea of Creation than from the particular handling. The relation of creativity to freedom is one of the fundamental axes of the poem and of the image of life that it contains. It is creative joy that makes danger worth while; and, if one is the consequence of the other, clearly both have to be accepted, for a life enslaved to benevolence is judged worse than a freely chosen Fall. Even in the commonest terms of human morality, the advice not to be joyful because tomorrow you die is a *non sequitur*. The creativity which God passes on to man at the Creation is not a good to be judged by results; the chance, even the necessity, that it will lead to the Fall is not sufficient to undermine it.

CHAPTER 9

The Heart of the Poem

(i) THE GARDEN: BOOKS IV AND IX

As I have noted above (pp. 48 ff) we reach the central situation of the poem, the Garden of Eden, and the protagonists, Adam and Eve, only after considerable weaving around this centre has prepared our minds for the complexity we meet there. We began the poem with a clear pointer to this centre. Milton tells his Muse to

> say first what cause
> Moved our grand parents in that happy state,
> Favoured of heaven so highly, to fall off
> From their creator. . . .   (I, 28–31)

But the process of exploring that question has taken us in a wide circuit away from Adam and Eve, and only in Book IV, after visiting Heaven and Hell, do we meet the objects of our eventual concern. And even then we do not see them with frontal simplicity; we see them through the oblique and voyeuristic gaze of Satan. The scene, when we get to it, is full of eyes pointing in different directions. Adam and Eve look up to God while we see Satan look at them. But Satan in his turn is not unobserved. Uriel looks down from the sun and sees the hatred that Satan cannot conceal when he sees Adam and Eve. A little later Gabriel is looking for Satan while Satan is looking for ways into the mind of Eve. Appearances offer us understanding, and we have little alternative but to follow them; but we have learned already that the tissue of appearances can be a tissue of lies. Satan, discovered as a toad, is forced by the angels to assume his 'proper' form, but the meaning of this form is seen differently by the angels and by Satan himself.

The Garden that Satan's gaze unfolds for us thus comes to us both as a goal and as a challenge. We have reached the place we were going to, and for a moment we pause from the forward movement of the poem and stare, like Satan 'stupidly good', 'with such delay/Well pleased', or else, trance-like 'journey on, pensive and slow'. The trance of balmy odours that Milton sets up for our final approach to Eden (156–65) describes, however, only one side of the Eden we reach. The Garden is a moral challenge as well as a resting-place; and Satan's response is used to give us both aspects. For Satan, the Garden is both what he seeks and what he cannot stand. The power of his reaction arises in large part, of course, from his likeness to the present inhabitants; he sees Adam and Eve as replacements for himself, 'Creatures . . ./Into our room of bliss thus high advanced' (359–60); Satan once lived thus, and Adam, we know, will in his turn become an intruder into bliss as Satan is now. The Eden we meet is charged with instability, sick with the future and overloaded with the past.

Milton first 'presents' Paradise to us as the cause of the powerful emotions that we see pass across Satan's mind – nostalgia, self-reproach, sentimental self-regard, new resolution quickly collapsing into renewed despair. Even when we move into what seems more like an objective description of the Garden, we move down from the vantage-point of Satan sitting as a cormorant on top of the tree of life. What we are shown is what 'he views/To all delight of human sense exposed . . . nature's whole wealth' (205–7). We ask if we are meant to align ourselves with the *human sense* or with the controlling view that looks down on human sense – Satan's. The lines that precede this suggest that the proper answer is: Neither. The value of things, we are told, lies not in themselves nor in the emotions they give rise to, but in their proper use. God, who alone knows how to 'value right/The good before him' (201–2), made the Garden, 'caused [it] to grow', but focused it not on beauty but on the idea of use, the act of choice.

I have discussed above, under the rubric of 'Style', some of the ways in which Milton dramatises the beauty of art in the presentation of the Garden of Choice; but it is worth while looking again at the key passage, Book IV, lines 216–68, where style, drama, doctrine and narrative combine to build up a density of apprehension. The poet or narrator can be seen to move through a series of alternative strategies of description. He moves from testable fact ('Wandering many a famous realm') to precious valuation ('How from that sapphire fount . . .') to a kind of throwing up of his hands over the inadequacy of his expressive means ('fed/Flowers worthy of Paradise'). But the contradiction between 'nature' in the Garden and the 'art' that Milton must use to describe it is not meant to be resolved by any of these methods. A simplification of Milton's technique would render the summing-up in line 246 as 'this was the place'; what Milton says is 'thus was this place', throwing the weight of our attention on the need of the artist as well as the inhabitants to contemplate the function of the Garden rather than relax in the fact of its existence. He displays the schemata of art as an earnest of his intention: the fount reminds him of *sapphire*, the sands are *gold*, the water is *nectar* (beauty rendered by valuation); the shade is a painterly *brown*, the fruit has *golden rind*, while the flocks are *interposed*, set in the way of an ideal point of view, as part of the deliberate composition of a landscape gardener. But the Garden itself is seen as a collaborator in this attempt to make sense of its objects. The scene rather self-consciously displays its wares: 'the mantling vine/*Lays forth* her purple grape', the 'irriguous valley *spreads her store*', the 'murmuring waters . . . /Her crystal mirror *holds*', the 'airs . . . *attune* their trembling leaves' (all italics mine). The verbs indicate the activity of the Garden in calling for response, in calling for man to notice and to use. Such activity is, of course, what we would expect, for the Garden was made for man.

The description of the Garden can be seen as a bridge passage between the two polarities that give it meaning, Satan and the human pair. It is interesting that Milton does not make Adam and Eve seem to grow out of the Garden like the trees and flowers, but at the point of introducing them returns our attention to the fiendish observer whose gaze began the description and who likewise ends it, with the remembrance that he

> Saw undelighted all delight, all kind
> Of living creatures new to sight and strange.   (286-7)

And so with a reminder that the value of the sight derives from the seer we finally meet the central characters of the poem:

> Two of far nobler shape erect and tall,
> Godlike erect, with native honour clad
> In naked majesty seemed lords of all,
> And worthy seemed, for in their looks divine
> The image of their glorious maker shone,
> Truth, wisdom, sanctitude severe and pure. . . . (288-93)

The repeated word *seemed* is particularly interesting here. Whether the viewpoint is that of Satan or of the narrator (and the question is an open one) the word tells us that something less than certainty attaches to the status of Adam and Eve. The present in which their innocent bliss is so movingly described is accompanied by the shadow of the choices within which they live, known to us from Satan's past and Adam's future. The two-dimensional dream of a wholly natural life is shown all the time from the third dimension of a fallen observer. They satisfy thirst and appetite with water and fruit; they work at gardening till they are warm and then they sit down on the grass; they wear no clothes; they exhibit no sexual shame – all this is shown from a point of view which explicitly or implicitly allows that mankind normally lives otherwise. The tension between their 'Simplicity and spotless innocence' and the fallen knowledge of good and evil that we bring to our reading is sometimes pointed up by the narrator, sometimes by Satan. With extraordinary skill Milton maintains a Satanic presence inside the framework of the idyll; the implacable foe to the blissful pair is always close but never in true contact with them. In his second soliloquy (358–92) he is reduced to the contemplation of future cruel pleasures. When he descends from his high tree he can stalk his prey more closely, but only within the frustrating disguise of one of the frisking animals who seek to please Adam and Eve after supper with an innocent parody of a court masque. The resonance that comes from those Elizabethan plays in which a court masque is a licence for disguised killings may be part of the effect intended here. But, if so, it is like other parts of the Satanic intention – glimpsed only in frustration. As a lion or a tiger he can rehearse the post-lapsarian ferocities of one 'who by chance hath spied/In some purlieu two gentle fawns at play' (403–4). But the post-lapsarian ferocity is visible only to the fallen – to the reader and to Satan himself. In the pre-lapsarian world the *gentle fawns* are invulnerable, and what Satan means as earnest is perceived only as play, as part of what Adam describes as 'all this happiness'. In the present tense of the Garden Satan's proximity to those he would destroy is torment to himself but no impediment to the undiluted joy the others know. Their happy ignorance that their enemy is beside them is in these terms a strength. But we cannot rest happy in the apprehension of such strength. Satan is ostensibly defeated; he turns aside and 'began/Through wood, through waste, o'er dale his roam' (537–8); but we the readers know that the villain who turns away at the first defeat will be back soon with a stronger assault, and that (in larger terms) the garden only has meaning when seen from the outside, while its values are being tested by non-beneficiaries.

The testing we see in the poem is not merely external; if so it would be wholly ineffective. The centre of the test comes from inside, for the Garden is, as I have said, more a moral gymnasium than a place of relaxation. For this reason any attempt to assimilate it to traditional pastoral requires elaborate qualification. It is not so much that Milton never shows us how it was with Adam and Eve before the arrival of Satan. The tree of the knowledge of good and evil is, we must suppose, created before the creatures who are to be tested by it. Pastoral often shows us an idyllic way of life under threat from external pressures; but the idea that there was a time when the pressure was not there, or that it may go away, serves to define what is, after all, more an idea than a reality. The idea that a life free of such pressures is a possibility seems essential to pastoral; and this we do not find in *Paradise Lost*. The real protection of the Garden does not lie in the wall or the angelic squadrons but in the perpetual vigilance of the human minds. This is the price of freedom, then as now. The pre-lapsarian and post-lapsarian situations are not, of course, identical. The fixing of human will in obedience to God's will was then all that was required to sustain blessedness. But God's will is not presented as simple or programmatic; it requires self-scrutiny and self-control to know how best to please the Father in Heaven and merit the advancement to a home in heaven with the angels that is the vaguely promised reward for a consistent performance in the early tests. 'Security' or overconfidence in blessedness, the failure to engage in strenuous enough self-scrutiny, was a much discussed sin in Protestant circles. Milton seems to allow that it was a danger in Paradise also; effort was a commodity that even there could not be spared. It was thus no accident that made Milton depart from the language of Scripture in his

> This Paradise I give thee, count it thine
> To till and keep, and of the fruit to eat.   (VIII, 319–20)

The Authorised Version does not use *till* here, but the milder word *dress*; it suppresses the idea of tillage until after the Fall. I have noted it elsewhere as a recurrent characteristic of Milton that he tends to stress the continuity in physical matters of life before the Fall and life after the Fall, just as he stresses the continuity between life on earth and life in heaven. The matter of work offers no exception. The curse of the Fall offers, of course, very specific statements about new conditions that attach to work. The soil is to become cursed; 'in sorrow shalt thou eat of it all the days of thy life . . . In the sweat of thy face shalt thou eat bread' (Genesis, 3 : 17–19). The implication is that something which was easy is cursed and so made difficult; the process of agriculture has been made a matter of sweat when it was not so before. Milton cannot deny this clearly stated Scriptural truth; but he can avail himself of the latitude that attaches to any definition of *easy* and *difficult*. He chooses, in the main, to gloss the *ease* of prelapsarian gardening in terms of emotional and social ease rather than of merely physical easiness.

When we first hear of work in the Garden it sounds more like healthy recreation than hard labour:

> after no more toil
> Of their sweet gardening labour than sufficed
> To recommend cool zephyr, and made ease
> More easy, wholesome thirst and appetite
> More grateful. . . .   (IV, 327–31)

A hundred lines later the attitude has not changed, though Milton raises (only to dismiss) the possibility that work is *toilsome*. Adam speaks of

> our delightful task
> To prune these growing plants, and tend these flowers,
> Which were it toilsome, yet with thee were sweet.   (437–9)

The hint given here is, however, the one that grows as the poem progresses. When we next hear of gardening, the tasks are seen as something imposed from outside rather than chosen from inside; Adam tells Eve:

> God hath set
> Labour and rest, as day and night to men
> Successive. . . .
> Other creatures all day long
> Rove idle unemployed, and less need rest;
> Man hath his daily work of body or mind
> Appointed, which declares his dignity,
> And the regard of heaven on all his ways;
> While other animals unactive range,
> And of their doings God takes no account.　　(612–22)

This is very far from describing work as a punishment (which is what the Fall decrees), since it makes specifically the point that man's dignity is shown by his sense of the propriety and meaningfulness of labour. In the sonnet on his blindness Milton tells us that he sees God as a taskmaster; but this is not to say that he sees him as a slave-driver who exacts day-labour at the end of a whip; rather, he is the tally-clerk who enters meaningful activity into his credit ledger, and rejoices to do so. None the less, some sense of tension between the external decree and the internal choice must be allowed to be present, in potential if not in actuality. *God hath set* man certain tasks, and His setting them is entirely logical; but the animals show an alternative that the vestiges of the pastoral tradition (which lurk behind what is said) reinforce as a possible human ideal. The pastoral tradition sets *otium*, or ease, against *care* or *busyness*, seen as the defining characteristics of courtly or metropolitan life. And into the life of dignified toil which Adam preaches something of the same sense of desperate busyness begins to intrude:

> Tomorrow ere fresh morning streak the east
> With first approach of light, we must be risen,
> And at our pleasant labour, to reform
> Yon flowery arbours, yonder alleys green,
> Our walk at noon, with branches overgrown,
> That mock our scant manuring, and require
> More hands than ours to lop their wanton growth:
> These blossoms also, and those dropping gums,
> That lie bestrewn unsightly and unsmooth,
> Ask riddance, if we mean to tread with ease.　　(623–32)

Man's *appointed work* is seen here, interestingly enough, as analogous to the work of God in the Creation. As that event put 'Like things to

like, the rest to several place/Disparted' (VII, 240–1), banished chaos
and by imposing order allowed the meaning of separate things to emerge,
so here, in their humble sphere, Adam and Eve 'Lop overgrown, or
prune, or prop, or bind' (IX, 210). The God-given creative impulse in
man should clearly rejoice to conform to the example of his Creator,
making sense out of nonsense and cosmos out of chaos. But there is an
important distinction. God's will created the universe in a flash of
energy unconfined by time; but the imposition of the human mind on
the brute material of the Garden is a process in time that tests love and
obedience at least as much as creativity. The love in which the Creation
fulfils itself returns to the Creator from the created, as I have argued
above; but man's creative love is only effectively returned in terms
of the mutual support that the human pair can give to one another. I
have quoted already Adam's 'Which were it toilsome, yet with thee were
sweet'. A little later the idea is given full-scale expression:

> we in our appointed work employed
> Have finished happy in our mutual help
> And mutual love, the crown of all our bliss
> Ordained by thee, and this delicious place
> For us too large, where thy abundance wants
> Partakers, and uncropt falls to the ground.
> But thou hast promised from us two a race
> To fill the earth, who shall with us extol
> Thy goodness infinite. . . .   (726–34)

The superfluous production of the Garden is here seen as a sign of
the overflowing abundance of God's goodness. Unfallen man can wait
for the coming of further hands with patient assurance in the completeness of God's providence. But such patient inclination of the will is by
no means the only possible response. At the beginning of Book IX, Eve
returns to the question, but with a different emphasis:

> Adam, well may we labour still to dress
> This garden, still to tend plant, herb and flower,
> Our pleasant task enjoined, but till more hands
> Aid us, the work under our labour grows,
> Luxurious by restraint; what we by day
> Lop overgrown, or prune, or prop, or bind,
> One night or two with wanton growth derides
> Tending to wild.   (IX, 205–12)

Eve's dutiful reference to 'Our pleasant task enjoined' hardly conceals
her alarm that the production norms are falling behind. The bliss of
mutual support that makes shared work the basis of social existence is

lost in the worry about externals. She asks Adam for a remedy, but before he can speak she offers her own one – they should work separately. It is not clear if Eve's proposal is to be read as part of a general search for greater independence, or as a genuine attempt to improve their economic performance (what Milton calls 'household good': l. 233). In either case it is clear that the accidents have been substituted for the essentials in God's will, the means turned into the ends. Social intercourse becomes the enemy rather than the necessary accompaniment (perhaps even the end) of human labour:

> For while so near each other thus all day
> Our task we choose, what wonder if so near
> Looks intervene and smiles, or object new
> Casual discourse draw on, which intermits
> Our day's work brought to little, though begun
> Early, and the hour of supper comes unearned.   (220–5)

The argument that follows can be seen to bring out into the open the ambiguities that attach to the idea of *work* in an unfallen society. Adam reiterates his view that work is not punishment:

> Yet not so strictly hath our Lord imposed
> Labour, as to debar us when we need
> Refreshment, whether food, or talk between,
> Food of the mind, or this sweet intercourse
> Of looks and smiles, for smiles from reason flow,
> To brute denied, and are of love the food,
> Love not the lowest end of human life.
> For not to irksome toil, but to delight
> He made us, and delight to reason joined.   (235–43)

The last two lines might be taken to be the crux of the matter. Man's chief end is not to clear up gardens but to glorify God and enjoy him for ever. Such tasks gladly undertaken are part of the glorification, but not the whole of it. When the idea of obedience is separated from the idea of love, then God becomes an oppressor and pleasure becomes the accompaniment of disobedience and so of guilt. Already, in these abstract terms, we have moved into a fallen world.

It is not accidental that Eve's argument about work shades imperceptibly into an argument about female independence. Eve sets joy against work; but the joy of work that Adam speaks about is the joy of equal labourers collaborating in the same work. The real meaning of work – real, that is, by the approval of God – lies in its expression of mutual need, mutual support, the direction of daily life towards a single God-pleasing end. When Adam reports to Raphael in Book VIII the

quality of his love for Eve he defends his joy in the relationship, seeing
it arise from

> Those thousand decencies that daily flow
> From all her words and actions mixed with love
> And sweet compliance, which declare unfeigned
> Union of mind, or in us both one soul;
> Harmony to behold in wedded pair
> More grateful than harmonious sound to the ear.
> Yet these subject not. . . .   (VIII, 601–7)

The perception that daily labour is the practical support of this *Union
of mind* is flatly denied by Eve's proposal that they will please God
better by fulfilling His work norms and labouring independently. In
these terms work is a wholly separate activity, measured by quantity
rather than quality. It is in vain for Adam to argue that other benefits
accrue:

> I from the influence of thy looks receive
> Access in every virtue, in thy sight
> More wise, more watchful, stronger, if need were
> Of outward strength. . . .
> Why shouldst not thou like sense within thee feel
> When I am present, and thy trial choose
> With me . . .?   (IX, 309–17)

For Eve the experience of mutuality has now moved from a sense of
joy to one of confinement and restriction. Perceiving herself strong she
assumes that any further support is not only superfluous but also insulting. In her final speech (322–41) she uses the plural pronouns *we* and
us only in the sense of 'one plus another' rather than in the mystical
sense of Adam and the marriage service, 'two persons joined in a singular
unity'. Her argument follows naturally from this: If *we* (you or me)
can only defeat our enemy by always remaining together, how intolerably
straitened is our condition 'thus to dwell in narrow circuit':

> Frail is our happiness, if this be so,
> And Eden were no Eden thus exposed.   (340–1)

In these lines *Eden* can only exist if it is compatible with self-fulfilment,
which is fulfilment through separation rather than via the achieved new
person of their common concern.

The answer to these arguments comes only dispersedly throughout the
remainder of the poem; but at crucial moments and with doctrinal
force. One might say that the most powerful moment is that in which

Adam is faced with the choice of rejecting the newly fallen Eve or choosing to let mankind fall with her. The fallen Eve is now an adept in the specious handling of the language of mutuality:

> Thee I have missed, and thought it long, deprived
> Thy presence, agony of love till now
> Not felt, nor shall be twice, for never more
> Mean I to try, what rash untried I sought,
> The pain of absence from thy sight.   (857–61)

Eve merely indulges in easy nostalgia for something irremediably lost. Adam, however, has to make real payment for the real choice that he would rather die with Eve than live alone. At a later point (pp. 196 ff) I shall discuss the nature of the values that this choice implies. Here I need only make the point that mutuality is seen as the most obvious of the unfallen virtues to last through the Fall and into the fallen world – which is proper enough if one remembers that it is the human reflection of the divine love. The nature of this continuation is spelled out at the end of the poem. When the curse is pronounced on Eve her first sorrow is for her home ('Thee native soil, these happy walks and shades/. . . flowers/That never will in other climate grow': XI, 270–4). Adam in the same situation laments over the places where God appeared, and is told that God can walk with man anywhere. In a parallel instruction Eve is told that the home of a loving wife is by the side of her husband; while she is with him she has not left her home:

> Thy going is not lonely, with thee goes
> Thy husband, him to follow thou art bound;
> Where he abides, think there thy native soil.   (290–2)

Eve is given no chance to respond to this instruction till some twelve hundred lines have passed. But when we hear her speak again she has not only absorbed the lesson; she has made it entirely her own. She tells Adam to lead her out of Paradise:

> In me is no delay; with thee to go,
> Is to stay here; without thee here to stay,
> Is to go hence unwilling; thou to me
> Art all things under heaven, all places thou . . . .
>   (XII, 615–18)

The aphoristic simplicity of these lines sums up what we seem meant to take as more than individual perception. As the Garden culminates in the pair who are its inhabitants, so the pleasures and temptations of the Garden culminate in the understanding that it is human mutuality that makes the blessing and the curse. It would be easy to sentimentalise this by overstressing the degree to which Eve and Adam have 'outgrown' the Garden; they are, after all, being driven out of it at the point of a flaming sword. The sense of loss and of the good use that may be made of loss are carefully balanced at the end of the poem. The capacity to deserve the Christ who is to come is carried out of the Garden between the pain of working together and the fulfilment inherent in the need to work together; but these two are so fundamental, in their co-presence and interaction, that the Garden itself might seem to be an incidental moment in their forward history.

(ii) ADAM AND EVE

The poem culminates, I am suggesting, in the relationship of Adam and Eve. This is again a matter in which Milton was both illuminated and restricted by the inspired words of Scripture. Genesis gives us information about Adam and Eve which is both clear (in its statement) and mysterious (in its meaning). With startling clarity we are shown what happened – 'And when the woman saw the tree was good for food . . . she took of the fruit thereof and did eat, and gave also unto her husband with her and he did eat'; but we are given no sense why it happened that way. It is the privilege of the method of a Bible to state and not to explain; but Milton's technique and his relationship to the reader do not allow him to evade the questions that attach to a statement of the facts; for the movement from Eve's eating to Adam's eating must be seen in *Paradise Lost* in the light of all the information we have been able to deduce about their relationship in the whole course of the poem. What does it mean to suppose that Eve is the kind of person who eats the apple first and then gives it to Adam? And how, above all, is it to be believed that Adam is the kind of person who takes it in his turn and eats also?

Certain characteristics of Adam's identity are shown to the reader of *Paradise Lost* as present at the earliest stages of his existence. As soon as he is created he begins to define himself by extending his consciousness out from his mind to his body, and from his body to the world around him:

> My self I then perused, and limb by limb
> Surveyed, and sometimes went, and sometimes ran
> With supple joints, and lively vigour led:
> But who I was, or where, or from what cause,
> Knew not; to speak I tried, and forthwith spake,
> My tongue obeyed and readily could name
> What e'er I saw.   (VIII, 267–73)

In natural communion with all around him Adam brings everything he sees into relation to his consciousness by his capacity to name it. But his primary drive is not to command the other but to understand himself:

> Ye hills and dales, ye rivers, woods, and plains,
> And ye that live and move, fair creatures, tell,
> Tell, if ye saw, how came I thus, how here?
> Not of my self; by some great maker then,
> In goodness and in power pre-eminent;
> Tell me, how may I know him, how adore. . . .   (275–80)

This assumes a reciprocity of knowledge which is, in fact, wholly justified. The instinct of his being is to ask questions, and the nature of his experience is to supply answers. In dream he is led into the Garden and shown the crucial feature of his life there.

> Each tree
> Loaden with fairest fruit that hung to the eye
> Tempting, stirred in me sudden appetite
> To pluck and eat; whereat I waked. . . .   (VIII, 306–9)

The strategic placing of the word *Tempting* here allows us to anticipate the repetition of '. . . plucked . . . ate' at the moment of the Fall in Book IX (line 781). But for Adam the tempting trees are only part of the unknown. His characteristic movement is not to satisfy carnal appetite but to begin searching once again:

> Here had new begun
> My wandering, had not he who was my guide
> . . . appeared. . . .   (311–13)

God's appearance stills the restless searcher. 'Whom thou sought'st I am,' says the Maker, with strong monosyllabic finality. It does not take Adam long, however, to recover his own nature and start asking questions once again, asking now the most sharply focused form of the question Who am I? The world around him, to which he originally addressed his questions, turns out to be dependent on him as he is not dependent on it; the pleasure of living with trees is a limited one. In his relationship to God there is a similar if opposite disparity. What his nature seeks for, Adam now sees, is something outside himself which is yet like himself. The animals have mates,

> but with me
> I see not who partakes. In solitude
> What happiness, who can enjoy alone,
> Or all enjoying, what contentment find?   (363–6)

It seems that we are not expected to find this questioning of God in any way offensive, or a sign of discontent. It moves naturally out of Adam's basic blessed humanity. God accepts the point without demur. Indeed, it produces one of His most humanely amiable moments. He replies playfully. It is, of course, as one would expect, a profound and serious playfulness:

> What think'st thou then of me, and this my state,
> Seem I to thee sufficiently possessed
> Of happiness, or not? Who am alone
> From all eternity, for none I know
> Second to me or like, equal much less.
> How have I then with whom to hold converse
> Save with the creatures which I made, and those
> To me inferior, infinite descents
> Beneath what other creatures are to thee?   (403–11)

The argument is not meant to be interpreted as a statement of doctrine. God tells us so ('Thus far to try thee, Adam, I was pleased . . . To see how thou couldst judge of fit and meet': 437, 448). But it reminds the reader that a good answer to Adam must be more than an indulgence of human weakness. The analogy the statement sets up between human and divine natures is carefully hedged around by Adam in distinctions that even God allows to be true, but it is not denied. God's perfection is in solitude; man is 'In unity defective, which requires/ Collateral love' (425–6). Love, society and the propagation of numbers are seen as means by which man advances towards perfection in the realisation of his own particular nature. Adam's desire for an Eve, and the cessation of his restless questioning about himself when she is created, even his willingness to 'die' with her rather than live alone, are all expressions not of his weakness but of his God-given nature. As created, he can only move towards perfection through means which are instinct with dangers and betrayals.

It is necessary to return here again to the difficulty of describing *unity* and *separateness* in the love of God (see above, pp. 68–70). Milton's ascription of unity to the Godhead here in Book VIII is the other side of the same difficulty. Fowler on line 420 properly rejects the idea that the assertion of unity shows us Milton's Arian disregard for the Son. But at the level of narrative rather than doctrine the line does make for difficulties. God is unlike Adam in that he *needs* no one else; but God's creative love as seen throughout the poem makes him the model of the lover who will not take No for an answer. In this respect God and Adam are alike, and the image of one provides the test of the other. God creates the Son, the angels and mankind as expansions from self to non-self, unity to otherness. He does this, we are told, not to 'break union' (VI, 612) but to expand unity by the free recirculation of love in the assertion of union by the other. Only the mystic otherness of the Son is able, however, to fulfil the system:

> O Father. . . .
> thou always seek'st
> To glorify thy Son, I always thee,
> As is most just; this I my glory account,
> My exaltation, and my whole delight,
> That thou in me well pleased, declar'st thy will
> Fulfilled, which to fulfill is all my bliss.   (VI, 723–9)

In becoming a third term between God and the angels (as subsequently a third term between God and man) the Son makes a preliminary move towards further expansion in the same terms. As Abdiel perceives, the Son's position as head of the angels makes the Father more accessible, more available to the circular process described above:

> he the head
> One of our number thus reduced becomes,
> His laws our laws, all honour to him done
> Returns our own.   (V, 842–5)

But what Abdiel sees one way Satan sees quite otherwise. Before we reach the Garden of Eden or hear the conversation bteween Adam and God we are aware of the potentials for good and evil that Adam's desire for a beloved other must set up.

Adam naturally desires the timeless response of 'harmony, true delight' in another creature like himself, and God performs all that could be expected of Him, creating for Adam 'Thy likeness, thy fit help, thy other self' (450) – what Adam less ambiguously calls 'bone of my bone, flesh of my flesh, my self' (495), and elsewhere 'Part of my soul . . . my other half' (IV, 487). Adam's love is expressed, like God's, by the desire to expand into an 'other self'; but the conditions of freedom require that such re-creation be distinguished from cloning; the 'other' is complementary rather than identical; it is another 'self' with a difference. When the newly created Eve sees herself in the mirror of a smooth pond, she discovers in the likeness she beholds 'answering looks/ Of sympathy and love' (IV, 464–5). The voice of God instructs her not to seek her own image (only a 'vain desire') but rather "he/Whose image thou art" (471–2). Love is naturally directed upwards to that which is like oneself but has priority, something extra, offering change and growth. The balance between diversity and hierarchy is difficult to define in what Milton says. Clearly both are involved; Eve has gifts that Adam lacks (see below), but Adam's gifts are seen to be, though incomplete in themselves, those of a leader. His joy in discovery is answered by Eve's gratitude for being discovered; and the two attitudes are meant (ideally) to hook together and hold the whole system in simultaneous unity and diversity. 'Obedience' is a word that Milton is too fond of for modern tastes, and the relationship between 'love' and 'obedience' in the poem is often misunderstod. Once again the Son offers the model by which all else has to be judged. When the Father condemns all mankind to die for disobedience, and the Son offers himself in ransom for their sin (III, 80 ff.), his attitude, it is said,

> breathed immortal love
> To mortal men, above which only shone
> Filial obedience: as a sacrifice
> Glad to be offered, he attends the will
> Of his great Father.   (III, 267–71)

As is evident here, love does not appear as the token of obedience, but obedience is the token of love, in a situation which is probably paradigmatic for Milton, between unequals. Modern critics are often too preoccupied with the ideal of equality to notice what Milton is saying inside the unargued framework of inequality, wishing above all to deny the premise and argue that true love 'ought' or 'must' be between equals. And, of course, when the premise is denied the consequents can hardly stand. To argue that without freedom there can be no true obedience sounds then like the last turn of the screw – the slave has to assert that he chose his prison, sing 'forced Hallelujahs', as Mammon puts it (II, 243). To argue that without love there is no true obedience sounds again like a demand for spiritless dependence.

It may, however, be worth while swallowing the premise (which contains no inherent absurdity) to see what Milton makes of it. The statement of woman's inferiority is certainly given with unambiguous clarity. Adam and Eve are

> Not equal, as their sex not equal seemed;
> For contemplation he and valour formed,
> For softness she and sweet attractive grace,
> He for God only, she for God in him.   (IV, 296–9)

The distinction as made is based on a distinction in faculty psychology I have already discussed the adventurous and aggressive rationalism of Adam, his restless search for understanding, as the basic quality of his nature. In received faculty psychology the reason was expected to 'rule' the emotions, to divert them from temporary satisfactions and to harness their power to the search for the highest good. But this degree of simplification would only be central if Milton were writing an allegory. He is content to leave this kind of diagrammatic distinction in the background of *Paradise Lost* while the foreground shows us believable human beings whose natures point them in different, though complementary, directions, so that equality is not an issue. Take the case of Eve's withdrawal from the astronomical dialogue in Book VIII:

> So spake our sire, and by his countenance seemed
> Entering on studious thoughts abstruse, which Eve
> Perceiving where she sat retired in sight,
> With lowliness majestic from her seat,
> And grace that won who saw to wish her stay,
> Rose, and went forth among her fruits and flowers. . . .
>   (VIII, 39–44)

It is easy for us to imagine that this is one of those received images in which the deep-browed husband sits in his study while the feather-brained wife simpers among the hollyhocks. Milton tells us explicitly, however, that Eve did not go because her mind was too weak for astrophysics:

> Yet went she not, as not with such discourse
> Delighted, or not capable her ear
> Of what was high. . . .
> Her husband the relater she preferred
> Before the angel, and of him to ask
> Chose rather. . . .   (48–54)

The contrast that is being established here is not a contrast of superior and inferior but of two different biases of character, each with its own splendour and its own danger. Adam's taste for abstruse speculation is part of the rationality we have already seen praised; but it is a source of moral danger, as Raphael spells out:

> Solicit not thy thoughts with matters hid,
> Leave them to God above, him serve and fear;
> Of other creatures, as him pleases best . . .
> In what he gives to thee, this Paradise
> And thy fair Eve; heaven is for thee too high
> To know what passes there; be lowly wise:
> Think only what concerns thee and thy being. . . . (167–74)

Eve meanwhile, we should notice, has been engaged in precisely the kind of activity that Raphael recommends to Adam. Even though she could enjoy the heavenly equations, she prefers to be *lowly wise* among the particular beatitudes of Paradise. Adam, we may say, is told to be more like Eve. And Eve, of course, would have been better protected had she been more willing to undertake intellectual analysis of the particular sensations the devil offers. Each is designed to depend on the other for completion; and within the protection of complete love and trust the questions of superiority and inferiority need never arise.

The practical expression of this mutuality in their daily work I have spoken of already. What needs to be discussed more is the way in which their mutual esteem obliterates the need to think about their comparative merits. As Adam tells the angel:

> well I understand in the prime end
> Of nature her the inferior, in the mind
> And inward faculties, which most excel,
> In outward also her resembling less
> His image who made both, and less expressing
> The character of that dominion given
> O'er other creatures; yet when I approach
> Her loveliness, so absolute she seems
> And in her self complete, so well to know
> Her own, that what she wills to do or say,
> Seems wisest, virtuousest, discreetest, best;
> All higher knowledge in her presence falls
> Degraded, wisdom in discourse with her
> Loses discountenanced, and like folly shows. . . .   (540–53)

For this Adam is rebuked by the angel 'with contracted brow'. But the point made is in itself innocent and natural. The key phrase, as I take it, is 'she seems . . . so well to know/Her own'. Her acts, her thoughts are so much a part of her beloved personality that it is impossible to condemn them. Perceiving with delight the absolute otherness of Eve, Adam has no sense that he ought to be changing her. 'Oft times nothing profits more/Than self-esteem,' Raphael replies (571–2). It sounds a dangerously priggish piece of advice. But read in context we can see that it is advice that comprehends and (within limits) allows Adam's delight:

> Weigh with her thy self;
> Then value: oft times nothing profits more
> Than self-esteem, grounded on just and right
> Well managed; of that skill the more thou know'st,
> The more she will acknowledge thee her head,
> And to realities yield all her shows. . . .   (570–5)

Raphael does not tell Adam to break down Eve's completeness or impose his personality on hers. The *acknowledgement* must be Eve's and must issue from the judgement of her nature. Adam's duty is to be no less himself than Eve is herself. Then his love of what she does, because she does it, will be matched by her love of his superiority, not because it is superior but because it is his. In this way love holds together the *realities* of reason and the *shows* of the senses, the mind and the body, the head and the limbs. Milton's language here reflects the mysterious sentence in 1 Corinthians, 11:3: 'The head of every man is Christ; and the head of the woman is the man; and the head of Christ is God' (with which one should compare Ephesians, 5:23: 'For the husband is the head of the wife even as Christ is the head of the church; and he is the saviour of the body'). In both these chapters Paul is (like Milton) explicit in stating the superiority of the man to the woman, but always in specific relationship to their joint duty to God through the Church. In that context each requires the other: 'Nevertheless neither is the man without the woman, neither the woman without the man, in the Lord. For as the woman is of the man, so is the man also by the woman; but all things of God' (verses 11 and 12). In the Ephesians chapter Paul takes up the words that Adam speaks when Eve is created ('they shall be one flesh': Genesis, 2:24), and again applies it to the relationship of the believer to Christ through the church: 'So ought men to love their wives as their own bodies. He that loveth his wife loveth himself. For no man ever yet hated his own flesh; but nourisheth and cherisheth it, even as the Lord the church. For we are members of his body, of his flesh, and of his bones' (verses 28–30). The superiority of the husband to the wife is thus closely and necessarily tied into the mutual membership of the Church and dependence on Christ, and has no simple relation to behaviour outside that context. 'This is a great mystery,' says Paul at the end of his chapter. 'But I speak concerning Christ and the church'. It has been thought that he is relating the mystery of two bodies becoming *one flesh* in marriage to the even more central mystery of the communicant and Christ becoming one flesh in the mystery of the Eucharist. Whatever the meaning it is clear that marriage, which Milton elsewhere calls 'the dearest league of love, and the dearest resemblance of that love which in Christ is dearest to his church' (*Colasterion*: CM IV, 253), is only conceivable to Milton in terms of the Christian institutions. Adam and Eve are not to be thought of as competing individuals but as partners in a Christian marriage, which 'is a great mystery'.

The Adam–Eve relationship can, of course, be seen reductively as can all the other mysteries in the poem – I have already spoken about the parallel relationship of the Son to the Father. For Satan, Christ's rule can only be known in terms of a scale of power: the more power he has, the less Satan can have. Eve is liable to the same kind of argument, even before Satan has put it in her mind. In the discussion with Adam about their separate gardening stints (considered above) love becomes an index of power. 'If you truly love me,' says Eve in effect, 'you will respect me enough to suppose me capable of resisting

Satan on my own.' Freedom becomes, as in Satan's argument with
Abdiel, a claim on enough space to exercise personal power, rather than
a loving choice to contribute to the power of the pair. In the ideal model
provided by the Father and the Son, love goes out as to the like ('All
hast thou spoken as my thoughts are': III, 171) and returns as from
the other, otherness rephrasing likeness, as Mercy rephrases Justice.
But Eve wishes Adam's love to go out to her not as she is like but as
she is other, so that she can pursue individual ends though protected by
their common purpose.

The central and most difficult expression of the relationship between
unity and difference, the self and the other, in the history of Adam and
Eve, comes at the climax of the poem. Eve, having chosen to eat the
apple herself, brings it to Adam and invites him to join her in the Fall.
Love and the sense of indissoluble unity invite him to fall; consciousness of superiority and of loyalty to God invite him to survive as the
perfect son, writing off Eve as a defective model. Obedience and love
thus appear on opposite sides of the dilemma. God states clearly the
error Adam makes in following Eve:

> Was she thy God, that her thou didst obey
> Before his voice, or was she made thy guide,
> Superior, or but equal, that to her
> Thou didst resign thy manhood, and the place
> Wherein God set thee above her. . . .
>   Adorned
> She was indeed, and lovely to attract
> Thy love, not thy subjection, and her gifts
> Were such as under government well seemed,
> Unseemly to bear rule, which was thy part
> And person, hadst thou known thy self aright.
>
>   (X, 145–56)

The doctrine reinforces what Raphael had already said. Clearly it is
the official line: Adam should have demanded that Eve's love produce
her obedience. But what this means is clearer as a static idea than as a
dynamic process. Even God himself is a poor advertisement for the ease
of keeping the freedom of the beloved free of insubordination. Neither
angels nor men prove willing (any more than Eve) to prefer the remote
and higher to the companionable and lower. And in neither case does
God act entirely in the spirit he recommends to Adam. His love still
follows the fallen (men if not angels), still accepting as unity what his
offspring act out as separation. The static doctrine does not seem
adequate in fact to describe what love implies for those who feel it
(whether divine or human). In the speech in which Adam debates and
accepts what has happened to Eve (IX, 896–916) he is presented by

Milton as if he is a man behaving not in error but in response to his own divinely created centre of being:

> with thee
> Certain my resolution is to die;
> How can I live without thee, how forgo
> Thy sweet converse and love so dearly joined,
> To live again in these wild woods forlorn? . . .
>   No no, I feel
> The link of nature draw me: flesh of flesh,
> Bone of my bone thou art, and from thy state
> Mine never shall be parted, bliss or woe.   (IX, 906–16)

Milton could easily have shown an Adam who was betrayed by fleshly weakness, unable to resist the seductive and carnally irresistible Eve. He did not. Adam's speech of resolution and tragic knowledge that he is to die is spoken, Milton specifically tells us, *to himself*, without persuasion or interruption from Eve. When he speaks to her his mind is already made up, and his business is then to evade, for their mutual comfort, the facts that his heart has received. But in the crucial decision he makes for himself there is no evasion. At that moment Milton gives Adam all the nobility in the world and makes him a model of the tragic hero whose *hamartia* is fatal to him, and necessarily so, but is an integral part of his human greatness.

It can be argued that Milton's art here fails him; he fails to embody in his poem what his doctrine and his avowed aim ('justify the ways of God to men') required of him and so relapses into mere humanity. Certainly if we suppose that doctrinal clarity and simplicity are the purpose of the poem, the means by which God's ways will be justified, then we must say that *Paradise Lost* fails. But if we say that the purpose of the poem is rather served by its power to evoke 'the burden of the mystery', then we must applaud the force that Milton brings to the tragic paradox of Adam's choice. Joseph Summers, who has written better on these matters than any other critic known to me, remarks that Adam errs in seeing his 'choice limited either to Eve and death or God and life without Eve. . . . But the very terms in which he conceives of his choice indicate that he has forgotten or dismissed God's providence. He assumes that God's will is inimical to his happiness. It does not occur to him to turn *to* God any more than it occurs to him to try to save Eve *from* the death to which he had exposed her' (*The Muse's Method*, 175). Given all the conceivable options inherent in the situation, I accept that this is true. But the poem hardly energises all the options. What the actual rhetoric points up is the sickeningly simple *It is too late,* represented not only as sinful but also as human. Adam waits, hopes for the best, fears the worst; Eve returns, blithe, chatty, pseudo-

confident, already damned. The scene is set, with maximum dramatic
tension, between the reasons of the mind and the reasons of the heart,
abstraction and concreteness, what separates and what is shared. Eve's
act, however crucial for the history of mankind, is not perceived as
making her different from Adam, offending his nature. The reminiscence
of the words that Adam spoke to God when Eve was created (VIII,
495) and so of Genesis, 2 : 23, and the oblique reference to the Marriage
Service in the last line quoted (IX, 916) – all this stresses the continuity
between past and present, the unbreached unity of husband and wife.
In speaking about the basic nature of Adam as the poem describes it to
us I have emphasized his restless search for understanding of himself,
awed but not satisfied by the revelation of God, and only stilled by the
creation of Eve. At an earlier stage all this was allowed; and what now
unallowable occurs is only a logical extension of what went before. 'I
feel/The link of nature draw me,' says Adam. By *nature* Milton must
intend us to understand human nature as found in the unfallen world.
The point of view is pressed close to these human realities. The presentation tends to exclude Summer's genuine alternatives. Adam's remark

> Should God create another Eve, and I
> Another rib afford, yet loss of thee
> Would never from my heart   ·   (911–13)

reflects accurately the reader's necessary priorities as well as his own.
As we read we cannot substitute for the presentness of the vivid scene
before us some abstract and hypothetical alternative. The idea of com-
panionship with God has to wait in the wings while the reality of human
relationship, with its specific priorities, occupies the stage.

Our desire to make a clear ethical distinction is further complicated by
the perception that the human love which makes Adam follow Eve rather
than reject her is a finite repetition of the pattern of divine love as well
as a betrayal of it. As noted above, God does not reject the estranged
and wilfully separated race of fallen men but joins himself (his Son)
to that fallen state as the supreme expression of his love. When Eve
cries out in response to Adam's decision to fall with her 'O glorious
trial of exceeding love' (961), despite the ambiguities in *trial* and
exceeding (see Fowler's note), we cannot fail to be reminded of the
angelic praise of Christ's self-sacrifice in Book III. The parody cannot
equal the original; but it draws strength from its genuine similarity to it.
Moreover, the doctrine that the Fall was 'fortunate', in that it caused
the Incarnation, and is therefore in its way a part of the planned
benevolence of the Creator, makes Adam's assertion of his humanity at
this point something like a *type* of Christ's self-sacrifice of Godhead to
human nature, effected in a parallel way by his embodiment of himself
in the life of a second Eve, the Virgin Mary.

Doctrine is obliged to call such matters *mysteries*. But poetry must do more than state mysteries; it must give us a sense of their emotional pressure even if it retreats from any explanation why such power is present. I have already mentioned the model of the tragic hero as a way of talking about the paradoxical relationship we have to Adam at this crucial moment of his choice. The outline story of the ritually polluted hero who is driven out of the place which he has desecrated is, of course, reminiscent of the most famous of Greek tragedies, the *Oedipus Rex* of Sophocles, and it may be worth while staying with that play to see how far the literary methods of Sophocles and Milton coincide, in their efforts to convey their very different senses of the human condition. Oedipus is, of course, a victim of a pagan pantheon which offers power rather than justice as the defining characteristic of the gods. But in human terms his fate offers a model of empathy, by setting the actions he undertakes (for the general good, for the city, for the truth) against the consequence for himself which they are seen to have. He is presented as *our* hero in the quality of response he achieves, for a destiny which is more terrible than ours, but not beyond our worst fears for ourselves, and so still our representative. In terms of his society he is a polluted person, corrupted and 'fallen', and must be driven out of the good life, ritually mutilated and deprived, made to show what he has become rather than what he was. But ritual expulsion 'from us' is seen as only a short-term expedient in the face of universal corruptibility and the hostility of the gods, not an answer to these facts. And so our sympathy for the polluted scapegoat draws strength from our knowledge that his sacrifice has only limited efficiency, that his happiness has been traded in, necessarily but without glory, for our short-term social security. The case of the Christian Providence which encapsulates Adam is, inevitably, rather different. But I suggest that the same emotional pattern of attachment and separation, guilt and glorification, remains. The balance between the things that make him like us and those which make it necessary for us to reject him seems the same, even though Adam's pollution arises from a freedom of choice that Greek heroes do not possess. Whether the gods simply destroy men, or make ethical demands on them which men cannot fulfil if they are to remain 'like us', in either case a sense of incommensurateness between what man is and what he is commanded to do creates a mystery between the doctrinal and the empathic poles of our response. We cannot, and yet we must, reject Oedipus, in the same way as we must, and cannot, reject our own natures; for his hubris is our humanity. And so with Adam, too. His decision to let 'the link of nature draw me' is one which even the language he uses to describe it makes inevitable; for how can one unlink the chain of being? And yet around our humanity, though incommensurate with it, there is another sense of self which seems to demand what we have no words to articulate, a dumb guilt that we cannot be other than we are. The idea that we can use such feelings to raise ourselves above Adam, exercise our superior sense of how much better we would have done must, however, remain an illusion, for humanity points in only one direction. We can condemn Adam by doctrine, and are, indeed, required to do so; but as we read along with him we cannot free ourselves from the link of nature any more than he can.

Critics often write about *Paradise Lost* as if the presence of doctrinal standards took away all creative freedom from the writer, except what he could smuggle in as the contradictory view of a secret atheist or Romantic rebel. This is to denigrate at once his capacities for belief and for humanity. The emotion of tragic mystery that Milton attaches to Adam's fate leaves doctrine where one might suppose it ought to be – as the highest expression of human capacity to understand. To accept, however fervently, the truth that Adam was wrong to follow Eve is not, however, to find him inhuman or unlike us, or to feel required to withold sympathy from him. Inside the framework of a true doctrine that no one can fulfil by mere humanity, man's tragic destiny must be to await the mystery of illumination by Grace. To follow Adam down the dark path he has to tread is not to defy God but to accept our place as human readers following the direction of the story.

CHAPTER 10
Critical History

To write a true critical history of *Paradise Lost* would involve writing a history of English taste, so central has the poem been to thoughts about poetry and culture in all succeeding generations. All that seems possible here is to point to a few well-known highlights, ignoring the shading and counter-currents that give history its body.

It is sometimes said that *Paradise Lost* was slow to make its way. This does not seem to measure anything more than naïve surprise that it was not an instant success; for within thirty years it was well established as an English classic. Given the inauspicious situation of the author when he wrote it (probably) and certainly when he published it in 1667, this success is remarkable. It is true that, in the earliest years, comment on the poem as a literary artefact can only be expected from those whose political principles allowed them to see Milton as more than a traitor and regicide. Andrew Marvell is an obvious figure of this kind; and his poem set before the second edition of *Paradise Lost* (1674) is the first notable critique to reach print. Marvell speaks of the immense ambition of the work and the improbability of anyone succeeding with such a subject. But

> Thou hast not missed one thought that could be fit.
> And all that was improper dost omit.[1]

In the Restoration mode he had become so expert in, Marvell's tribute is mainly concerned with the contemporary literary scene. He picks up Milton's defence of blank verse, but uses it not to describe the poem but to attack John Dryden, who had obtained Milton's permission to 'tag' (render into heroic couplets) such parts of *Paradise Lost* as could be turned into an opera, *The State of Innocence and Fall of Man* (published 1677 but written 1674). Dryden's co-adjutor, Nathaniel Lee, thought that the couplets ('tinkling rhyme' is Marvell's phrase) had refined Milton's 'golden ore', civilised his rusticity:

> You . . . to court this Virgin brought
> Drest her with gems, new weaved her hard-spun thought,
> And softest language, sweetest manners taught.[2]

Dryden in his preface to the opera declines the compliment, saying that
the original is 'one of the greatest, most noble, and most sublime poems
which either this age or nation has produced'.[3]

The view that Milton's vocabulary and blank verse – 'numerous prose',
the Earl of Roscommon calls it in 1685[4] – are old-fashioned, harsh and
uncivilised remained an obvious difficulty for readers of *Paradise Lost*
until the end of the eighteenth century, even for those who wished to
praise the poem. In 1693 Dryden explained Milton's usage by the
tendentious words 'rhyme was not his talent; he had neither the ease
of doing it, nor the graces of it; which is manifest in his *Juvenilia*'.[5]
A more fruitful explanation of Milton's disregard for neo-classical
decorum was already emerging by this date. This was the invocation
of the *Sublime*, a mode whose effects were to be achieved by bursting
asunder the rules of correctness. The application of this to Milton
becomes obvious in an essay in the *Athenian Mercury* for January
1692. This is concerned to compare Milton and Waller – a comparison
that would occur to very few critics today, but obviously designed to set
correctness and incorrectness in relation to one another. The conclusion
is that 'Milton was the fullest and loftiest, Waller the neatest and most
correct'.[6] Thus a space is made for eccentric genius, and in a mode
that allowed *Paradise Lost* to be seen alongside Homer and Virgil. As
we have noted already, this is a context that Milton deliberately invoked.
Once the mists of political and literary prejudice began to clear, this is
the light in which the poem was generally received – as a classic
monument of English culture. And slowly but surely the mists did
begin to clear, aided by political as well as literary change. It is not
presumably an accident that 1688, the year of the 'Glorious Revolution'
and the re-emergence of anti-Stuart Whiggery, saw the printing of
Paradise Lost in the format usually reserved for classics, in folio, with
engravings and an impressive list of subscribers. Tonson the printer tells
us that this edition (the fourth) had been supported by Lord Somers,
the Whig grandee and engineer of William III's accession. Because of
Lord Somers's good opinion says Tonson, the poem 'has been so well
received, that notwithstanding the price of it was four times greater than
before, the sale increased double the number every year'.[7]

Twenty years after its first publication the poem had achieved the
status of being the first English poem printed by subscription; some of
the responsibility of this must be Milton's, even if Lord Somers did have
a part to play.

The classic status of Milton's epic was finally sealed by the first great
critical exercise upon it – probably the first great critical exercise on any
English poem – the eighteen papers by Addison (another notable Whig)
published in *The Spectator* between 5 January and 3 May 1712,
reprinted at least thirty times in the course of the eighteenth century.

Addison rescues *Paradise Lost* from the severest charges of 'irregularity' ('the most lofty but most irregular poem that has been produced by the mind of man', said John Dennis in 1704).[8] He compares Milton's epic, in detail and in general, with the epics of Homer and Virgil and invokes the critical canons of Aristotle. From this inquisition the poem emerges with many beauties and few blemishes; it is 'a work which does an honour to the English nation'.[9] Another consequence of Milton's classic status is found in the edition of 1732, undertaken by Dr Richard Bentley, probably the greatest classical scholar England has produced. Bentley formed the opinion that *Paradise Lost* was so nearly a great classic poem that some explanation had to be invoked why it was blemished at some points by 'lapses in taste'. It was the great editor's business to detect these, explain them and then rectify them. Milton was blind when he wrote *Paradise Lost*, Bentley noted; his poem must have been seen through the press by another person, clearly a person who 'did so vilely execute that trust that *Paradise* under his ignorance and audaciousness may be said to be *twice lost*'.[10] This person also 'had a fit opportunity to foist into the book several of his own verses'.[11] Bentley thus set up a situation in which his own taste was the arbiter for Milton's text. What is interesting to us today is the extent to which the 'classic' taste of the eighteenth century seeks to clarify and simplify the dazzling complexity of Milton's style. Though Bentley was immediately and vociferously attacked for his meddling, his critics found it just as hard as he did to detect what Milton was actually saying.

Bentley's edition had the great merit of directing attention towards the detail of Milton's writing. Thomas Newton's edition of 1749 undertook to present the text 'as the work of a classic author *cum notis variorum*'.[12] Newton (one of the many bishops who concerned themselves with Milton – Burnett, Atterbury, Pearce, Warburton, Hurd, come to mind) remains even today one of the most acute and dependable commentators on *Paradise Lost*. His theological learning was still in the mode of Milton's own, and makes him aware of nuances that subsequent readers have ignored or been unaware of. Newton's 'Life of Milton' became, like the edition, the standard one for the rest of the century. It had the great advantage that it was written from a position of orthodoxy, even though the orthodoxy of the 'true Whig principles' he mentions in his dedication to William Pulteney, Earl of Bath. The danger of Milton studies less circumspectly handled (Newton calls Milton an enthusiast rather than an infidel, and 'as enthusiasm might make Norris a poet, so poetry might make Milton an enthusiast')[13] is evident from the Life of Milton that Newton's replaced – that of John Toland. Toland, one of the most notorious Deists of his day, originally (1698) set his 'Life' in front of his edition of the prose works, but later it was printed separately. The association of the two names, Milton and

Toland, did Milton's reputation no good. The literary establishment's never deeply buried feelings about the Commonwealth, Milton's religious and political position, and so his personal life, rose to the bait. William Warburton suggests that it is typical of Toland's 'malignity and folly' that he 'represents Milton's moral character as a member of society to be excellent, which was certainly the most corrupt of any man's of that age'.[14]

Samuel Johnson's 1779 'Life of Milton' (from *The Lives of the English Poets*) is the last great monument of the passion and prejudice which Milton's political existence continued to excite. Johnson had shown himself unusually malignant towards Milton by his defence (though anonymous) of William Lauder's trumped-up charge that Milton was a plagiarist. Like Warburton before him he could not deny what was by his time incontrovertible – that *Paradise Lost* was England's greatest poem; he speaks of it as one 'which, considered with respect to design, may claim the first place, and with respect to performance the second among the productions of the human mind'.[15] None the less he felt it his duty to moderate enthusiasm, allowing that: 'The everlasting verdure of Milton's laurels has nothing to fear from the blasts of malignity; nor can my attempt produce any other effect than to strengthen their shoots by lopping their luxuriance.'[16] So he proceeded to lop: he not only gives us splendid evocations of Milton's 'gigantick loftiness', 'imagination in the highest degree fervid and active', 'sublimity of mind', 'sanctity of thought and purity of manners', but also implies that all this is a bit much for the human mind: '*Paradise Lost* is one of the books which the reader admires and lays down, and forgets to take up again (none ever wished it longer than it is). Its perusal is a duty rather than a pleasure. We read Milton for instruction, retire harassed and overburdened and look elsewhere for recreation.'[17] The most famous and most discussed of Johnson's objections to the poem are those which deal with its style and vocabulary: 'Of him, at last, may be said what Jonson says of Spenser, that *he wrote no language*, but has formed what Butler calls a *Babylonish Dialect*, in itself harsh and barbarous, but made by exalted genius and extensive learning the vehicle of so much instruction and so much pleasure that, like other lovers, we find grace in its deformity'.[18]

What we begin to see in Dr Johnson, and more fully formed in Thomas Warton, whose objections to 'the glaring picture of Paradise'[19] interestingly anticipates Leavis, is a retreat from the critical category of the sublime. The 'Miltonics' that were available to eighteenth-century poets, as one variant of the classical mode, came to rest on a poetry of contemplation and the description of nature rather than anything more astonishing and active. Wordsworth is the natural inheritor of this vein of writing, using the generalising power of Milton's vocabulary and the slow music of his blank verse paragraphing to hold together the object seen and the mind that sees it. The idea of Milton the man as a solitary and austere patriot contributes also to this absorption of his identity into Wordsworth's self-image of the poet as a man settled in the unchanging rural pieties, free of the vanities of fashion and competitiveness. The quotations from Wordsworth painstakingly assembled by J. A. Wittreich seem to show, however, that Wordsworth's primary response was to the minor poems of Milton, to the 'republican austerity' of the sonnets, and the elegaic control of 'Lycidas'.

The reputation of *Paradise Lost* was receiving, however, about the same time, a new access, and from a very different source. The spread of a new non-conformist and evangelical piety gave 'the poems of this divine enthusiast',[20] as William Hayley calls them, a sudden relevance to individual experience. Blake (and Shelley in his very different way) find in the Milton who excoriated priests and 'hirelings' an enthusiastic rebel of their own stripe. The man Milton becomes as important as his writings; or, rather, the writings are responded to as the natural expression of that kind of man. The Satan who stands alone against the anathemata of Heaven starts out of the story and becomes the shadow of Milton himself, the enemy to tyrants and censors. Hence Blake's famous remark: 'Milton wrote in fetters when he wrote of Angels and God and at liberty when of Devils and Hell . . . because he was a true poet and of the devil's party without knowing it'.[21] Milton the *true poet*, it seems, was an apocalyptic visionary like Blake. Such sentiments are startling because extreme, but do not easily enter the mainstream of criticism, because extreme. But the combination of a reverence for Milton's piety together with a distaste for the detail of his theology appears in general criticism also, though in different forms. The discovery in 1823 of the manuscript of the *De Doctrina Christiana* and the printing of it in 1825 was an event which in an earlier period would have produced a furore; but, as it was, the critical reputation of Milton's poetry was little affected by it. The investigation and understanding of seventeenth-century theology became in fact a matter of antiquarian research rather than individual belief. David Masson's great Life of Milton ('narrated in connexion with the political, ecclesiastical and literary history of his time'), published in seven volumes between 1859 and 1894, may be taken as confirming the view that Milton's writings are historical phenomena, belonging to the past rather than to the present. The immediacy of the poetry of *Paradise Lost* can come to seem in the context of such an argument the triumph of a powerful individual soul over everything about it that belongs to the seventeenth century and be taken to show the limitation of that parochial and confining background. It is only one step further to find that the poetry or literary art of *Paradise Lost* is the only thing that saves it from obsolescence. Sir Walter Raleigh's famous remark that the poem is 'a monument to dead ideas'[22] throws the burden of interest on the shape and carving of the monument.

In these terms the attitudes of the nineteenth century can be seen to lead directly to those of the twentieth. The description of the poem as sonorous and artful prepares us for the chop that Pound, Eliot, Leavis and Waldock were not too reluctant to deliver. The new demand that true poetry be toughly self-aware was able to draw on current defences of *Paradise Lost* to show that the poem failed the test. It has taken the defenders some time to regroup. But one line of stylistic revaluation appears as early as 1935, in William Empson's brilliant essay 'Milton and Bentley', though as a defence it is a little compromised by its suggestion that Milton wrote 'better' (more like Donne) than he had intended. This line of defence has recently been extended by Christopher Ricks and by Donald Davie (in Kermode's collection). R. M. Adams and F. T. Prince have also helped us to understand Milton's style in different terms from those presented by Modernism.

The mainly Cambridge attack on Milton began with style, but style is only the surface of belief, and its logical conclusion is William Empson's virulent attack on Christianity, *Milton's God* (1961). The first Oxford High Anglican counter-attack took its explicit stand on Christian premises. In Charles Williams's preface to the Oxford 'World's Classics' edition of Milton's poetical works (1940) and in C. S. Lewis's *A Preface to 'Paradise Lost'* (1942) the hieratic style of the poem is seen as the necessary expression of a joyfully ordered, ceremonial and hierarchical view of life, to which the Christian imagination naturally responds, and in whose terms Satan cannot be a hero but must be seen to be self-obsessed, absurd, boring. One certainly sees that he would have been excluded from a number of high tables.

The other movement in twentieth-century criticism of *Paradise Lost* which is sufficiently unified to deserve an outline description is that which picks up the line of historical research already described. A new attitude to theology as mythical and descriptive rather than dogmatic and prescriptive has allowed a succession of scholars to reanimate the 'dead ideas' of Miltonic theology, even if only as 'ways of describing' our experience of external reality. The structure of Milton's doctrinal learning and the tradition of the *hexaemera* or methodised creation, have been explored by (among others) Denis Saurat (a venturesome pioneer), Grant McColley, Sister Corcoran, G. N. Conklin, Arnold Williams, Howard Schultz, R. H. West, R. M. Frye, C. A. Patrides, J. M. Evans.

NOTES

1 'On Paradise Lost', 11. 27–8 (printed, for example, in *The Poems of John Milton*, ed. Carey and Fowler, pp. 455–6.

2 *The Works of John Dryden*, ed. Scott and Saintsbury, V (Edinburgh, 1883), 109.

3 *The Essays of John Dryden*, ed. G. Watson, I (London, 1962), 196.

4 *An Essay on Translated Verse*, 1. 377. See Shawcross, *Milton: The Critical Heritage*, I (London, 1970), 92.

5 Dryden, *Essays*, ed. Watson, II, 85.

6 *Critical Heritage*, I, 98.

7 Tonson's dedication in the seventh (1705) and subsequent small-format editions.

8 *Critical Heritage*, I, 128.

9 Joseph Addison, *Criticism of Milton's 'Paradise List'*, ed. Edward Arber (London, 1898), 151.

10 *Milton's Paradise Lost. A New Edition*, by Richard Bentley, DD, sig. a1v.

11 Ibid. sig. a2v.

12 Preface to *Paradise Lost*, ed. Thomas Newton, 2 Vols. (1749), sig. A7 in 2nd edn., Vol. I (1750).

13 Ibid., I, lxxvi.

14 Letter to Thomas Birch, 24 Nov. 1739; *Critical Heritage*, II, 89.

15 'Life of Milton', in *Lives of the Poets*, ed. G. B. Hill, 3 Vols. (Oxford, 1905), I, 170.

16 *The Rambler*, no. 140, in *The Works of Johnson*, Yale edition, IV, ed. Bate and Strauss (New Haven, Conn., 1969), 383.

17 'Life of Milton', 183–4.

18 Ibid., 189.

19 *The Adventurer*, no. 101: *Critical Heritage*, II, 228.

20 'Conjectures on the Origin of *Paradise Lost*' (1769): *Critical Heritage*, II, 381.

21 *Marriage of Heaven and Hell* (1790), plates 5–6.

22 Sir Walter A. Raleigh, *Milton*, 88.

BIBLIOGRAPHY

The following is a list of the basic works of Milton scholarship, together with a select list of the critical books most likely to be interesting and rewarding to the serious student of literature.

(i) *Editions*

The current standard complete edition of Milton's works is the Columbia edition of *The Works of John Milton*, ed. F. A. Patterson, *et al.*, 20 Vols (New York, 1931–40). The text is without commentary but the two final volumes (the index) provide a rich topical survey of all Milton's references. This is referred to throughout as CM.

This edition was boiled down into a massive single volume, *The Student's Milton: Being the Complete Poems . . . with the Greater Part of His Prose Works*, ed. F. A. Patterson (New York, 1930; 1933); referred to throughout as SM.

A later edition of the prose, now nearly completed, is the Yale edition of *The Complete Prose Works of John Milton*, ed. Don M. Wolfe, *et al.*, due to be completed in 8 Vols (New Haven, Conn., 1953–). Each work is given a long introduction, and annotations of great amplitude; referred to throughout as YM.

H. F. Fletcher has edited *John Milton's Complete Poetical Works Reproduced in Photographic Facsimile*, 4 Vols (Urbana, Ill., 1943–8). The Trinity College, Cambridge, manuscript of Milton's poems and drafts was edited by W. Aldis Wright in collotype facsimile with facing transcriptions (Cambridge, 1899). It is printed in CM, XVIII, and photographically reproduced (paper-bound) by the Scolar Press (Menston, Yorks, 1972).

There are innumerable simple reliable texts of Milton's poetry available, edited, for example, by Douglas Bush (1949; 1969), J. M. Shawcross (1963), B. A. Wright (1959).

Adequately annotated editions of Milton begin with Thomas Newton's edition in two volumes (1749). The notes are largely absorbed into *The Poetical Works of John Milton in Six Volumes, with the Principal Notes of Various Commentators* (1801). Merritt Y. Hughes's edition of the poetry (and some prose) (New York, 1957) has been standard in America since that time. In Britain the edition of A. M. W. Verity (Cambridge, 1910) has been superseded by that of J. Carey and A. D. S. Fowler (London, 1968) – Fowler being the editor responsible for *Paradise Lost*. This section is now issued separately in paperback. A useful edition with brief to-the-point notes and an appendix of background materials and critical extracts is *Paradise Lost*, ed. Scott Elledge, Norton Critical Editions (New York, 1975).

A series of volumes compiling the comments of all the commentators is in preparation under the general editorship of Merritt Y. Hughes. The volumes concerned with *Paradise Lost* have not yet appeared, but the precedent created by the other volumes suggests that they will be unwieldy and indiscriminate, but also essential.

Concordances to Milton's poetry have been compiled by John Bradshaw (New York, 1894; 1977), Laura E. Lockwood (New York, 1907; 1968), W. Ingram and K. Swain (Oxford, 1972).

(ii) *Life and Reputation*
David Masson's huge *Life of Milton Narrated in Connexion with the Political, Ecclesiastical and Literary History of His Time*, 7 Vols (London, 1859–94; Vol. I revised 1881), is not likely to be replaced. W. R. Parker, *Milton: A Biography*, 2 Vols. (Oxford, 1968), is an excellent supplement, a spare narrative supported by a mass of detailed evidence. J. M. French has edited *The Life Records of John Milton*, 5 Vols. (New Brunswick, NJ, 1949–58).

Helen Darbishire has introduced and edited *The Early Lives of Milton* (London, 1932; 1965). Christopher Hill, *Milton and the English Revolution* (London, 1977), discusses fully the unorthodox political and religious pressures around Milton. D. L. Clark, *John Milton at St Paul's School: A Study of Ancient Rhetoric in English Renaissance Education* (New York, 1948; 1964), presents the implications of the school curriculum. H. F. Fletcher, *The Intellectual Development of John Milton*, 2 Vols. (Urbana, Ill., 1956–61), takes Milton through school and university.

Brief accounts of Milton's life appear in most standard general introductory books about him, for example, Muir (1955), Daiches (1957), Wright (1962).

W. R. Parker has compiled *Milton's Contemporary Reputation* (Columbus, Ohio, 1940). John T. Shawcross's two volumes of *Milton: The Critical Heritage* (London, 1970, 1972) print critical references to Milton from 1628 until 1801. A third volume is said to be in preparation. J. A. Wittreich, *The Romantics on Milton* (Cleveland, Ohio, 1970), collects the multitudinous opinions of Blake, Wordsworth, Coleridge, etc. J. G. Nelson, *The Sublime Puritan: Milton and the Victorians* (Madison, Wis., 1963), has chapters on key aspects of the Victorian attitude to Milton. Raymond D. Havens, *The Influence of Milton on English Poetry* (Cambridge, Mass., 1922; 1961), charts the absorption of the Miltonic mode in poetry by the poets of the eighteenth and nineteenth centuries.

Brief surveys of the course of Milton's critical reputation appear in the preface to Shawcross, Vol. I, and in the preface to J. T. Thorpe, *Milton Criticism: Selections from Four Centuries* (New York, 1950; 1965).

Accounts of twentieth-century criticism appear in chapter 1 of B. Rajan, *'Paradise Lost' and the Seventeenth Century Reader* (London, 1947; 1962). See also B. Bergonzi, 'Criticism and the Milton controversy', in F. Kermode, *The Living Milton* (London, 1960), and Patrick Murray, *Milton, the Modern Phase: A Study of Twentieth Century Criticism* (London, 1967).

(iii) *Reference Works*
J. H. Hanford, *A Milton Handbook* (New York, 1926); latest edn. (5th) with J. G. Taaffe (New York, 1970).

C. Huckabay, *John Milton: An Annotated Bibliography, 1929–1968* (Pittsburgh, Pa, 1969).

W. B. Hunter, Jnr., *et al.*, *A Milton Encyclopedia*, 4 Vols. (Lewisburg, Pa, 1978).

(iv) *Critical Studies*
 (a) *Collections*
There are useful anthologies of modern essays in A. E. Barker, *Milton: Modern Essays in Criticism* (New York, 1965); L. L. Martz, *Milton, 'Paradise Lost': A Collection of Critical Essays* (Englewood Cliffs, NJ, 1966); C. A. Patrides, *Milton's Epic Poetry: Essays on 'Paradise Lost' and 'Paradise Regained'* (Harmondsworth, 1967); Alan Rudrum, *Milton*, Modern Judgements Series (London, 1968); A. E. Dyson and Julian Lovelock, *Milton: 'Paradise Lost'*, Casebook Series (London, 1973). There are also collections of specially commissioned essays: F. Kermode, *The Living Milton* (London, 1960), and C. A. Patrides, *Approaches to 'Paradise Lost'* (London, 1968).

 (b) *Books*
R. M. Adams, *Ikon: Milton and the Modern Critics* (Ithaca, NY, 1955).

J. B. Broadbent, *Some Graver Subject: An Essay on 'Paradise Lost'* (London, 1960).

D. H. Burden, *The Logical Epic: A Study of the Argument of 'Paradise Lost'* (London, 1967).

J. Carey, *Milton* (London, 1969).

G. N. Conklin, *Biblical Criticism and Heresy in Milton* (New York, 1949).

Sister M. I. Corcoran, *Milton's Paradise Lost with Reference to the Hexaemeral Background* (Chicago, Ill., 1945).

D. Daiches, *Milton* (London, 1957).

T. S. Eliot, 'Milton I', 'Milton II', both reprinted in *On Poetry and Poets* (London, 1957), the former from *Essays and Studies by Members of the English Association* (1935), the latter from *Proceedings of the British Academy* (1947).

R. D. Emma, *Milton's Grammar* (The Hague, 1964).

W. Empson, *'All* in *Paradise Lost'*, in *The Structure of Complex Words* (London, 1951).

W. Empson, 'Milton and Bentley', in *Some Versions of Pastoral* (London, 1935).

W. Empson, *Milton's God* (London, 1961; 1965).

J. M. Evans, *'Paradise Lost' and the Genesis Tradition* (Oxford, 1968).

A. D. Ferry, *Milton's Epic Voice: The Narrator in 'Paradise Lost'* (Cambridge, Mass., 1963).

S. E. Fish, *Surprised by Sin: The Reader in 'Paradise Lost'* (Berkeley, Calif./London, 1967).

Northrop Frye, *Five Essays on Milton's Epics* (Toronto, 1965).

R. M. Frye, *God, Man and Satan* (Princeton, NJ, 1960).

R. M. Frye, *Milton's Imagery and the Visual Arts* (Princeton, NJ, 1978).

M. Kelley, *The Great Argument: A Study of Milton's 'De Doctrina Christiana' as a Gloss upon 'Paradise Lost'* (Princeton, NJ, 1941).

R. W. Kirkconnell, *The Celestial Cycle: The Theme of 'Paradise Lost' in World Literature, with Translations of the Major Analogues* (Toronto, 1952).

F. R. Leavis, 'Milton's Verse', in *Revaluation: Tradition and Development in English Poetry* (London, 1936); first published in *Scrutiny* in 1933.

F. R. Leavis, 'Mr Eliot and Milton', in *The Common Pursuit* (London, 1952); first published in *The Sewanee Review* in 1949.

C. S. Lewis, *A Preface to 'Paradise Lost'* (London, 1942).

Isabel G. Maccaffrey, *'Paradise Lost' as 'Myth'* (Cambridge, Mass., 1959).

Grant McColley, *'Paradise Lost': An Account of Its Growth and Major Origins* (Chicago, Ill., 1940).

L. L. Martz, *The Paradise Within* (New Haven, Conn., 1964).

Kenneth Muir, *John Milton* (London, 1951).

C. A. Patrides, *Milton and the Christian Doctrine* (Oxford, 1966).

Ezra Pound, 'The Renaissance' and 'Notes on Elizabethan Classicists', reprinted in *The Literary Essays of Ezra Pound*, ed. T. S. Eliot (London, 1954); first published in *Poetry (Chicago)*, 1914, and *The Egoist*, vols. IV–V (1917–18).

F. T. Prince, *The Italian Element in Milton's Verse* (Oxford, 1954).

B. Rajan, *'Paradise Lost' and the Seventeenth Century Reader* (London, 1947).

Sir Walter A. Raleigh, *Milton* (London, 1900).

Christopher Ricks, *Milton's Grand Style* (London, 1963).

Denis Saurat, *Milton, Man and Thinker* (London, 1925; 1944).

Howard Schultz, *Milton and Forbidden Knowledge* (New York, 1955).

J. H. Sims, *The Bible in Milton's Epics* (Gainesville, Fla, 1962).

J. M. Steadman, *Milton's Epic Characters: Image and Idol* (Chapel Hill, NC, 1968).

Arnold Stein, *Answerable Style* (Minneapolis, Minn., 1953).

Arnold Stein, *The Art of Presence: The Poet and 'Paradise Lost'* (Berkeley, Calif., 1977).

J. H. Summers, *The Muse's Method* (Cambridge, Mass., 1962).

E. M. W. Tillyard, *Milton* (London, 1930).

A. J. A. Waldock, *'Paradise Lost' and Its Critics* (Cambridge, 1961).

R. H. West, *Milton and the Angels* (Athens, Ga, 1955).

Arnold Williams, *The Common Expositor: An Account of the Commentaries on Genesis 1527–1633* (Chapel Hill, NC, 1948).

A. S. P. Woodhouse, *Milton the Poet* (Toronto, 1955).

B. A. Wright, *Milton's 'Paradise Lost'* (London, 1962).

INDEX